The Art of Selling Intangibles:

HOW TO MAKE YOUR MILLION($) BY INVESTING OTHER PEOPLE'S MONEY

LeRoy Gross

New York Institute of Finance

Library of Congress Cataloging in Publication Data

Gross, Leroy.
    The art of selling intangibles.

    Includes index.
    1. Brokers. 2. Selling. I. Title.
HG4621.G77   332.63'2'0688   81-11349
ISBN 0-13-048777-5   AACR2

This publication is designed to provide accurate and authoritative information in regard to the subject matter covered. It is sold with the understanding that the publisher is not engaged in rendering legal, accounting, or other professional service. If legal advice or other expert assistance is required, the services of a competent professional person should be sought.

—From a Declaration of Principles jointly adopted by a Committee of the American Bar Association and a Committee of Publishers and Associations

Printed in the United States of America

10   9   8   7   6   5   4   3

Contents

Immunizing Against Stock-Broker Diseases, 92

Making Research Reports Produce Orders from Prospects, 97

Using the Mail Effectively, 101

Cold Calling Successfully, 107

Foreword

I'm sure you have heard the saying, "Those who can, do; those who cannot, write books about how to." If there is such a rule, LeRoy Gross is the perfect example of the *exception* to it. LeRoy has been a successful salesman, sales manager, and sales trainer for most of his adult life. He has personally used the sales approaches and techniques he discusses in this book, and he has used them successfully. In the years he worked as a securities salesman, he became one of the top producers in his company and in the industry. Not content with that achievement, he created the National Option Sales Department and later became the Director of Marketing for Reynolds Securities Inc., one of Wall Street's leading investment and securities brokerage firms.

I first met LeRoy in 1964 when he was seeking a securities sales career. He had left a successful business in his home town of Asheville, North Carolina, and had moved his family to Charlotte. Having pondered his future, LeRoy decided to pursue a career in the securities business. He joined the Reynolds & Company Account Executive Training Program in April 1964.

It was my privilege to be LeRoy's training director. From the outset it was clear that he was a unique trainee. Though he had the same conventional investment and market interests as his peers, he had some unconventional ones, too. For instance, on many of his lunch hours you could find him at Filer, Schmidt & Company's option trading desk learning everything he could about options. Remember, this was 1964, many years before listed options and the CBOE. In the evening hours, if an investment seminar was being given in or around New York City, he attended, learning everything he could about the right and wrong ways to conduct seminars. Also, his training period was shortly after the Keogh Act (Individual Self Employed Retirement Tax Act) was passed by Congress, and few people in Wall Street understood the intricacies of the act and how to market and sell Keogh plans to the self-employed. LeRoy researched the field on his own and discovered that an executive of one of the large mutual funds was the leading expert on the act and on how to set up and market Keogh plans. He arranged numerous meetings with this gentleman and by the time he left New York for Charlotte, LeRoy was as knowledgeable in setting up retirement plans as anyone in the industry.

Behind this all-out effort to develop unusual expertise in such products as options and Keogh plans was a carefully thought-out game plan. LeRoy reasoned that if he became more knowledgeable in selected products than any other brokers in the Charlotte investment community, it would help him to quickly establish an identity as a professional. Also, as a stranger to Charlotte, he properly reasoned that the investment-seminar approach would be the best way to develop personal visibility and credibility.

The fact that he was a rousing success is history. In his first year he sold more Keogh plans than all of the other account executives in Reynolds & Co. combined. He became THE expert in the company on organizing and giving seminars. And, because of his knowledge and success in options he was asked, as of January 1, 1970, to move to New York company headquarters and establish a National Option Sales Department.

Packaging his own option selling strategies and using his rare communications skills, company-wide option sales were soon booming. In fact, after only a few months in his new role, LeRoy had built option sales to a level that was straining the then-existing operational processing capability. The managing partner asked him to direct his sales-development talents in other areas while the option operation was being expanded. We agreed that one of the most constructive things he could do would be to put together his many sales ideas and techniques for use in training both our new account executive trainees and experienced brokers throughout the country. These ideas, which have been honed, refined, expanded, and continuously field-tested over a 10-year period, are the foundation of this book. Frankly, in my 30 years of experience in training securities salesmen, I have not known anyone who has better credentials for writing it.

I foresee the book having an appeal well beyond the obvious audience. Anyone now selling securities and/or related products will find it a gold mine of income-producing sales ideas and techniques, as will anyone involved in any selling of intangibles. Moreover, I think it will be read and appreciated by salespeople of all descriptions. And for those contemplating a career in the challenging world of financial and intangible sales, the book gives a very practical insight into the job requirements and demands. It will help these people make the right career decision.

Glen E. Givens

First Vice President
Director of Training
Dean Witter Reynolds, Inc.

Preface

My hope is that many readers of this book will find in it ideas they can use and reuse to help their earnings grow to a highly satisfying level.

Selling intangibles can be an exciting, rewarding profession for those who like challenges, adventure, and annual incomes *with no upside limit*!

To succeed in selling, it is necessary to master certain fundamental selling skills. This book was created to help people acquire tested selling skills.

Successful salespeople recognize that it is far easier to emulate successful ideas than it is to reinvent the wheel: striving to reach sales success following your own thoughts is very difficult and can be fraught with failure.

This book contains hundreds of workable ideas. Open-minded people seeking sales success should be able to select one, two, or more ideas that will be of substantial help as they strive for a desired degree of success. Those who find my ideas productive can encourage me by writing me a note.

I am grateful to the many people who helped in formulating the final manuscript. To these wonderful friends, I owe deepfelt thanks (and an autographed copy!): to Glen E. Givens, Alan C. Snyder, John Olson, Bay Gruber, for their constructive critical reading of the manuscript. To Joanne Marinello and Barbara Heintzelman, for their typing skill. And to Debra Teel Carpenter for her artful caricature. Finally, to Joyce Perkins, for her thoughtful editing.

LeRoy Gross

The Making of "Born" Salespeople

Everybody is a salesperson in the sense that we all must persuade others to buy or pay for the products or services we can provide. This is true of secretaries, carpenters, doctors, CPAs, teachers—of everyone who *earns* money. Understanding and practicing selling fundamentals can substantially improve the incomes of people who never think of themselves as salespeople.

The making of a "born" salesperson involves instilling pride in being a salesman. Selling is a respected profession without which our society would be much less affluent. Without salesmen we would not enjoy the many fine luxuries and "necessities" that Americans are so envied for around the world. Yes, selling for a living is honorable, respectable and a prideful occupation that should be as sought after as zealously as that of a doctor, lawyer or engineer.

Do you know the one objective all employers seeking people to sell their product or service have in common? To hire "born salespeople." The instruction to do that is blithely given to personnel directors, who then try to teach their subordinates how to recognize, interview, and select this highly desirable, much sought-after commodity, the "born salesperson."

Written tests are devised to unearth this precious creature. Video- and audio tape instruction suggests what to look for in appearance, in verbal responses to questions, and in answers on written tests. Numerous articles and books detail innumerable questions and information-extracting methods that supposedly make it easier to select the "born" prize from all the applicants for the sales job. Special seminars are frequently available, at high cost, that promise to make selectors of salespeople more proficient in their hiring role. Some hirers, on the other hand, simply rely on "gut feel" or look for qualities most like their own.

Unfortunately, as most employers of sales forces have discovered, the "born" salesperson is elusive, difficult to pick out from the throng clamoring for the job opportunity. Effective salespeople come in all sizes and shapes, arrayed in all modes of dress. They may be educated or uneducated, articulate or inarticulate. In voices high pitched or low, they are equally likely to use impressive vocabularies or one-syllable words, including expletives. These highly desirable and much-sought-after salespeople have no distinguishing markings at all! So there's a problem in finding them, right?

There *is* a problem, but it may not be the one you suspect. The real problem with searching for/and selecting the "born" salesperson is that no such person exists! This search is fruitless, like the search for the Holy Grail or the pursuit of the Abominable Snowman. The simple fact is that outstanding salespeople are *made—developed—trained*—not born!

Selling is an *acquired skill*, and one that can be developed, at least to some degree, by anyone. People who acquire a high degree of proficiency in the skills of selling are often said to be "born salespeople." They have so smoothly practiced their art that it appears inborn to observers; they seem to have a natural talent. But such skilled salespeople are no more born to their profession than are accountants, doctors, lawyers, engineers, athletes, or other professionals. Top salespeople acquire their skills through study, reading books and articles, attending seminars conducted by talented professional sales trainers. They learn the tools and techniques of selling from films, video-tapes and audio tapes, and other teaching aids. They learn from close observance of other selling professionals. Trial and error is one of their greatest teachers; nothing teaches so quickly and so well as performing the task. Even better is performing the job function under a trained person who watches every movement and listens to every word with an attentive ear and then offers constructive help.

Yes, top salespeople are made, molded, developed, trained; they are *not* born at the top. Almost anyone can sharpen their selling skills through good sales training, once the realizations dawn that no one is born to sell, that selling is a learned skill like any other, that proficiency comes with constant practice of fundamental selling techniques. Naturally, some will develop into better salespeople than others. Skill levels will vary from high to low, just as they do in all other professions.

You can read this (or any) book on selling, but that won't make you into a good salesperson any more than reading a book on tennis, golf, or bridge will turn you into a top player. What makes anyone excel at tennis, golf, bridge, or selling is diligent, consistent practice of fundamental techniques. What you *can* gain from reading this book is an understanding of the many fundamentals of selling skill needed to become a top salesperson.

Even the best security salespeople often don't recognize a good opportunity until they see it working for a competitor!

TWO THINGS YOU CAN DO TODAY TO MAKE YOUR BUSINESS GROW!

1. **Check every aspect of your personal appearance and manner that might keep some prospect from giving you an order. Use this list and grade yourself.**

hair_____	clothes_____	smile_____
nails_____	posture_____	breath_____
shoes_____	handshake*_____	jewelry**_____

   *not too hard nor too limp

   **not too much/too splashy, or too cheap

2. **Know and present four compelling reasons to buy now for any product you are selling today. Clearly state any risk or sales cost early in each presentation. Do this and watch your percentage of "yes" answers grow.**

If you practice these skills and if you have the desire to reach the top, you may become one of those so-called born salespeople. Some of you may become so proficient that your earnings will double, triple, or even grow to a sum beyond your present ability to imagine.

With the perception that salespeople are *made*, not born, gradually becoming clear at corporate levels, a rather simplistic wishful thought often follows: "If salesmen are made, developed, trained, molded into producing entities, let's do it quickly." The idea sounds so good that great sums of money and countless hours are spent in developing programs, workshops, and seminars designed to produce trained salespeople.

The time allotted to getting this wondrous creature, the "trained professional salesperson," into a production mode may be one day, two days, three days, a week, a month, three months, or, infrequently, six months to a year. The length of training depends upon many factors, including the corporation, the product or service, industry requirements, licensing or regulatory requirements, and, perhaps most influential, the corporate need to have the salesperson in place trying to get orders.

Despite salespeople's obvious importance, their rate of turnover in cornerstone industries like insurance and securities is almost incredible—and frightening to management. Insurance industry statistics purport to show that nine out of ten who enter this field in sales *fail* within three years! In the securities industry, approximately two out of three who enter the industry in sales fail within three years.

The high dropout rate in these and similar industries has two main causes. One is the poor selection of the candidates hired for the job. The second is the lack of high-quality, on-going, training in sales techniques. In my opinion it takes *years* to develop a skilled salesperson. Normally, training cannot be accomplished quickly, no more than one can quickly become a doctor, a dentist, a lawyer, a professional athlete. And without such training, not only will one fail to produce top salespeople, but the turnover rate will stay high, robbing corporations that sell of their greatest potential asset.

Tested under field conditions, the ideas proposed in this book can be used by sales trainers or salespeople themselves to produce more and bigger sales. Reading them once and trying out one or two ideas will not turn a below-average salesperson into a star, however. To achieve star sales status, the sales principles described herein must be applied with disciplined and consistent *long-term* dedication.

Achieving Sales Success: 7 Basic Rules

Based on my years of selling and of observing top salesmen, I have formulated seven rules that can help make the salesperson of intangibles a success. Put these rules to use and watch your earnings increase.

Sounds facetious, capricious, but once you understand the reasons for this particular suggestion, you may agree that it is one of the most valuable in helping achieve sales success. When newly trained completely registered brokers (or sellers of insurance, tax shelters, bonds, or other intangibles) return to the office (assuming they were trained someplace other than at the branch office), they will normally be warmly welcomed by the office manager as well as by their selling coworkers. Everyone wants to hear the latest rumors afloat at the home office as well as wanting to bring the returning salesperson up to date on local happenings. These people all appear to be friendly and nice, and that makes it difficult to refuse the time to carry on those oh, so interesting discussions.

New salespeople, not wanting to make enemies or hurt anyone's feelings, often surrender a good part of their potentially productive work time carrying on discussions that cannot lead to a commission! These friendly overtures are so insidious that neophytes rarely realize so-called friends are *stealing* that most precious commodity, selling time.

New salespeople may accept lunch invitations from office

Rule 1:
Learn to "Hate"
Other Salespeople
in Your Office!

"buddies" (during which neither can earn a dime in commissions) and so successfully kill an hour, maybe two. Or perhaps a colleague will extend an invitation to have a drink late in the afternoon, further robbing the new salesperson of valuable selling time.

Successful professional salespeople know that selling time is their most valuable asset and must not be recklessly squandered on non-prospects! A difficult but crucial lesson to learn is how to abbreviate time spent with coworkers and maximize time spent with prospects and clients.

New salespeople must constantly be aware that their most ferocious competitors for business are often their own associates on the sales force. Such people are looking for, fighting for prospects in the same market area. Secretly, the older salespeople root for the new ones to fail. And why not? Every failure lessens the competition and offers positive proof to the manager, spouses, and higher-up of how tough it really is out there. Besides, should a new salesperson succeed, that very success might suggest that the older, more experienced people on the sales force aren't working hard enough, might even cause some people to think that the old pro's should be replaced!

Each multi-manned office usually contains bitter, unhappy, and relatively unsuccessful salespeople *who can infect others* with their bearish opinions and outlook if given the opportunity. Often they even try to create opportunities to spread their "disease."

Understanding the "learn to hate the other salespeople "concept, taken in the sense that your coworkers are really not your friends but are often (subconsciously if not consciously) seeking your failure, can be a life-saver. Be courteous at all times, of course, but learn to say "good morning" and "good evening" at the appropriate times and spend the rest of your time making prospecting calls and sales attempts.

Rule 2: Work Long, Effective Hours

Sales success rarely comes easily in the field of selling intangibles. Sales of securities, insurance, tax shelters, mutual funds, commodities, and so on, can often be consummated early in the morning or at night, before or after the normal working day.

Aggressive, eager-to-make-it salespeople normally pay a price for success. The price is that precious commodity, time: time spent away from family and from recreation, time spent planning, arranging appointments, seeking prospects, calling prospects. It is not unusual for a new broker to log sixty or more hours each week, month in and month out, trying to get a foothold in the community. The nine-to-five mentality usually does not find success in the brokerage business or in any sales business where the income potential is unlimited but depends solely on sales commissions.

Just putting in the hours, however, does not insure success.

Top security salesmen know that continual prospecting is the key to the continued success of their brokerage business. Twenty-five percent of the average AE's accounts are "lost" each year to attrition. Prospecting at every opportunity is the only way to overcome this normal occupational hazard. Do you have 1600 prospects in your file? Are they regularly contacted?

TWO THINGS YOU CAN DO TODAY TO MAKE YOUR BUSINESS GROW!

1. Try to get the local bank to sponsor your giving a course: "Teaching Your Wife How To Be a Widow!"

2. Call ten strangers (business people) to tell them about the Liquid Asset Fund and the short-term CD unit trust.

Many people work long, hard hours and earn very little for their efforts. It is what you do with your time that counts. Many so-called salespeople fritter away valuable selling time—reading, filing, doing many varieties of nonselling activities so that they can fool themselves and their supervisors into thinking they are working. The true measure of the value of hours worked is eventually counted in commission dollars earned, in actual sales presentations made, and in "asked for" orders. Reading, studying, keeping informed is very valuable and necessary, but these activities do not produce sales. What produces sales is the calls you make *asking for the order.*

Work *is* a four-letter word, but not a dirty one. It's the kind of four-letter word that can put big dollars in the commission salesperson's pocket. Work in the sales game is the *constant* day-in, day-out solicitation of orders from prospects and clients.

Rule 3: Keep Good Records

If you aspire to success, to sales stardom, you must discipline yourself into being a good record keeper. Records must be kept on each prospect. Information must be recorded when the prospect is called, sent mailings, seen. You should note what was discussed and when the next contact is to be made. All transactions, consummated or proposed, must be carefully recorded and filed so as to be easily recoverable. All signed documents necessary to each account must be copied and retained in a file in the event that the client or the home office misplaces their copies. All verbal or written commitments concerning future service must be placed in a "tickler" file or entered on a desk calendar so that they are not forgotten. Your efficiency and attention to detail breeds confidence and loyalty in your customers, and pleasing clients helps to develop referrals.

Any complaints or errors should be promptly written up, with copies of pertinent documents for the file or to the local manager. Uncorrected problems or adjustments that drag on uncorrected in your customer accounts drive business away. Prompt notification to the right authority, along with correct documentation to support the claim, speeds the process and makes for happier clients and more business.

Top salespeople want to know how they are doing, so they constantly keep records of their own progress. Daily commissions, monthly commissions, monthly new accounts, and daily sales calls are the minimum of personal records to maintain. Typical record-keeping includes the following to be kept.

1. Prospects: names, addresses, phone, occupation, income
2. Prospect contacts: mail, phone, in person
3. Documents: authorizations, agreements
4. Complaints
5. Errors
6. Customer statements and order confirmations
7. Commission statements

Rule 4:
Develop Enthusiasm
and Confidence

Developing enthusiasm and confidence in the product or service is one of the most important factors in determining the future success of the seller of that product or service. Getting that enthusiasm and confidence is not such an easy task, however, especially for stock or commodity brokers who deal in risk investments. Adverse markets *do* occur, and they can cause the best-researched, most carefully thought-out investment position to deteriorate and, at least temporarily, erode a client's capital. How do brokers stay confident, and show it, when a price move against their recommendations make their judgment look bad? How do brokers get enough enthusiasm and confidence to make even make risk recommendations?

Perceptive, successful account executives at some point in their career realize that they can obtain more results from time and energy spent getting business from existing clients than in seeking new clients.

TWO THINGS YOU CAN DO TODAY TO MAKE YOUR BUSINESS GROW!

1. *Set up a special seminar exclusively for CPAs and attorneys. Invite attendees (wedding type, R.S.V.P. invitation), topic to be "Today's Viable Tax Shelters"—everything you always wanted to know about tax shelters. Selected expert panel—oil and gas professionals, real-estate professional, plus your own in-house, tax shelter department head.*

2. *Contact your tax-shelter department head. Sell him on the idea. He will be able to select panel speakers whose firms most likely will pick up all expenses for dinner, cocktails, and even the direct mail. Shoot for a turn-out of 50 or more. Beef it up with special invitations to the super-wealthy in your area. This could be a yearly event that could produce big $ for you.*

> Top security salespeople understand the importance of good communication. They make more and bigger sales through their mastery of the three communication skills: (1) simplicity; (2) conciseness; (3) clarity. These apply to phone calls, memos, or letters.

TWO THINGS YOU CAN DO TODAY TO MAKE YOUR BUSINESS GROW!

1. *Put all tax shelter information into a 3-ring binder for quick reference.*
2. *Call 5 people about the next available shelter and its benefits.*

Confidence and enthusiasm are created through *in-depth knowledge of the product or the service* being sold. That knowledge is often obtained by attending product seminars conducted by experts, from extensive reading of analyst reports, or through contact with a knowledgeable industry executive.

Thorough study of the investment situation, along with the strong opinion of a recognized expert, gives broker salespeople the enthusiasm and confidence necessary to sell their viewpoint to others. The more you know about the proposed investment, the more confidence you will have. Natural enthusiasm will then grow from your knowledge. Regardless of what people purchase, they feel more comfortable and reassured if the seller is enthusiastic and confident. Customers also tend to buy more and refer friends to a confident, ebullient salesperson.

The study involved in building a *story book* is one of the greatest ways for stockbrokers to obtain knowledge and confidence and increase sales. A story book is simply a three-ring binder containing the annual report, the quarterly report, the Standard & Poor's sheet, and, if available, the Valueline report. You should also include your firm's research report, newspaper clippings, the prospectus (if any), and the company's brochures on its products. This book should be compiled on those stocks you truly believe to be suitable recommendations for a large percentage of investors. The objective is to build a large position that will eventually be sold at a profit, making available proceeds to put toward another chosen situation.

Once compiled, the story book is a powerful tool to help close face-to-face sales, for prospects get the opportunity to see the story as well as hear it. It also provides instant reference on a company, and serves it a compliance function by proving that you have done your homework.

Story books can also be compiled on a variety of other products, such as options, tax shelters, annuities, municipal securities, mutual funds, commodities, life insurance, and financial planning. They are wonderful aids in achieving sales success. They take time and effort to build and maintain, but you will find they pay back golden dollars for your investment.

SALES TIP

Don't go anywhere without a story book under your arm. Whenever you meet anyone, a friend or a stranger, work the conversation around to your profession—investments. Inevitably you will be asked, "What looks good now?" With the ammunition in your story book, you are on your way to a show and tell session that can lead to an order.

Rule 5:
Complete 30
Selling Phone Calls
Per Day

The measure of how hard you work in selling investments is not how many piles of mail are addressed and sent out each day, nor how many minor details have been attended to, nor how much reading and filing has been finished. The sole measure is how many calls were made asking for orders.

Your goal is to build a clientele whose commission-generating business will propel you into the ranks of high earners. Except for those rare few whose prior connections provide an almost immediate pool of clients and prospects, salespeople starting out have no clientele. Similarly, many older salespeople have lost clientele through normal attrition, poor judgment, or adverse markets. In either case, the answer to achieving high income lies in *contacting strangers daily* and asking them to buy a product or service on the first contact.

If you want high income, strive *each day* to reach 30 new people and ask each for an order. That may sound brash and nervy. Many people find it difficult to understand how people can be expected to entrust their money to a completely unknown—

Good security salespeople would love just once to be as sure of anything, as their manager is of everything!

TWO THINGS YOU CAN DO TODAY TO MAKE YOUR BUSINESS GROW!

1. *Ask at least 10 different clients/prospects to buy 1000 shares of your favorite (under $20 stock. One extra yes per day can really up your production. More than one can put you in the super-star category. (Remember, you have to make every one 1000-share-conscious-everyday!*

2. *Be sure you are "in love" with an under-$20 stock that is highly recommended currently by research. Put together a show-and-tell story book (3-ring binder) containing the research report, the annual report, the S&P, the ValueLine, plus the quarterly report and any pertinent news items or competitors' write-ups.*

Good security salespeople know they have no time to waste: they have to arouse interest immediately. Their first words and actions must be planned to capture the prospect's complete attention. Options, with limited risk and unlimited profit potential for buyers, can capture the prospect's attention perhaps better than any other product!

TWO THINGS YOU CAN DO TODAY TO MAKE YOUR BUSINESS GROW!

1. **Call 2 of your firm's top producers to see if you can get an idea—psyche yourself up.**

2. **Meet with the Mercedes salesman. You might exchange leads and get access to their list of late model foreign car owners.**

and unseen—salesperson and, moreover, to do it at the first phone contact. But that scenario of first contact-first order is replayed daily. What you must realize is that selling is a numbers game. The more contacts made and the more orders asked for, the greater the possibilities for success.

Many salespeople are hard workers who make the suggested number of calls and still fail. One reason for their failure may be that their verbal and selling skills are not great. Most often, however, they fail because they are *timid*. The reluctance to ask for an order still exists in many salespeople. They want the client to make the decision to buy, to roll over or play dead, to place an order and hand over their money voluntarily. Salespeople who think that way are usually destined to remain at lower earning levels. Making the daily quota of calls is not enough unless you can state after the call is completed, "I asked for an order, and I asked for an appointment."

Each day of 30 completed selling phone calls should produce one or more "live prospects" who will eventually become clients, if not at the first contact.

Take the pledge:

1. Complete 30 calls each day to strangers for 30 consecutive business days.

2. Ask each person for an order or an appointment.

At the end of 30 days, review your results in terms of new accounts and business done, and I believe you will find the effort paid off, especially when compared to any previous effort. I predict you will make the 30-call practice a daily habit.

Constantly trying to create sales and develop prospects through phone contact alone eventually becomes boring. Besides, many salespeople are better at "one on one" than they are

**Rule 6:
See Two Prospects
Each Day**

at making their sales points over the phone. To create a mental uplift and provide new vigor to the task of prospecting, create a daily discipline of seeing *at least quality prospects* face to face each day. Please note that I said "prospects," meaning people who are not yet your clients.

These "face to face's" can be accomplished during lunch hour, on the way to or from work, or on a simple prospecting tour of the other business places in and around your office. Meeting people face to face tends to pump up your enthusiasm, and it provides you with an opportunity to use your story book to get the order. Good salespeople also recognize that many wealthy prospects *only* do business with people they have met and with whom they feel comfortable.

In addition to providing a breather between phone calls, face-to-face meetings can be made to produce referrals, and they typically result in larger initial orders than those gained through phone prospecting. These face-to-face presentations can be of three types:

1. Scheduled appointments in your office
2. Scheduled appointments in the prospect's office or home
3. Nonscheduled appointments in the prospect's office

Establish a goal of meeting at least two qualified prospects face to face each day and asking each to do business with you. If you do so, you will be amazed at how rapidly your business and referrals grow.

SALES TIP

Make time for daily "facials," not excuses for avoiding them.

Rule 7: Send Out 10 to 20 Personalized Mailers Each Day

Salespeople well versed in selling fundamentals constantly try to keep a steady stream of prospects coming to them to seek advice and place orders. A great aid in strengthening the flow of incoming calls and requests is in the proper use of direct mail.

Mail-produced leads, in my experience, consistently produce more and better-qualified prospects than do newspaper or magazine insertions. Mail can be pinpointed to a narrow geographic area densely populated with the affluent investors who are the desired targets.

Using the mail to produce a sufficient supply of qualified prospects at a low cost requires a lot of thought and planning, as follows:

1. The area to receive mail coverage should have a demonstrable concentration of wealthy prospects.
2. The area should be close enough to the office to enable you to visit the prospect easily and for the prospect to visit you at the office.

Calvin Coolidge should have been a sales trainer for stockbrokers. Following his immortal words could make every AE an outstanding success:

"Nothing in the world can take the place of persistence. Talent will not. There are many unsuccessful men with talent. Genius will not. Unrewarded genius is prevalent. Education will not. The world is full of educated derelicts. Persistence and determination are omnipotent."

TWO THINGS YOU CAN DO TODAY TO MAKE YOUR BUSINESS GROW!

1. *Check out the costs of leasing (new or used) a computer typewriter. The memory unit could hold all names of prospects and approved letters in a variety of topics. This tool, properly used, can double a good producer's income.*

2. *Learn all the various applications of this immensely helpful tool. The salesperson may also become your client and a referral source.*

   If the cost per month is too much for you to bear, test your sales ability. Try to get the manager or other aggressive AEs to split costs and share in use.

3. Send no more mail than you can follow up with a phone call approximately one week after the mailing. Mass mailing is an expensive burden on the office and will not normally be tolerated by the local manager unless sales results can be documented. It is also a waste of time, because you cannot possibly follow up on each piece.

4. Each piece of mail should have a business card attached or be stamped with your name, address, and phone number. (If you stamp, use red ink. It is a better attention-getter than the typical black ink.

5. Personalize each piece of mail with a *handwritten note* block-printed in large, easy-to-read letters. (Again, the use of a thick-writing pen with colored ink helps gain readership and lessens the chances of your mailing becoming a quick throwaway.)

A typical general use personalization might read:

> *Dear Leroy:*
> *Call me right away as soon as you have read this.*
>
> *(Your name)*

6. Never send out *any* direct mail unless you enclose *at least two response cards* for the prospect to complete and

return. Response cards that request a specific item are the most rewarding, because they pinpoint an area of interest that you can zero in on. You should further instruct your assistants to include two or more sales darts in all your outgoing correspondence that, when returned, can lead to an order or new client.

7. Log all outgoing mail for a follow-up phone call one week later. Use the phone call to make sure the information was received and to solicit the order. (Never forget that getting the order is the object of the game.)

To make your mail program work, you must always have on hand a supply of response-card enclosures of various types to appeal to any interest. Samples of tested reply cards are shown in the back of this book. Use paper in different colors; bright, light shades of yellow, blue, green, and pink are recommended.

Don't leave the office each day until at least ten "somethings" are in the mail, personalized, containing sales darts.

Do see that preaddressed return envelopes that carry your name or identifying number are enclosed to ensure that any leads generated get directed to you. If the response card needs no envelope and is preaddressed, mark your initials or identifying number on the card to properly ensure the lead assignment.

Setting Time-Limited Goals

In working toward that powerful measure of sales success, high dollar earnings, you will have to establish goals. Goals serve as prods to spur you onward and upward. Goals serve as measures of attainment—monitors of performance. Goals are instruments in determining accountability. They are invaluable as guides along the pathway to success.

In order to be truly helpful as you climb upward, goals *must have a time limit.* You should establish for yourself three sets of goals: (1) near-term goals, (2) intermediate-term goals, and (3) long-term goals. Each goal should have specific benchmark dates to determine progress.

Goal-setting does entail two warnings, however. The first is this: do not set goals so high that they border on the impossible to achieve. Too high a goal is likely to discourage you when you perceive it cannot be accomplished. Take a lesson from professional high jumpers and pole vaulters: they gradually inch up the bar when they find they can easily clear a lower setting. If you find you are easily reaching your goals, simply make an adjustment and raise your sights. Keep stretching and seeking higher levels and you will be on your way to attaining them.

The second warning is to set a time limit for achieving a goal. Without the time limit, it is easy to procrastinate and you lose the impetus that meeting a deadline gives. This pressure and sense of urgency is something that most salespeople need and thrive on.

Here are some goals that stockbrokers should consider establishing at the beginning of a career. Experienced brokers or sellers of other investment products can readily adapt the suggestions to fit their particular focus.

Goal 1: Establish a daily minimum goal of phone contacts asking for orders. Don't leave the office until this goal is reached.

Goal 2: Establish a daily minimum goal or direct mail contacts seeking appointments or asking for orders. Don't leave the office until this goal is reached.

Goal 3: Establish a daily minimum goal of seeing at least two people face to face and asking for the order. Don't go home until this goal is reached.

Goal 4: Establish weekly, monthly, and year commission goals. After a regular clientele has been built up, establish a narrower goal of daily commission.

Goal 5: To keep enthusiasm high, every month stockbrokers should "fall in love" with a stock that they want to buy for accounts. A goal must be set as to the minimum number of shares to be positioned in a selling period of 20 business days.

Monthly sales goals should also be set for other products: for example, perhaps $50,000 each month for tax-deferred annuities, a specific dollar volume in municipal securities, individual bonds, or unit trusts, closing one tax-shelter sale each month, and so on.

A goal for opening new accounts must also be set. The target I recommend is a minimum of ten new accounts per month. This is the minimum even for established salespeople, who presumably benefit from referrals. Seekers of superstardom should double or triple that number.

Discuss your goals with your manager and with your family. Their knowledge of and interest in what you are trying to do can

Top security salespeople know that Wall Street has many brilliant AEs who start out in a blaze of glory but lack the sticktuity to be a continuing success. Their accounts and business are eventually taken by patient, hardworking AEs who never stop prospecting and asking for orders regardless of market conditions!

TWO THINGS YOU CAN DO TODAY TO MAKE YOUR BUSINESS GROW!

1. *Review your cross-reference file and see how many people you can get to trade up to 1000-share positions from lower amounts.*

2. *Send a note with new information to each holder of shares in your biggest position.*

help you on the road to doing it. Let them know your progress frequently; they may offer some good positive suggestions. The more people you can interest in your progress, the better chance you have to progress.

Creating Success: 6 Surefire Ideas

Stockbrokers seeking to make it big should recognize that the great majority of the industries' big producers create significant portions of their revenue from "position building." They zero in on a particular stock, research it carefully on their own (even if the stock is extensively covered by their own research departments) and become sold themselves before recommending a single share to clients. Once having found a desirable stock, they tell and retell the story about that stock to as many people as possible each day. Of course *they ask each listener to buy!*

Top producers know that they have a responsibility not only to select suitable recommendations but also to follow them until the position is eventually sold. Good salespeople also know that they can know really well and follow only a limited number of issues. Knowing this, they carefully restrict the number of stocks they follow usually to no more than 10 or 12 in any given year. All of which leads to the six surefire success ideas.

Success Idea 1:

Familiarize Yourself With Products

Each month, *select one stock* to learn thoroughly, and then sell the story to as many people as possible. The natural enthusiasm generated by a new idea builds sales quickly. However, any story you tell and retell dozens of times every day will become old and boring to you. After a time, your enthusiasm wanes, and along with the decline in enthusiasm, sales begin to slow. After a period of concentration on the chosen stock, *stop actively promoting it!*

18

Top security salespeople constantly have to guard against cheating themselves—by wasting time. They alone know how many sales calls they made, how long they took for lunch, how hard they really work. They know their income and future rest on how well they use their daily time.

TWO THINGS YOU CAN DO TODAY TO MAKE YOUR BUSINESS GROW!

1. **Set up 3-ring binder for company policy memos and Compliance bulletins. File them by date.**
2. **Now read them!**

Learn a new stock. Follow the procedure for researching and documenting. You will find the constant need to keep your enthusiasm at a high level. One way to ignite enthusiasm in yourself and in others is to learn something new each month. This procedure keeps position-building within reasonable compliance limits and also permits prudent diversification among holdings in clients accounts.

Success Idea 2: Ask for Referrals

Nothing warms salespeople's hearts so much as the account and commissions earned through a referral. Having a friend or client refer another prospect to you not only brightens the day but usually so charges you up that you will probably find yourself making more calls and selling more enthusiastically. Salespeople *love* referrals, yet many are so timid that they will not directly ask for a referral. They want their judgments—their stock, option, or commodity recommendations—to perform so impeccably that satisfied clients will automatically disgorge an unending stream of referrals.

What a wonderful dream world! The real world, however, is full of risk as well as the possibility of profit. No matter how carefully a situation is chosen or researched, it can deteriorate substantially after the client has invested. Erosion can occur with a general market fall or because of unforeseen circumstances affecting the particular situation. Certainly a loss in value won't help make the client eager to recommend others to the same broker's ministrations. Sometimes, as in 1973–74, a protracted stock market decline dries up referrals. So much for referrals generated by the broker's flawless recommendations to clients.

If you know anything about investor psychology, you should understand that the best way to get referrals in regular, large numbers is to ask for them. The two best times to ask for and get referrals are as follows:

REFERRAL TIME 1

Ask for a referral when you report the executed price of a transaction in a stock, option, or commodity. Once investors know they are "in," their natural instinct is to root for that position to move favorably and produce a profit. They also realize that the greater the number of people assuming the same side of that trade, the more pressure is brought to move the position in the desired direction. If asked for referrals at the time of a price report, these clients are likely to surrender two, three, or more names of people who might want to test the same water. Investors' enthusiasm is high at the time of entry into an investment; good salespeople press this advantage and ask for referrals at this point.

A typical price reporting conversation might go like this: "You bought 300 ZXY at $18. The outlook really looks great for increased earnings, a dividend increase, and a higher stock price. I have three extra reports on my desk right now. Who do you suggest I mail them to, people who might also be interested in this excellent opportunity?"

REFERRAL TIME 2

Whenever you have investors enjoying a winning recommendation, ask for referrals. Call each winner and say that you can handle a few additional accounts and would like to place selected friends of theirs on your mailing list. This approach is usually very effective and helps build a prospect file.

Sometimes prospects will allow you to use their names in contacting others (most desirable, of course), and sometimes not. Always ask permission *after* you have the referral names.

Don't put off asking for referrals. The market action of your recommendation may do you in. An immediate decline may occur even before settlement, creating a "nonreferral" situation that may last for a long time—maybe forever.

I once sold the bulk of an entire syndicate new issue stock offering just by asking for referrals. The issue was "cold," "sticky," hard to move at the $12.50 per share offering price, enabling interested salespeople to get a lot of stock and earn a good commission for each share placed.

With the prospectus information in hand, I called a local merchant, a stranger to me, who handled the products sold by the particular company making the offering. I extolled the potentials (and outlined the risks), stressing that it was an opportunity to purchase shares at the same price available to any public investor, no matter how wealthy. I also stressed the "no commission to the buyer" aspect of the newly issued shares. The

Top security brokers keep looking for additional products and services to help clients fulfill their financial goals. By doing this in-depth work, they get more and more of a client's business—and their competitors get less!

TWO THINGS YOU CAN DO TODAY TO MAKE YOUR BUSINESS GROW!

1. *Visit the business editor of your paper. Take him or her to lunch. Develop rapport and the possibility of becoming the subject of article later in paper. Get a personal account, no matter how small. Your name frequently in the paper is great public relations (referrals can be big and continuous).*

2. *Visit a veterinarian. They are big $ earners. Seek information from him or her about the biggest $ expense for drugs. Maybe the supplier's stock might be attractive. Get the account! They meet and know all the well-to-do people, can be great prospecters for you (they might even cure some of your "dogs").*

prospect, who was thoroughly acquainted with the company and its products, gave me an order to buy 100 shares at the $12.50 offering price. No big deal, sure, but a new account was on my book and a commission in my pocket.

I then asked this prospect for the names of people he knew who might want these new shares. He suggested a cousin and a friend in different towns. I called them and opened an account for each, using my new client as a reference. Each of my new clients then gave me several other names to call, which I did. The chain of referrals and orders grew and grew. I eventually opened 45 new accounts in seven different states and sold over three quarters of our entire syndicate allotment myself. All as a result of asking for referrals!

Seek referrals from these main sources:

1. Existing clients
2. Close friends
3. Acquaintances
4. Other salespeople not in competition with you

Finally, always remember that "no sales," people who do not buy, for whatever reason, can still give referrals.

The *apology sales technique* is a sales fundamental that can add thousands of dollars in commission income each year to its skilled practitioners. Here is the principle behind the apology sales technique: when salespeople obtain an order for an investment (stock, bond, annuity, life insurance, mutual fund) and confirm the price to the investor, they normally experience a moment of joy (sometimes exhilaration, depending on the size of the order), and then continue their routine of calling other

Success Idea 3:

Learn the "Apology" Sales Technique

clients and prospects, having "finished" with the client who gave the order. What many salespeople fail to understand, however, is that clients, particularly new ones, rarely place an initial order representing all, or even a significant part, of their available cash or assets. First and second orders are usually tests. If the salesperson's recommendations work out favorably, more orders, and larger ones, will be placed. Initial orders are trial votes of confidence in the salesperson's story.

You can often get increases in initial order sizes with the apology sales routine. Assume the following scenario: Joe Salesman calls John Prospect about a research-selected stock, XYZ, selling at $20 per share. The stock is rated A-plus and currently yields 10 percent from a dividend that has been raised annually for 20 consecutive years. The future outlook for more dividend and earnings increases looks good. John likes what he hears and agrees to buy 200 shares at $20. After executing the order and reporting the purchase price, Joe feels great. His hard prospecting work has paid off with a new client and an order.

The next morning, just before the market opens, Joe calls John: "John, this is Joe. I'm calling to *apologize* about your purchase yesterday of 200 XYZ at $20." Joe then pauses while his words sink in.

Typically, John Prospect is jarred. He might stutter: "What happened? How far down is it?"

Joe continues: "Don't get upset. Nothing bad has happened. *I just wanted to apologize to you* for my poor sales presentation. Yesterday I told you about the attractive features of XYZ and you did buy 200 shares. I must not have made clear to you that this stock is rated A-plus by Standard & Poor's—that is the highest possible rating. It yields 10 percent from a dividend that has been regularly increased for 20 years. The future is bright not only for the payment of higher income, but this stock offers potential capital gains as well. My story was so poorly delivered that you only bought 200 shares. I am calling this morning to make up for my lack of enthusiasm yesterday and see what else you might have that you could transfer into 300 (or 800) more shares while the price is low and the yield high. If you place an additional order right now before the opening, you might be able to get shares at or near where they closed."

A conversation of this type usually brings a response from the prospect such as "You really must like this stock to call me back so soon after my first purchase. If you are really that strong on it, get me 300 more shares."

Experienced sellers of investments know that frequently people understate, misrepresent, or lie outright about the funds they have available for investment. But at the drop of a good investment story, they suddenly "discover" or remember about money available. By calling the same client back the day after a purchase and forcefully, enthusiastically presenting the same sales points, an original order frequently can be "lifted" to a much higher level.

I conducted a sales meeting early one morning in Syracuse,

Top security salesmen know that many other Account Executives have good ideas and work plans but fail to achieve good results. The big producer understands that success stems from following through on a work plan for today...tomorrow...next week...next month?

TWO THINGS YOU CAN DO TODAY TO MAKE YOUR BUSINESS GROW!

1. **Put all the annuity information into a 3-ring binder for quick reference.**
2. **Call 5 people to tell them how to:**
   - **—earn high untaxed interest**
   - **—run no principal risk**
   - **—have all principal $ available on demand**

New York, for 16 established salespeople. The apology sales technique was one idea that attracted Mike C. He said, "LeRoy, that sounds terrific. I'm going to try it today!" Mike went to his desk and called a client to recommend the purchase of 200 shares of Continental Telephone. He stressed the high yield, the dividend increase record, the quality. Mike got the order for 200 shares.

Mike then asked if I was going to be around the next day to supervise him in the implementation of his first try at using the apology sales technique. I told him I was leaving that day after the market close. Mike was disappointed that I would not be around to monitor his attempt at apology selling. He frowned for a moment, and then his face lit up: "Hey, I'll just *wait an hour* and call my client back and try the apology sale while you're here and can watch me."

An hour went by, and Mike called the client who earlier bought 200 Continental Telephone: "John, this is Mike, and I want to really apologize to you about the 200 Continental Telephone you bought this morning."

"What happened Mike?"

"Nothing yet. The stock is just where you bought it. But I really must not have turned you on. You only bought 200 shares. Maybe I didn't make clear to you that the dividend has been raised each of the last 10 years, the yield is high, and your opportunity for a future profit looks great. If I were any good as a salesmen you would have gotten at least 500 shares. I am calling back while the stock is still low to try to get you to buy 300 more shares of this high-quality, high-yield stock."

"You really must like this stock to call me back only an hour after I bought!"

"You know I believe it or I wouldn't be trying so hard to get you to buy more," Mike replied.

Said John, "Well, if you feel that strong about it, buy me another 300."

The apology sale worked for Mike as it has for me. The second request for an order soon after the first creates the client's conviction that the salesperson really believes in the recommendation!

Mike was so excited about this success that he excitedly exclaimed, "I am going to wait another hour and try it again with the *same client!*" Another hour went by and Mike called the client who had twice that day bought Continental Telephone shares: "This is Mike again. I want to apologize to you. In my hurry to encourage you to buy more Continental Telephone because of its high quality, high yield, and capital-gain potential, I forgot to tell you that if you buy 1000 shares today, you are entitled to a much lower commission charge per 100 shares. With a conservative investment like this, one that offers the potential for more income each year plus the opportunity for a capital gain, you should put more dollars in it now while the price is low. What do you have that you could transfer into another 500 shares and take advantage of our lower commission rate?"

Mike's client, certainly surprised at the third call that day, exclaimed, "Well, if you really like it that much, sell 500 XYZ and get me 500 more Continental."

Mike hung up the phone, wrote the orders with a big smile lighting his face, and said, "LeRoy, you taught me a lesson I will remember all my life."

The apology sales technique worked for Mike and it can work for you, too. Give it a try! Let it help you make big sales out of little ones.

Most salespeople's commissions are greatly affected by their mood. When they feel up, they can close sales, prospect enthusiastically, do the work of several people. But when they feel down, salespeople can't even sell the best quality investments at sacrifice prices.

Top security salespeople know that prospecting efforts have to be doubled in bear markets. They also know that loss-burdened investors are more receptive to new ideas from other brokers in depressed markets. Are you contacting 10 new prospects daily?

TWO THINGS YOU CAN DO TODAY TO MAKE YOUR BUSINESS GROW!

1. **Set up a 3-ring binder to hold a form file and procedures for handling estate securities.**

2. **Call on 3 attorneys in person to show this estate security valuation service, and seek their personal and estate business.**

Use ingenuity when times get tough, and you can build your sales back to where they should be. Option knowledge can build your sales and make you a better broker for your clients!

TWO THINGS YOU CAN DO TODAY TO MAKE YOUR BUSINESS GROW!

1. **Call 5 civic club presidents and try to get yourself scheduled as a speaker at a meeting. (Also try to get the president's account.)**

2. **Call the muni bond desk trader to get a current idea of a heavily available discount—quality muni bond to merchandise this week.**

Nowhere is this mood swing clearer than in stockbrokers who trade securities for a significant portion of their income.

In euphoric periods like the late 1960s and up-market times in the 1970s, brokers excitedly sold new issues, little-known secondary stocks, and established growth stocks to eager investors. They convinced themselves and others that 30, 40, 50, and even 60 times the latest 12-month earnings was a "cheap" price to pay for shares. Prestigious institutions, pension plans, and investment advisors also participated in the frenzy. The up mood created by large profits caused large and small investors alike to pay little heed to risk. It was easy to make sales due to the mood of the moment.

When down markets hit in 1969–70 and 1973–74, brokers in general could not get up enough courage to recommend A-plus utility shares yielding 15 percent, even when they were offered at a net price to the client and the salespeople paid double, even triple, the normal commission rate. Brokers made only faint-hearted efforts to sell old clients and prospect for new ones. People were reluctant to buy well-known companies like EXXON and General Motors, even though their shares sold at historic low prices.

Learning how to psyche yourself is a fundamental selling skill that you must develop in order to reach the income level you desire, no matter what the selling climate. All the above is background for my next idea.

Selling face to face requires different skills than selling by phone. Personal appearance becomes an important factor, as do exhibits and documentation that can be used as convincers to close the sale. Also helpful are attractive surroundings, a professional-looking office.

In addition to using all the foregoing to your advantage,

Success Idea 4:

Plan Appointments for Big Ticket Sales for Friday Afternoon or Saturday Morning

make the appointment for a Friday afternoon or a Saturday morning. If the appointment results in a sale, your weekend mood will be elevated.

You'll feel great! Even though the rest of the week may have been torture, ending the week with a good sale helps create a better, happier weekend environment for you and the people you're close to. When Monday morning arrives and you enter the order ticket for the good sale, you will feel much more up than those associates struggling for the first order of the week. The up feeling will provide some equanimity in the event that Monday's market moves adversely for your special situations. The feeling you get from the weekend close is that you have the new week made. Feeling that way enables you to seek more orders and make more appointments on the wave of optimism caused by the sale. Making weekend sales is one of the best morale boosters in the world! I must warn you, though, they're addictive. But that type of high is entirely beneficial.

Success Idea 5: Prospect 7 Days a Week

Sellers of intangibles understand the necessity for getting new accounts. They know that new accounts are their life blood, and in order get new accounts on a regular basis, one or another form of prospecting is necessary. Salespeople who don't make it fail because they have not made themselves prospect-conscious 100 percent of their waking hours.

Always be on the lookout for prospects. Search for new clients among friends, acquaintances, strangers. Always keep your eyes, ears, and mouth open. Trying to open up a stranger and get the conversation turned toward investments is a constant challenge.

If you are looking for them, prospects can be encountered almost everywhere you go. You can strike up conversations in airplanes with a captive audience. In restaurants it is often possible to strike up a conversation with a prosperous-looking fellow diner and steer the conversation to investing. Bars may be productive meeting places. Cocktail parties and other social functions like wedding and birthday parties are great for meeting new people who are prospects for future solicitations for business. Always be alert for prospecting opportunities at civic affairs, church-group meetings, club functions. Let people know what business you are in, what services you can render. Don't be afraid to start and steer conversations toward your favorite topic, investing!

Wherever good sellers of intangibles spend money, they concentrate on trying to get some of it back by selling to the salesperson, the manager, or the owner. For example, when you buy a car, get the salesperson (who earned a commission from selling you the car) to become your client for investments. The folks are usually talkers and, as clients, are likely to refer a stream of others to you.

Eliminate the thought that prospecting is done only during

Top security salespeople understand that bad markets create sale declines. To break a sales slump they plan a specific course of action and let nothing deter them from the completion of the planned program.

TWO THINGS YOU CAN DO TODAY TO MAKE YOUR BUSINESS GROW!

1. Visit "cold" two hospital administrators (they earn $ and know all the doctors) and see if you could speak at their monthly meetings on TDAs (or some other topic).

2. Spend some time in the hospital coffee shop trying to strike up conversations with doctors. Have in your briefcase all types of sample literature.

working hours. All your waking hours can be prospecting hours, and the sooner you realize this and eagerly pursue the opportunities to present yourself and your ideas wherever and whenever people congregate, the quicker your commission checks will increase.

Success Idea 6:

Set Up "1000 Up" Prospect Files

Getting accounts on the books is the necessary beginning to building a large production base. In order to develop a book of accounts quickly and maintain a high level of opening new accounts, skilled salespeople establish a prospect file.

I have come in contact with thousands of salespeople seeking to climb the ladder of success who are not yet successful. These people invariably buttonhole me and ask me to review what they are doing and perhaps put them on the path to sales stardom. My first question to these success seekers is, "Could I see your prospect file?" More often than not, they don't have a prospect file. Many who do show me a file box or rolodex on a shelf or in a drawer that is sparsely filled with some heavily notated, soiled cards. Others drag out coffee-stained lists from seldom-used drawers. Still others offer up as prospects old coupon leads heavily inscribed with hieroglyphics of some type.

Here are my ideas of what a prospect file should consist of and how it should be maintained:

Qualified names only: Each name that goes in the prospect file should represent an investor with potential as determined by either of two things: where he or she lives (in an affluent area) or what he or she does. Don't waste time and money calling or mailing prospects with little buying ability.

Screened names:	Have your local manager screen each name in your prospect file prior to your making a sales effort, to prevent time wasted in your prospecting an associate's account.
Lined cards:	Use lined cards only, so that all information can be neatly aligned. *Unlined* cards encourage sprawling, illegible note-writing. Make sure the card is sufficiently large to contain a lot of information and that the back of the card is lined also. (See the exhibit section.)
Quarterly purge:	Every three months the entire prospect file must be reviewed card by card. Prospects repeatedly contacted and found to be unresponsive or deemed to have low potential should be culled and put into a special file for an annual mailing (the "dead" sometimes do come to life!).
Weekly additions:	To keep a prospect file "live," it is necessary to feed it new names. A minimum of ten new prospects a week must be placed in the file in order to keep it up to strength, since the quarterly purge weakens it.
Placement near phone:	To be effective the prospect file should be situated next to the phone as a constant reminder that there are calls to be made, appointments to be sought. The prospect file that is hidden from view is a file that never lives up to its potential for getting business. The file constantly in sight puts subtle pressure on you in dull or despondent moments: it reminds you constantly that there is sales work to be done!

A prospect file that is too small is quickly used up and seduces you into slowing down your efforts to seek new

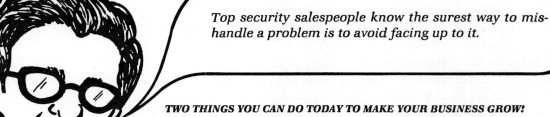

Top security salespeople know the surest way to mishandle a problem is to avoid facing up to it.

TWO THINGS YOU CAN DO TODAY TO MAKE YOUR BUSINESS GROW!

1. *Get out of the office and see "face to face" two affluent businesspeople or professionals and ask them for an order.*
2. *Call a local charity, such as the YMCA or United Way, and volunteer your services as a solicitor. This gives you the opportunity to meet new people and do a civic good deed.*

28

accounts. That is why building the file to large numbers is important. Then the excuse "I don't have anyone to call!" can never be used truthfully. Contact each name in the file at least once a month by phone, by mail, or in person. *Consistent prospect contact builds clients.*

Finding Money, Moving Money, Placing Money

To people who have never sold intangible investments but think they'd like to, the idea of talking to others about money and how to use it to better advantage has great appeal. Possibilities for talking about unlimited earning potential, avoiding ditch-digger callouses and mechanic's grease, and so on, make the salesperson's work seem attractive and somehow easy.

However, experienced purveyors of stock, commodities, bonds, insurance, tax shelters, mutual funds, and other investment products know that getting and keeping a clientele is not easy. The failure rate is high, and a substantial number among those who survive more than three years do not earn attractive incomes.

An important cause of the high failure rate and low earnings is the failure of many in the field to grasp what their job entails. The investment salesperson's job has three main aspects:

1. Finding money
2. Moving money
3. Placing money

Properly understanding these three aspects of the job can help propel you toward the higher earning level you desire.

Finding Money

The first task is finding money—locating the pockets of wealth in the community you serve. (Remember that with the

A wise man once said:
Anyone who stops learning is old, whether this happens at 20 or 80.

TWO THINGS YOU CAN DO TODAY TO MAKE YOUR BUSINESS GROW!

1. *Review all the names in your prospect file. Have you called each or written each within the last 30 days?*
2. *See that all recent names of prospects from ad leads or whatever source are properly placed on prospecting cards in your desk-top file.*

help of the phone, the community you serve can actually be nationwide.) Finding money is a never-ending quest for aggressive, high-income-seeking salespeople. They constantly have to find more and more money from which commissions may flow, to replace dollars that get frozen or flow away. The building of a prospect file, as previously discussed, is the first step in the money-discovery process. The second step is contacting individual prospects to ascertain whether investment dollars are actually available, either in cash-equivalent forms or in other liquid assets. Prospects that have neither cash equivalents or liquid assets may still have the use of money by means of their borrowing power.

The best place to search for money is among the *known* wealthy. Attendees at investment lectures, or direct-mail respondents are sometimes extremely wealthy. People who have acquired wealth through marriage, divorce, or inheritance are fine prospects. Such people may live in areas that seem unpromising, so you must have an eye open and an ear tuned to every individual with whom you come in contact. Money is often discovered where you least expect it. Furthermore, people who *don't* have investment dollars may lead to and influence those who do.

Once you locate money, you must make your strongest effort to move it under your control. Moving money is the objective of all the selling skills discussed in this book. Moving money may require home or office appointments that take hours and hours of your time. Conversely, money sometimes moves quickly by phone, with just a nudge from you, because the prospect has been thinking about moving money and is simply activated by the timeliness of your call.

In order to turn a prospect into a client, the *money must*

Moving Money

move. However, just finding and successfully moving money do not *always* insure sales success in respect to commissions earned. I met a broker once who was not doing well enough although the total capital represented by accounts on his books was over $5 million! He had been successful in finding money and successful in getting the money moved to his firm. Yet all that work and effort was rewarded with very little in the way of commission dollars. One client kept over $1 million in a money-market fund because it was convenient and earned high interest. Nice for the salesmen's firm, but no immediate commission for the salesmen and only the hope that some day some of those dollars might flow to a commission-producing product.

Another of his clients had transferred a portfolio from another firm to his. Here was a $1 million stock account with a $300,000 debit balance. The salesman had worked hard to find this money. He worked even harder to convince the individual to give up allegiance to the other broker and transfer the account. The big sales hook to influence the transfer was one-half-percent lower interest charge on the client's debit balance. What a joyful day for my friend when that account transfer was effected. A million dollar client was his, all due to hard work in prospecting and employing selling skills to cause the money to move.

A year later the salesman had not earned one cent in commissions from this account! The portfolio consisted of stocks, each with an extremely low cost basis—stocks the individual *never intended to sell.* The total dividend income was being used to pay the interest and reduce the debit balance. A good account for his firm because of interest profits the firm might earn, but not a winner for the broker.

It's not enough, then, to find money and make it move. The money must be so positioned as to create a commission flow.

Placing Money

One of the great secrets to selling securities successfully is the concept of money placement. Many salespeople flunk out of the industry because they are simply poor at placing money. After working hard to find and move money, they either lock it up in one-time commission sales or select investments that lose a significant portion of their client's assets, thereby turning off not only future commission flows but referrals as well.

I believe that ambitious securities brokers should concentrate on trying to place the bulk of a client's money in products that will deliver repeat commissions. If the money you find can be made to turn over periodically, each turnover creating a commission, you get an earnings-producing effect denied to our friend above with the virtually useless million-dollar client.

It goes without saying that the client's account should not be churned. Within the bounds of prudence and good money management many opportunities for beneficial changes dictated by the various investment markets as well as by changes in

Top security salespeople know they are not paid for having brains. They're paid for using them!

TWO THINGS YOU CAN DO TODAY TO MAKE YOUR BUSINESS GROW!

1. **Spend 10 minutes with your manager, seeking ideas, new leads, or the right to contact some names from the "kill" file.**

2. **Stop by the Chamber of Commerce to see the manager (you might get his account) and to pick up copies of their free lists of civic-club presidents, and so on.**

client circumstances will arise. These occasions should be utilized. Sometimes, brokers are governed by fears generated by their compliance departments that they fail to recommend appropriate changes; as a result, their clients are not well served.

The same reluctance to suggest changes often causes security salespeople to lock up money in the purchases of mutual funds, utility stocks, long-term bonds, or unit trusts. All of these may or may not be "good" investments, but they reduce the turnover of money to a base trickle, necessitating the finding and moving of *new* accounts in order to earn commissions.

My concept of building success in the securities industry revolves around the development of repeat commission business. Try to place found money into the four categories discussed below: Note that the percentages suggested are for the *total* money under your control, not the money in each individual account. The percentages recommended can be altered to suit the individual salesperson's preferences.

MONEY-PLACEMENT PLAN

Covered call writing: 25 percent. Approximately one-quarter of all the money you can find and influence to follow you should be placed in a covered-call-option-writing program. This placement generates *repeat commission business* from that same money as stocks are sold due to exercises of the calls, as calls expire and new ones are written, as calls are purchased, and as new calls are written at higher or lower strikes or for longer time periods.

Covered call writing is one of the simplest-to-understand option activities and, if properly conducted, is quite often recognized as prudent by investors, brokers, and compliance departments.

Customers to whom you recommend this activity must, of

course, be suited to it and the type to be satisfied with seeking a high annual return. The proper prospect for covered call writing is a percentage-minded securities-oriented, active investor who enjoys following the market and is content not to try to get rich quick.

Experience leads me to suggest the following guidelines for the writing of covered calls:

1. *Recommend the purchase of quality stocks that pay at least 4 percent in annual cash dividends.* Make sure that the dividends have been maintained or increased over the most recent five years and that the outlook for future increases looks good. Clients find it easier to retain their equanimity in falling markets if their unrealized losses are eased with the balm of receiving dividends and premiums. Panic action is lessened by this steady influx of money to the client.

2. *Recommend the writing of the longest-term call possible.* (Sometimes the middle month is acceptable if there's not a respectable differential in time premium of the far month over the middle.) I recommend this practice, first, because writing the far-out call brings in the greatest number of advance premium dollars, which gives more instant stock downside protection while lessening the amount of dollars the client invests in the position. Second, writing far-out calls normally reduces the number of decisions required of the investor, which tends to make the procedure more attractive to the busy, sometimes unavailable investor. Third, writing far-out calls sharply reduces the overall commission dollars in comparison to the commission dollars for a consistent investment practice of writing near calls. Finally, writing far-out calls generally results in fewer completed transactions that must be reported for federal taxation purposes. Consequently, the long-term call writer's transaction recording is simpler and potentially less expensive. These four advantages, to my mind, more than offset any potentially slightly higher annualized gain from writing near-term calls.

3. *Recommend writing out-of-the-money calls.* By establishing for the call written a strike price above the stock purchase price (usually the nearest strike over the stock purchase price), the combination of cash dividends, premiums, and favorable strike price differential increases the potential for profit.

Special situation common stocks: 25 percent. Approximately one quarter of the money you find and influence should be committed to special situation common stocks that investors buy intending to sell at a profit some time after holding them

Good security salespeople spend time and effort preparing their sales presentations to make them effective. They have learned to adhere to the three important rules for successful sales presentations: (1) prepare a good opening; (2) prepare an excellent close; (3) keep the two very close together!

TWO THINGS YOU CAN DO TODAY TO MAKE YOUR BUSINESS GROW!

1. Get approval to take the 144 examination.

2. Read the 144 material so that you can become a "miner" of 144 gold.

longer than one year (the period currently necessary to gain long-term capital gain tax treatment).

Position building for a broker is an important ingredient for success. The security business holds no greater thrill for a broker than building a large (100,000 or more shares) position in a stock, watching it reach a target profit level, and then calling clients and saying those soothing words: "Let's sell now and take a profit!" The clients are served well, and they enjoy the money made, as well as the successful completion of their venture. And the broker has earned a well deserved commission. Funds from the sale can then be put to work in a new special situation. And hopefully so on ad infinitum.

Such common stocks should be well chosen, research-endorsed, and merchandised in a way to build a significant position. The expectation of a future sale at a profit should be built into the sales presentation. When you truly believe in such a stock and are yourself sold on the recommendation, build into your presentation the recommendation of a future purchase at a lower price if the stock goes down for market reasons (as opposed to a fundamental change in the outlook for the company). Averaging down is not always an investment no-no, many times it results in lowering the average cost of a position that later works out.

Special situation stock investors are often itchy, anxious for the expected force to come and move the stock up. If the stock simply remains stable or drops a little, many investors become bored with the insignificant price fluctuation and want a new recommendation. The turnover occurs, and along with it commissions.

Knowledgeable brokers teach their clients not to fall in love with stocks per se, but to understand that they are simply pieces of paper by means of which profits are sought. Teach your clients to understand that changing one piece of paper for another may provide tax benefits, better profit possibilities, lower risk potential, or higher annual income.

In selecting special situation common stocks for position building, the focus should be on low-risk, high-potential situations as opposed to high-risk, high-potential situations. Why? One reason is that no broker really enjoys the commissions earned from clients' losses, especially those derived from the broker's suggestions. The more important reason is that losses, although traumatic events to the broker and client alike—part of the game—reflect the everpresent risk of being "wrong."

Diversification in an individual's account is also important. If no situation represents a large part of an investor's assets, then a single declining stock—even if not sold in time to prevent a major loss—will not greatly affect the overall portfolio.

Clients will stay with a broker year after year and provide a steady stream of commissions if they make a lot of money or make a little money or even *lose* a little money. But they will leave a broker and cut off commissions *if they lose much money.* Investors stay with brokers often because stock trading provides an interest, excitement, a feeling of involvement outside their usual sphere of activity that can last long *as long as the major part of the capital is not lost.* Good brokers avoid high risk. Stock risk cannot always be measured in advance to determine the exact degree of risk to the share buyer. But reasonably accurate downside calculations can be computed for many stocks widely held. Mental (or actual) stop-loss points can also be used as exit points for stocks that fail to move favorably.

Managed money: 25 percent. A third 25 percent or so of the money you find and influence should be placed in managed-money accounts. Guided commodity accounts are a typical depository for a small percent of a *wealthy investor's assets.* A $1 million portfolio might have $50,000 dedicated to a guided commodity program where commodity experts provide a diversified commodity portfolio seeking a high annual return. Guidelines about leverage, stop-loss points, breadth of diversification, and order entry procedure are all provided by the manager. You are free to prospect and find new money instead of being tied to the desk watching pork bellies fry or orange juice get squeezed.

Other managed-money accounts are available for equity investments, for option writing, and for risk arbitrage. Commissions from these accounts flow in whether you are sick or well, on vacation or in the office. Commissions generated on a regular, recurring basis provide some degree or security in a very insecure business.

Typically, a broker who places 20 accounts, averaging $50,000 size, with commodity advisers would normally receive $150,000 to $200,000 in annual gross commissions and normally would obtain pretax earnings of $60,000 to $80,000 *each year* the money stayed in the advisers' hands. The potential for even greater commission flow exists if the assets increase substantially in value. The one-time sale of the idea coupled with on-going commissions is a pleasant conjecture and even more pleasant when realized.

One million dollars placed with professional money managers in a normal call writing program might be expected to provide you $50,000 a year in gross commissions (pretax income approximating $17,500). Before you conclude that commodity managed-money accounts in commodities are so lucrative that you should concentrate your efforts in money placement solely in that area, let me hasten to assure you that the risk associated with commodities makes them much more difficult to obtain. Moreover, there are fewer suitable candidates for managed accounts in commodities than for managed accounts in equities. Generally, the amounts placed in equity managed accounts represent a much greater portion of an investor's assets.

Single commission sales: 25 percent. The fourth quarter of the money you find and can influence should go into a potpourri of single-commission sales that pay a handsome one-time commission and normally result in the money's being locked up in that investment for a long, long time. Such sales are not likely to produce more sales commissions from that same money.

In this category I lump tax shelters, mutual funds, tax-deferred annuities, unit trusts, and long-term bonds (occasionally tax swaps can cause these to turn over). All are good products and certainly play a part in a broker's product mix. They frequently provide additional commission revenue from add-ons or additional purchases, but not from the initial investment dollars.

If you try to build a business on the fourth 25 percent (making it a more dominant factor in your product mix), you will be dependent on constantly finding new clients and new money. If the emphasis is placed on putting money into products that generate repeat business, like those in the first three money placement suggestions, you are likely to remain in the industry and develop into a large producer.

Making a Sale: The 4-Gs Method

In order to sell an investment product, there are four simple steps to master.

Step 1:
Get Someone
to Listen

This, of course, is the step on which most failures or low producers stumble. They don't get enough people each day to listen to their sales pitch. You can't expect to achieve sales success unless you talk about the merits of your investment products to a large number of prospective buyers—either current accounts or new prospects. Without an audience no one can build sales success. If you really want to make it big, be sure each day you get 20 or more people to *listen to you* tell them about an investment idea.

Step 2:
Get Their Interest

Just talking to a large number of prospective buyers each day will not produce substantial sales unless the salesperson gets their interest. The biggest interest-getting device available is the idea of the prospect's potential profit as a possible result of the investment you recommend. The appeal to greed still is the most powerful sales approach, and the one that most often works. Staying within compliance guidelines, point out the profit potential and you will rivet the prospect's attention. Any risk associated with the proposed investment should be presented fully and clearly, but that does not mean you have to

The secret of selling is to show prospects that your product could help them obtain something they really want.

TWO THINGS YOU CAN DO TODAY TO MAKE YOUR BUSINESS GROW!

1. **Select a heavily available muni bond and fill out 10 muni bond mailers to mail to prospects. Be sure to record their names to follow up with phone calls in one week.**

2. **Call 10 clients to sell them about the muni bonds that you are going to suggest to prospects.**

"Tax-free" is a magic phrase!

deemphasize the profit potential. To make the sale, prospects must be made to see sugarplums dancing in front of their eyes.

Prospects who invest hard-earned, retained dollars want to reassure themselves of the correctness of their judgment in making the investment. The reassurance is gained from the salesperson's concise, accurate, enthusiastic presentation of *the facts* about the investment and listing *the benefits* that may accrue to the buyer. Constant repetition of the facts and benefits is usually necessary to make an imprint on the prospect's mind. Give the benefits and facts many times over in a single sales presentation. Follow up by asking the prospect to repeat the salient facts and benefits. Selling is not a one-sided undertaking. Get the prospect involved in the conversation by asking questions and you will be on your way to making sales.

Step 3:
Give Facts and Benefits

No matter how many people listen to an investment idea, get their greed level up, and understand the benefits and facts, *no* commissions are earned unless an order is obtained. Many salespeople do a fine job in advancing through the first three steps to sales success but then trip and fall on the fourth step. Getting the order is the objective, yet many salespeople fail to get orders because they (1) are afraid actually to ask the prospect to buy, (2) they wait for the prospect to voluntarily commit funds, and/or (3) they don't know the many different techniques for asking for orders.

The fear of being told "no" influences many sellers of investments to talk too long or to become repetitious to the point that they actually alienate would-be buyers. The trick is *always* to ask for an order after making sure that the prospect clearly under-

Step 4:
Get the Order

stands the facts and benefits of the proposal. (Asking for an order more than once is a selling fundamental).

In order to accomplish these four steps, you must become a good question asker. Politely asking pertinent questions may open up a prospect who will disgorge reams of information that you can file in your memory bank (and later on the prospect information card) to use in getting the order.

Here are some great questions I have used or seen others use that help loosen the prospect's tongue. Listen carefully to the answers; they will give direction to your sales effort.

SUPER QUESTIONS FOR PROSPECTIVE INVESTORS

1. Can you use *tax-free* income?
2. What stock worries you the most right now?
3. What is your tax bracket?
4. What was the most profitable security investment you ever made?
5. What do you think a really good broker should do for you?
6. Are you satisfied with the return you are getting on your investments?
7. Would you like to pay less in income taxes?
8. Would you like a Standard and Poor Sheet on every stock you *now* own?
9. What are you doing to protect your assets against inflation?
10. Would you like a free portfolio valuation?
11. Would you like to have all of your municipal bonds priced at current market and graded as to quality?
12. How did you get where you are today?
13. When you retire how much do you think you will need each month in *after-tax* dollars?
14. Do you have enough insurance to take care of your loved ones adequately when you die?

Your own ingenuity can add to the above list. The main idea is to learn to ask questions bearing on the needs and wants of the prospect's investment program.

Be a good listener. Prospects' responses will guide you concerning the products they might need and their receptiveness to a proposal. The more you can learn about prospects, the easier it will be for you to sell, and the very best way to learn is to *ask questions!*

Selling Savvy: 6-Way System

One of the more difficult things salespeople have to learn in order to ply their trade successfully is to organize the sales presentation in a logical sequence so that it becomes easy for a buyer to say yes. Selling investments, intangible products that put the client's own savings at risk, requires a subtle approach. It takes careful conceptualization and speech to gain that wanted order. Making your sales presentation conform to the six-part format discussed below can improve your average at getting the buyer to say yes.

Point 1:
Point Out a
Profit Potential

The preceding chapter emphasized trying to get a prospect interested in the offered product. *Nothing* captures interest faster or keeps it at a higher level than the mouth-watering thought of a profit. If the potential gain is large, your prospect's interest focuses sharply on your next comments.

Be sure that you lead off with your big gun in the sales pitch: the possible profit for the prospect. Do not, however, overstate the possibility of gain. To stay in business you must build credibility and live within the boundaries established by compliance departments, regulatory agencies, and simple good business ethics.

Here are some typical interest-generating openers:

ILLUSTRATION 1: COMMON STOCK

"John Prospect?"
"Yes."

"This is Joe Salesman with [the firm]. Our Research Department has just come up with an idea that *might make money for you—maybe as much as 50 percent or more* over the next 12 months. I need just a couple of minutes to tell you why our analyst strongly recommends that this high-quality stock be bought now."

ILLUSTRATION 2: TAX-DEFERRED ANNUITY

"John Prospect?" "Yes." "This is Jill Saleswoman with [the firm]. We have an idea that might make money for you. Many of our clients are now earning over *10 percent annually, free from current income taxes*, without risking a single dollar of principal. You might want to learn what they are doing to legally avoid current taxes while keeping their *savings safe from risk.*

Point 2:
State Three
Essential Facts

Unless you back up your talk about profit potential with some supporting facts, prospects will normally not believe you. They will just dismiss the potential, and you, from their presence and from mind.

In order to soften the direct approach of pointing out the profit potential, it is absolutely necessary to furnish the prospect with at least three incontrovertible pertinent facts to add believability to what you say about the reward potential. These facts must quickly follow your statement of the profit possibility.

ILLUSTRATION 1: COMMON STOCK

"Here are some of the reasons why our analyst likes the stock right now. *The shares at 20 are selling 30 percent below book value* and near the low for the year. *The earnings have been higher each year for the past ten consecutive years. And the dividend has been raised each year for ten consecutive years.*"

ILLUSTRATION 2: TAX-DEFERRED ANNUITY

"Our clients, who hate paying current income taxes as you do, like the fact that they *can earn currently untaxed income, at a high rate [specify the rate] guaranteed for at least one year.* In addition to avoiding current taxes and getting high interest, they love the security of knowing that they can get all or part of their money on demand to meet any sudden need and that they are *guaranteed against loss of principal.* A lot of people today are earning taxable interest at a rate lower than they could earn in currently untaxed interest. They pay more in taxes simply because they are not aware of how to pay less, earn more, yet be absolutely safe."

Good security salespeople know that success comes in can's, failures in can'ts!

TWO THINGS YOU CAN DO TODAY TO MAKE YOUR BUSINESS GROW!
1. *Call the convertible trader for a possible merchandisable idea about a good value or new risk arbitrage opportunity you could sell to suitable investors.*
2. *Call at least 10 people with a convertible arbitrage idea while its fresh and you are enthused.*

Point 3:
Give 2 Primary Benefits

After carefully imprinting on the prospect's mind a few key facts about the product being offered, shift the flow of conversation to the benefits that will accrue to the prospect once the money has been turned over to you. In stressing the benefits strive to speak *slowly, distinctly, forcefully* so that the message really gets across to the prospect.

Remember, *repetition* helps the prospect understand and become convinced! See that the benefits are voiced at least twice in each sales presentation and you will be on your way to more closes.

ILLUSTRATION 1: COMMON STOCK

"Getting the stock at this low level will provide a *real benefit to you* in terms of locking in a *high return on your money of 10 percent* from a dividend that has been increased in each of the last 10 years. Another benefit to you is the *potential low-taxed, long-term capital gain* should the stock reach our analysts' target."

ILLUSTRATION 2: TAX-DEFERRED ANNUITY

"Putting money into this tax-deferred annuity right now provides a real benefit to you in being able to *get a 10-year guarantee* that your money can *never* earn you less than 8 percent a year but *could* earn you more. Another benefit to you is in *not having to have to pay federal or state taxes on your interest earnings* while your money is at work."

Point 4:
Point Out Risk

In selling intangible products it is paramount that you avoid damaging your credibility. To develop repeat commission and a flow of referrals, you must give the prospect confidence in you. Prospects must feel that what you say is honestly presented without omitting any possible negatives. Failing to note any potential risk adequately is a flaw that is most often found in sales presentations made by losers.

Most salespeople mistakenly believe that pointing out risk or disclosing a sales charge will kill the prospect's interest. Nothing could be farther from the truth. A prospect who has been properly educated as to the risks as well as the reward potential is always a more satisfied client. (Such prospects also have little basis for complaints or lawsuits.)

The message should be quite clear: point out all the risk you can foresee under the the *worst imaginable circumstances*. The worst-case possibility can then be softened by restating the potential profit probabilities based on your own or your firm's best guesstimates.

ILLUSTRATION 1: COMMON STOCK

"The risk looks low as the shares are *selling near their lowest price of the last 10 years,* while the per-share earnings are highest in their history. No one can guarantee any stock's future price, but judging from historical price action your downside risk looks minimal if you buy now."

ILLUSTRATION 2: TAX-DEFERRED ANNUITY

"Very few areas are available where you can put your money to work at a high rate of interest, avoid paying current income taxes, yet *run no risk of losing even one dollar of principal.* Yes, you heard me correctly! With a tax-deferred

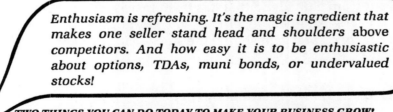

Enthusiasm is refreshing. It's the magic ingredient that makes one seller stand head and shoulders above competitors. And how easy it is to be enthusiastic about options, TDAs, muni bonds, or undervalued stocks!

TWO THINGS YOU CAN DO TODAY TO MAKE YOUR BUSINESS GROW!

1. **See that all of your prospects are on cards in desk file—not on lists in your drawer or file cabinet. Remember, out of sight—out of mind.**

2. **Delete names from your prospect file of the deceased, moved, or just no possibility. A prospect file, to be rewarding, must be filled with real possibilities.**

Good security salespeople talk to their prospects about the prospects' needs, wants, and problems. They don't talk too much, for they know it's what you say that makes a sale, not how much!

TWO THINGS YOU CAN DO TODAY TO MAKE YOUR BUSINESS GROW!

1. **Meet with the leading Cadillac salesmen (maybe you can exchange leads—or get an account). Ask for a copy of their list of late-model Cadillac owners. They have it! Your job to get it.**

2. **Same as above with the Lincoln Continental salesman.**

annuity, your principal is absolutely guaranteed safe against loss by the issuing insurance company."

When investing money, careful investors try to assay the potential risk versus the potential reward. If the foreseeable risks are greatly outweighed by the potential benefits, an order is more easily obtained.

Visually or verbally offer the prospect a comparison, a comparison that *fairly* shows all degrees of risk that might exist and then compares the potential loss to the potential gain. This approach tends to clarify in the prospect's mind the wisdom and prudence of the suggested money placement (assuming, naturally, that the comparison points out a clear case for accepting the risk).

Point 5:
Compare the Benefits
Potential Versus Risk

ILLUSTRATION 1: COMMON STOCK

"When you weigh our *downside risk estimate of approximately 15 percent, based on historical prices, versus the potential gain in value, over the next year or two, of 50 percent or more,* you might want to buy more than 1000 shares. Consider also the fact that you would *be getting 10 percent in annual dividends* versus the *5 percent you are now receiving* on your bank savings."

ILLUSTRATION 2: TAX DEFERRED

"I want to *compare for you the difference,* in your 50-percent tax bracket, in *earning 7¼ percent in taxable interest* on your time deposit *versus earning 7¼ percent in untaxed interest* from a tax-deferred annuity. Using the $20,000 you have available now, in 20 years you would have over $100,000 more, all without undertaking any greater risk."

Point 6:
Ask for the Order

Salespeople dependent upon commissions know that in order to survive and thrive, they must get orders. Skilled sellers of intangibles understand that to get orders, they must ask for the order rather than wait and pray for the prospect to buy. A concept that seems difficult for many people to accept is that most securities and insurance contracts are *sold by the efforts of the sellers*, not passively selected by prospects.

In learning the selling process and in developing and delivering sales presentations according to the system set forth in this chapter, you can perform well in the first five parts and then dissipate the value of your effort by not boldly asking for the order.

Prospects like to be sold! They like being asked to buy, encouraged to make decisions. Don't blow future sales simply because you get cold feet at the very end and lack the courage to ask for an order. A useful technique is to ask for an order several times during a sales presentation. Many sales are closed only after asking the client to buy two or three different times in the same selling interview.

ILLUSTRATION 1: COMMON STOCK

"Now that you have carefully weighed the potential in this stock versus the risk, *do you want to get 2000 shares or 1500 shares*? Keeping in mind the annual yield of 10 percent as well as the gain potential, I would suggest that you acquire 2000 shares. Which quantity is better for you right now while the stock is low?"

ILLUSTRATION 2: TAX-DEFERRED ANNUITY

"Judging from your comments, you clearly understand that your money in this tax-deferred annuity will earn high interest untaxed until you later take it out. Knowing that your money is guaranteed safe and available, would you prefer to transfer $50,000 or $40,000 from your savings to take advantage of the current high rate? Which amount do you think is best for you right now?"

Putting It All Together

Now let's put all six parts of our illustrated sales presentations together and observe the flow, the continuity. The proper

Top security salespeople have learned the value of their time. They segregate their work into two categories: (1) sales activities, (2) nonsales-producing duties. All items in (2) must be done before the selling day begins or after the selling time is over.

TWO THINGS YOU CAN DO TODAY TO MAKE YOUR BUSINESS GROW!

1. **Clean up your desk area! Throw away old, out-dated papers. You will feel better and work better.**
2. **Check your prospect file to see that it contains at least 1000 names and phone numbers on cards. If not, start building that number.**

construction and sequence of a sales presentation greatly improves the possibility of getting the order. Good preparation followed by a good delivery will provide commission dollars (the level of commission dollars determined generally by the number of presentations given). The more you talk about your products to qualified prospects, the greater your opportunity for success.

ILLUSTRATION 1: COMMON STOCK

Broker: "John Prospect?"

Prospect: "Yes."

Broker: [Potential Profit] "This is Joe Salesman with [your firm]. Our Research Department has just come out with an idea that might make money for you, maybe as much as 50 percent or more over the next 12 months. I need just a couple of minutes to tell you why our analyst strongly recommends that this high-quality stock be bought now.

Prospect: "All right. I have a couple of minutes."

Broker: [Facts] "This stock is LRG Corporation. Here are the reasons why our analyst likes the stock right now. The shares at 20 are selling 30 percent below book value. The earnings have been higher each year for the past 10 consecutive years, and the dividend has been raised each year for 10 consecutive years."

Prospect: "That sounds pretty good."

Broker: [Benefits] "It is good, in my opinion. Getting the stock at this low level will provide a real benefit to you in terms of locking in a high return on your money—10 percent—from a dividend that has been increased in each of the last 10 years. Another benefit to you is the potential low-taxed, long-term capital gain should the stock reach our analyst's target."

Prospect: "Look, it sounds okay, but I've heard good stock stories before. What's the risk?"

Broker: [Risk] "The risk looks low to our analyst and to me as the shares are selling near their lowest price of the last 10 years, while the per-share earnings are the highest in their history. No one can guarantee any stock's future price, but judging from historical price action, your downside risk looks minimal if you buy now."

Prospect: "You make it sound very attractive."

Broker: [Comparison of Risk versus Benefits] "It not only sounds good, John, but it is good when you compare our downside risk estimate of 15 percent versus the potential 50 percent or more gain over the next year or two. Consider also the fact that you would be getting 10 percent in annual dividends versus the 5½ percent you are now receiving on your bank savings.

Prospect: "What are the shares selling for now?"

Broker: "The last sale was at $20."

Prospect: "And what did you say the dividend rate was?"

Broker: [Asking for Order] "Two dollars per share annually and paid fifty cents quarterly. I want you to keep in mind the annual yield is 10 percent plus the capital gain potential. Now that you have carefully weighed the potential benefits versus the risk, do you want me to try to get you 2000 shares or 1500 shares while the price is low? What quantity is better for you right now?"

An unknown sage remarked:
"Those who insist upon seeing with perfect clearness before they decide, never decide. Accept life, and you must accept regret."

TWO THINGS YOU CAN DO TODAY TO MAKE YOUR BUSINESS GROW!

1. **Call the Unit Trust Department to find out what secondary units are available at less than 1M. You might be able to sell some to new clients or average down with old customers.**

2. **Check the daily option wire for a good covered call write. Recommend the strategy to at least 5 people.**

48

Top security salespeople have had to learn one of life's most valuable lessons: "Lost money may be recovered but lost time is gone forever!"

TWO THINGS YOU CAN DO TODAY TO MAKE YOUR BUSINESS GROW!

1. *Try to meet with the* Welcome Wagon *or* New Neighbor *hostess in your area. She may become an account and could refer you to lots of people. Try to speak at a monthly luncheon.*

2. *See two attorneys face to face to show them the benefits of an estate security valuation report.*

In the second illustration the product is entirely different, yet the six-part sales presentation is the same. Once you have learned the six-part presentation, you can make it fit any product or service that you have to sell. It takes a little planning and effort, but the payoff is easily measured in commission dollars you can earn.

ILLUSTRATION 2: TAX-DEFERRED ANNUITY

Broker: "John Prospect?"

Prospect: "Yes."

Broker: [Profit Potential] "This is Jill Saleswoman with [your firm]. We have an idea that might make money for you. Maybe a lot of money. Many of our clients are now earning over 10 percent each year free of current income taxes, without risking a single dollar of principal. You might want to learn what they are doing to legally avoid current income taxes while keeping their savings safe from risk. I need just a few minutes to give your the basic information that might help your dollars earn a lot of money for you."

Prospect: "Okay. It sounds interesting but make it quick. I am busy."

Broker: [Facts] "Our clients, who hate paying income taxes like you do, like the fact that they can earn untaxed income at a high rate, guaranteed for one year. They love the security in knowing that they can get all or part of their money on demand. They also like being guaranteed against loss of principal.

Prospect: "I like the thought of not paying current income taxes and being guaranteed against loss. But it really sounds too good to be true. What are you talking about?"

Broker: [Benefits] "I am talking about your putting money to work in a tax-deferred annuity where the benefit to you would be in getting a 10-year guarantee that your money could never earn you less than 8 percent a year but could earn you more. Another benefit to you would be in not having to pay income taxes on your interest earnings while your money is at work."

Prospect: "What is the catch? There must be some risk?"

Broker: [Risk] "You heard me correctly. With tax-deferred annuities your principal is guaranteed absolutely safe against loss by the issuing insurance company. I am sure you know that there are very few investments available where you can put your money to work at a high rate of interest, avoid paying current income taxes, yet run no risk of losing even one dollar of principal."

Prospect: "I like that safe aspect because I have lost plenty of money in speculation. That's why I am out of the market now."

Broker: [Comparison of Risk versus Benefit] "When you compare the difference in earning taxable interest on your money versus earning this percentage of tax-deferred interest, you will want to transfer a significant dollar amount of your savings into a tax-deferred annuity. The dollars you won't pay Uncle Sam can earn thousands of extra dollars for you to spend later, when you need them. This extra benefit is all earned without incurring any risk."

Prospect: "What is the minimum amount I can invest and what sales charge do I have to pay?"

Top security salespeople have learned how to defeat the four biggest time wasters: laziness, procrastination, distraction, impatience. Make up your mind to join the ranks of top producers and conquer these four enemies.

TWO THINGS YOU CAN DO TODAY TO MAKE YOUR BUSINESS GROW!

1. *Send each phone prospect contacted a note (enclose a return info request card).*

2. *Offer a free S&P sheet on every stock owned by any prospect you have solicited for the first time. This service can lead to an appointment or an order, and it also extracts the number of holdings.*

Broker: [Asking for order] "The tax-deferred annuity I am recommending is no-load! That means you do not have to pay anything initially in order to put your money to work. The minimum amount you can purchase is $5,000." Judging from your comments you clearly understand that your money in the tax-deferred annuity will earn high interest untaxed until you later take it out. Knowing that your money is guaranteed safe and always available, would you want to transfer $40,000 or $30,000 from your savings to take advantage of the current high rate? Which amount do you think is best for you right now?"

Closing: How and When

Salespeople who aren't doing as well as they believe they should from the number of sales calls they complete often tell us that they are uncertain about how to close and when to close. Many people selling intangibles really don't understand that to close you have to *ask the prospect to make a decision*. Their selling skill may enable them to outline all the features, give facts, and detail benefits; but unless they actually *ask for an order* they are unlikely to be rewarded by earning a commission.

How to Close

How do you close? Simply ask the prospect a question! Try to phrase the question so that the prospect is presented with a choice of two positive courses of action, either of which could well result in an order. Be sure *never* to ask a question that can be answered "no!"

Here are some "choice-of-two-positives" questions:

1. Would you like to get $20,000 worth of these tax-free municipal bonds on the offering or $15,000? Which quantity is best for you?

2. While the stock is low do you want to enter an order for 1000 shares at $20 or 800 shares?

3. Do you want to place $25,000 in this tax-deferred annuity while we can get you a guaranteed *minimum* interest rate of 9 percent or $20,000? Which amount is best for you??

52

Goethe really understood security salespeople, as evidenced by his observation: "One of the greatest things in this world lies not so much in finding out where we are, but in what direction we are moving." Which way is your production heading?

You always want to make the prospect dwell on the choices you select and choose one.

Never give the prospect the choice between *buying and not buying!* As you can imagine, given that choice, quite often the prospect chooses not to buy. This is the wrong way to ask for a decision: "Do you want to buy 100 shares?" The way the question is phrased leads many prospects to say "no" almost automatically.

When to Close

When to ask for an order? Many sellers of intangibles worry constantly about when they should directly ask the prospect to buy. Should it be at the end of their sales presentation? Should they try to close near the end? In the middle?

Ask for an order as soon as you notice any buying signals. You may ask for the order early in the sales presentation, you may ask for the order in the middle, or you may ask at the *end*. As a matter of fact, in the world of skilled selling you may ask for the order *several times* during the sales presentation, not just once.

Just make sure you do ask for the order!

A good selling skill to develop is being smooth in asking "testing" questions that normally a prospect answers with a yes. Testing questions are what my good friend Lee DuBois, Birmingham, Alabama, calls trial closes. Lee is one of America's top sales trainers and one of its most skilled sellers, too. Trial closes, says Lee are "opinion-asking" questions so phrased that the answers help you determine whether the prospect is ready to be closed. Here are some closing questions to put in your sales arsenal:

1. "In *your opinion* do you feel that investing is *low-risk, high-potential-gain* stocks is in line with your particular objectives?" (If you get anything but a yes answer I will be shocked.)

2. "In your opinion do you feel that investing *without risk* and earning high *untaxed current interest* is in line with your particular objectives?" (Tax-deferred annuities)

3. "In your opinion do you feel that earning *tax-free interest* at a *high rate* is *important to you?*"

When you get that yes answer to a trial close, then follow through and ask for an order. Remember to present the prospect with a choice—a decision to make between two attractive offers. Help the prospect arrive at a decision by repeating facts and benefits.

If the prospect fails to buy when asked to make the decision, just go back and try another trial close, reemphasizing your main sales points.

This process can be reiterated in the same sales presentation. Don't expect the miracle of getting an order every time. It just doesn't work that way in the selling world. What you want to do is improve your batting average by getting *more orders, bigger orders.*

Closing frequently, whether early or late, often will help make your paychecks grow.

Fighting the Word "No!"

Any commission-paid salesperson who makes a real effort *each day* to get orders or appointments from prospects (as well as clients) is going to get a lot of "no's." "No's" are part of a salesperson's life, and you should learn to expect that answer the majority of the time you ask for an order or an appointment.

Many sellers of intangibles quit because the "no's" get under their skin and become unbearable, almost painful. Rather than accept the pain, they tend to lessen their daily potion of "no's" by making fewer calls or trying to substitute other work (such as paperwork or reading) for the gut-wrenching effort involved in asking strangers to do business.

Don't Take "No" as a Personal Rejection

The seller of intangibles, must fully understand that the wealthy prospect is a target, literally besieged with all kinds of sellers trying to get some of the prospect's dollars. Car dealers want the wealthy person to trade frequently, buy second or third cars, give a car as a present. Real-estate sellers always have a wonderful opportunity available, a self-liquidating, tax-saving apartment or shopping center, possibly requiring little or no money down if the prospect assumes all obligations. Sellers of all kinds are after the well-to-do individual, and especially anybody selling anything high in price is hot on the trail of the rich. The very well off are constantly under attack, badgered and besieged from all sides by a myriad of sellers.

"No!" spoken harshly to those solicitors is a potent weapon

to rid oneself of those unwanted, undesired sellers and their pitches. "No!" uttered forcefully, even snidely, does its job well in turning sellers away.

A good salesperson must understand this aspect of a prospect's psychology. The loudly spoken, positively uttered "no!" *is simply a prospect's capital defense.* Prospects who do not say no to over 90 percent of the sales pitches they receive will *soon have no money!*

If you are going to make your living selling intangibles you have got to learn to deal with "no!" Understand that no-saying prospects are not rejecting you personally; they are simply putting a shield around their money. You, of course, will try to penetrate that shield. In order to make your goal attainable, learn to prepare a *counter* for the expected "no." Develop automatic strategy that gets you temporarily by the "no" and leaves you in the game of trying to make a sale.

You Can Fight a "No"

Program yourself to respond to the word "no" by asking a question. If you are convinced that the product or service that you offer is a good value, you can train yourself to respond something like this: "This value looks so attractive for you right now. What are your reasons for saying no?" Get the prospect to respond and disclose objections. Once prospects get into the conversation and voice the reasons for not buying, you may learn what they *do* want (a different product or service) or what additional information you should present to convince them about the proposed transaction.

My premier sales training friend Lee DuBois (the Birmingham, Alabama, patriarch of good salespeople) has taught thousands of attendees at his training sessions to respond to the word "no" with a memorized phrase: "Obviously you have some reason for saying no. Do you mind if I ask what it is?" According to Lee, once the objections are voiced there is a good chance that you can whisk them away by using a couple of other "commit-to-memory" phrases (no one said gaining selling skill was going to be easy!). Sometimes, you can brush objections away with the help of this particular calming comment: "Suppose everything was just the way you want it, and you had money to invest right now."

That lovely phrase is then followed with Lee's trial closing favorite: "Then in your opinion do you feel you would buy this low-risk, high-gain-potential stock that pays a high dividend?" A "yes" to that question is a clear signal to try again for the order.

Persist Past the "No"

To succeed in selling intangibles, you must learn to sell past the first "no," the second "no," and even the third "no!" Stick it out through several "no's" and you'll wind up with orders that the less determined, less skilled sellers miss. You will get orders

A great truth can be learned from top security sales-people in the Confucian age: "He who loses his temper, loses the order."

TWO THINGS YOU CAN DO TODAY TO MAKE YOUR BUSINESS GROW!

1. *Turn your focus on tax-deferred annuities for the entire day. (I assume you are licensed—if not—start today the procedure for getting licensed). Call every client and prospect you can and point out the dynamite features in TDAs that make them needed in every portfolio: no principal risk, high untaxed interest earned (until later withdrawn), ready access to all or part of your money just as if it were in a bank. Set up an appointment for every day next week.*

2. *Learn the features of a particular tax-deferred annuity available for sale in your state. Choose a no-load, disappearing withdrawal charge for easier sales. Be sure you have plenty of brochures to enclose in all outgoing mail for the coming 2 weeks. Each brochure must be accompanied by a return card to be completed by the prospect.*

from strangers, who may develop into long-term, repeat-business clients who are obtained because you understand the client's point of view and the reason for the first "no," as well as the rationale behind asking why. Continuing the selling process by *repetition of facts and benefits* after hearing "No!" makes for many a sale.

Ignore "No"

A second way many skilled salespeople fight the word "no" is to ignore it. They simply act as if they do not hear it. New features, facts, or benefits not given to the prospect initially are brought up as additional ammunition. Even repeated "no's" may be brushed aside by presenting additional evidence to make the prospect ready to buy. Never allow the talk to be one-sided. Continually involve the prospect deeply in the sale by asking questions, trying to elicit opinions from which you can glean an opening to drive home a key point that could lead to the order.

Telling Stock Buyers What They Want to Know

Salespeople working for brokerage firms should, after careful research and approval from research and compliance departments, try to build positions in favored stocks. Too often I have seen account executives spin their wheels, wasting time researching and recommending stocks that for one reason or another were not suitable for developing into a large position. This bring's me to LeRoy's maxim: "If it isn't good enough to build a big position, it isn't good enough."

With proper guidance and a good understanding of investor desires, stock-oriented salespeople can become tremendous producers with a reservoir of repeat commission clients.

In order to sell as much as you can, as quickly as you can, to as many people as you can—that is every salesman's objective—it is important to understand what turns people on to a common stock. You must know what investors everywhere want to know before purchasing a stock.

Beware of Common Turn-Offs

Many would-be big producers never make it because they sell the wrong features of the investment. They may be right on their judgment of value in the stock, but they fail in getting enough people to go along with their opinion. Some account executives are so steeped in knowledge about their chosen company that they flood the prospect with trivial information, but instead of making the sale, they *lose it*.

Others use brokerage jargon that confuses uninformed in-

Top security salespeople stay tops because: (1) they welcome responsibility and (2) seek help when they need it. Are you working at becoming a top *security salesperson*?

TWO THINGS YOU CAN DO TODAY TO MAKE YOUR BUSINESS GROW!

1. **Check the broad tape for any news causing sharp ups or downs in stock positions recorded in your cross reference. If quickly communicated, the news might produce more business—either add-on buys or sells.**

2. **See that your cross reference is up to date! This is a gold mine; don't fail to keep it current.**

vestors and bores sophisticated ones. By jargon I mean terms like *debt/equity ratio, P/E ratio, capital structure, outstanding shares, fully diluted earnings,* and so on. All high-falutin' terms designed to impress rather than sell.

Still other brokers try the ouiji board approach, featuring the technical position of the shares. They try to overwhelm prospects with words like *pennant formation, rounding bottom, head and shoulders, resistance level, support level,* and *long base.*

Once in a board room I overheard a broker talking excitedly to a prospect. The conversation went like this:

Broker: "Mr. Jones, you really ought to buy some shares now, at the market! It's just had a break-out from a long base!"

Prospect: "Huh?"

Read the broker's pitch again. Do the words, no matter how enthusiastically uttered, make much sense to the average investor? Are they a turn-on to anyone, except perhaps a very limited few who will risk their capital without knowing or caring about fundamental things like earnings and dividends? The broker may have selected a winner, but the chances of using that selection to make this sale were nil. He completely failed to understand certain selling techniques that would have enabled him to build a following for his idea.

I observed that broker as he breathed his excitement over the phone. He extended one arm horizontally outward and upward in a swoop, to help clarify his exclamation, "It's just had a break-out from a long base!" The only problem with that emphatic gesture was that there was no picture phone, and the prospect *didn't* get the message. Are you sending out messages neither seen nor understood by your prospects?

Investors everywhere want to know three simple, basic things before buying a common stock. Let's examine them one by one.

PROFIT POTENTIAL

What's in it for the investor? *That's* what an investor wants to know most of all. The broker earns an immediate commission from the share purchase, but the client wants to have a target profit possibility pinpointed. The temptation offered the prospect of having more money later gets investors in the state of mind to spend dollars now on a recommended stock. If you want to make more sales to more people, zero in on the profit potential to them (estimated from analysts' projected targets.)

Don't overstate the potential, for that can lead to lawsuits and compliance problems. But within prudent guidelines, ensure that prospects understand the earnings potential of the capital they are thinking about investing.

TIME PERIOD FOR EXPECTED PROFIT

Setting a time period for the expected profit is important to encouraging the investment. The profit prospect may look good for doubling a client's money, but if the time period for the estimated doubling is 50 years, no sale is going to result! If the estimated time period for the potential value increase is one, two, or three years, the prospect can imagine its happening and can anticipate being around to collect if the payoff is realized. When pitching a common stock to a prospect, be sure to set a target price and a target time frame. You will sell more to more.

RISK ESTIMATE

One sure way to lose the clients that your hard work has obtained is to fail to point out the risk being undertaken. Clients can accept losses and still be clients—commission givers—as long as they have been properly alerted to any and all risk *prior to entering into the investment.*

Good salespeople seeking to build long-term relationships make an appeal to the profit motive, of course. But just as surely, they adequately alert clients to the risk undertaken. The opportunity then exists for the client to compare the risk estimate against the hoped-for profit. After comparing and relating to the time period recommended as the holding period, the client can fairly quickly form a judgment on the investment.

Think about these three things I've said clients want to know, and ask yourself if those aren't really the important things that you would want to know before investing your money in a common stock.

Top security salespeople are sincere to all. They know even the tough ones will do business with this approach.

If you zero in on these three fundamental desires, you will make more sales and make them quicker. Your stock position building will grow, and so will your income.

The following illustration of a typical stock solicitation between broker and existing client can easily be slightly modified to a broker/prospect scenario. Note carefully the absence of trivial information and the accent on the three things all stock buyers want to know.

Broker: "Let me speak to Ann Client right away please."

Client: "Ann Client speaking."

Broker: "Ann, this is Joe Salesman. We have just now received a research report on ZXY Company, a company that I am really excited about. The stock is rated A-plus. Our analyst believes if you buy now there is an excellent opportunity for you to make 50 percent or more from the current level of about 17."

Client: "That sounds good."

Broker: "Not only does the potential profit look great but the analyst thinks a price rise could take place within 18 months. The shares are depressed, along with the market, and are selling below book value."

Client: "Does it pay any dividends?"

Broker: "Not only does it pay dividends, but it has raised its dividend every year for the last ten. The current yield is 7.2 percent. In addition to getting a good return on your money while waiting for a profit, we believe if you buy now at the 17 level you won't be running a great risk. The lowest price the shares have sold in the last ten years is 15½, and that low was reached at the bottom of a bear market when the earnings and dividends were lower than they are today."

Client: "That sounds like my kind of stock. Send me the report."

Broker: "I'll put the report in the mail today. The problem is that opportunities sometimes get away from you, as others quickly recognize the bargain value. This looks so attractive that you ought to get some today while the price is low. After you receive the report and read it, you might want to buy more if it is still available near today's price."

Client: "You really think it might move that quickly?"

Broker: "Look, Ann, this report is just out. A lot of brokers like me are going to recommend it. Other firms may also be attracted on their own or because our analyst has spotlighted the value. Maybe it will be the same price when you get the report, and maybe it won't. There are no guarantees in common stocks. Why don't you try to buy 500 or 1000 shares at the last price? I don't want you to miss out completely on this opportunity while you're waiting for the mail. Which quantity is right for you now, 500 or 1000?"

Client: "Okay, see if you can buy me 500 at the last price. If it starts to move or pick up volume just buy at the market."

Getting the Order:
4 Kinds of Helpful Evidence

In trying to persuade prospects to commit money to the offered product or service, skilled salespeople bring in all the evidence they can muster. Yet the sellers of intangibles face peculiar problems when presenting a specific type of evidence. Their problems are different from those facing sellers of autos, houses, boats, typewriters, television sets, and the like. Yet if the evidence is strong and logically presented, more orders will result.

Evidence comes in several varieties. For the seller of intangibles, some types of evidence are more effective than others. These are the main types of evidence that can bring the prospective buyer of an intangible to a successful close.

1. Samples of the products
2. Anecdotes about users of the products
3. Statistics
4. Endorsements from third parties

Samples of the Products

Sellers of tangible products get terrific mileage from demonstrating their product to prospects. They want prospects to get their senses involved. The smell of new leather, the feel of seating comfort, the beauty of a paint job, the sound, the look and feel of fabric all are artfully presented to make prospects want the offered item more than they want to hold onto their money. Demonstrating investment products is not so easy, but it can be done.

If you can involve prospects in using their senses, even intangibles become more "real" and thus more likely to interest prospects.

When I was a broker trying to establish a large position in a common stock, I would contact the company and ask for samples or miniatures of products they made or sold. I used these in demonstrations to my prospects. Most companies are extremely cooperative; after all, they want to acquire more shareowners.

At one point Cooper Tire and Rubber company shares looked very good. Our analyst loved the company, earnings were good, and the dividend yield was high. But I was having difficulty in getting investors to purchase shares because the name Cooper was just not as familiar as General Tire, Goodrich, and Goodyear. I called the company and asked the public relations people to send me a cross-section of a belted bias tire, at that time a hot item in the replacement tire market. Familiar as I was with Cooper's financial data, I wouldn't have known a belted bias tire if I'd tripped over one!

A few weeks after my call, a truck pulled up to the front of the office and the driver entered, announcing, "I have a delivery for Mr. Gross!"

The receptionist pointed me out, and the driver asked, "Where do you want it?"

I pointed to a spot near my desk. He went out and came back rolling a dolly holding a huge, six-foot-high wooden crate! He rolled this monster off the dolly, placed it on the floor near my desk, got his receipt, and was on his way, leaving me to struggle with my "demonstrator." With the help of a chisel, a hammer, and three friends, I was able to uncrate it and view my lovely piece of evidence.

There it was! A life-size new tire mounted on a wooden

Good security salespeople are well aware that the adage "Buy low—sell high" is the secret to stock-market success. Never in recent market history has it been so easy to aid clients and prospects in achieving the first half of the success formula.

TWO THINGS YOU CAN DO TODAY TO MAKE YOUR BUSINESS GROW!

1. *Assess your personal appearance. Is your hair neat? Are clothes cleaned and pressed, not frayed or badly worn? Do you look conservative?*

2. *Get the current tax table. Ask each client or prospect their tax bracket; tell them that this info can be of help in deciding to transfer to muni investments or from mini investments.*

Top security salespeople have learned to be concerned about clients rather than competitors. Competitors don't give orders, clients do!

TWO THINGS YOU CAN DO TODAY TO MAKE YOUR BUSINESS GROW!

1. *Review all of your month-end statements for accuracy of positions.*
2. *Call everyone who has an odd-lot position to round out if possible, or sell to consolidate. Upgrade holdings to higher quality and to those recommended by research.*

display emblazoned with the Cooper name! The top part of the tire was cut away to show different colored belts, each clearly labeled and self explanatory.

What a piece of evidence! You could see it! Touch it! Smell the new rubber smell! At a glance you could understand what the company made and how the tires were constructed.

With some rearranging I was able to keep that display near my desk. As prospects and clients came to my office for appointments, they would look at this awesome piece of evidence—feel it—sniff it—look at the various colored belts. When I then told them the financial data about Cooper, they bought the shares, for they had gained an immediate understanding of belted bias tires and the replacement market. The product sample helped get orders that words or fact sheets alone could not.

Showing a product sample has subsequently been used to market hundreds of thousands of shares of different stocks.

Think about how a piece of evidence relating to the intangibles you sell—evvidence that can be felt, tasted, heard, smelled, or seen. Product samples are one of the most powerful forms of evidence and should be used at every opportunity in trying to make a sale.

User stories are another powerful form of evidence put to work by sellers in all fields. Telling true stories about how others have benefited from a particular product goes a long way toward convincing new prospects to buy. Buyers everywhere want to know that others have bought, used, and are satisfied with a product they are considering. Buyers are usually aware that there are dissatisfied owners of the suggested product, but the reassurance of hearing about the good experiences of others is often the evidence necessary to close the sale.

Anecdotes about Users of the Products

Brokers featuring stocks will benefit any time they can relate user stories about investors who bought ZYX when it was low and are now sitting on a handsome profit. Or they do well to point out an analyst's past recommendations that brought success to those who followed the advice.

The seller of tax shelters should gather a collection of user stories built around dollars saved for particular clients and potential profit possibilities retained. Prominent sports figures and other nationally known investors who committed some of their funds to these investments are often mentioned in magazines. Local buyers often give permission for their stories to be used.

Sellers of insurance should store up a supply of user stories, such as those about people who bought policies providing certain policy benefits that were later paid as promised. People who are being encouraged to buy an intangible need, want, and love the support of user stories. The stories are pieces of evidence that make sales presentations more credible.

WARNING:

User stories properly presented build sales, but false user stories lead to loss of credibility, order cancellations, even law suits. Make sure any user story you relate is accurate, true, and supportable. Equally important is adequate stress on any risk of loss. Selling fairly is the only mode to pursue in building a quality, long-lasting business.

STATISTICS

As long as people have been selling, statistics in one form or another have been a highly favored type of evidence. Statistics are the chief weapon in the arsenal of the seller of intangibles.

Top security salespeople know that a Saturday morning session is necessary to get caught up with reading and selling ideas after a busy week.

Top security salespeople have learned to do what they can with what they have in their particular location. They know that business is available if they work hard enough.

TWO THINGS YOU CAN DO TODAY TO MAKE YOUR BUSINESS GROW!

1. Put all tax shelter information into a 3-ring binder to serve as a reference.

2. Make a face-to-face visit to two accountants with your binder. Point out the benefits and features of a coming tax shelter. They may refer you some of their clients.

By themselves, statistics can be boring, meaningless, and actually counterproductive. If you jam too great a volume of numbers into the prospect, a turn-off is the most likely result.

To be effective, pertinent statistics must be separated from nonpertinent surrounding masses of data. The statistics you show to a prospect must be easily understood, clear to the ear or eye. If you are using printed data, make sure they appear in bold, easy-to-read numbers.

Charts, fact sheets, income statements, balance-sheets, earnings, dividends, hypothetical proposals, and past results are all statistical evidence available to help you in your search for that "yes" answer to a proposal. Colorful, large, clear illustrations bearing on a single point are usually the most effective.

Used in conjunction with the other selling-skill techniques, statistics help make sales come easier, but don't become so statistic-conscious that you deliver numbers and facts machine-gun fashion to the point that little actually gets through to the prospect. Under these conditions, what does get through is often negatively received.

Keep statistics simple and few in number. Use them judiciously to spice up your presentation. Use statistics to quantify *the benefits* and *respond to the needs and desires of your prospects* so that the prospect can justify spending money.

When you are presenting statistics for the prospect to read, make sure they meet the following conditions:

1. Bold, easy-to-read type
2. Color contrasts
3. Spotlights on single statistics
4. Simple to understand
5. Relevant to the product being offered

When you are telling the prospect statistical evidence, make sure it meets the following conditions:

1. Clear and easy to understand
2. Concise (brevity makes for a more receptive client)
3. Relevant to the product
4. Narrowly focused on a specific topic or feature
5. Stated slowly and forcefully

Endorsements from Third Parties

The endorsement of a product by some third party, preferably a person or source well known to the prospect, is powerful evidence.

The third-party endorsement is often a written testimonial by a happy user or a favorable article by a writer in a prestigious magazine or newspaper. Evidence of this type usually stresses all key points and advantages (sometimes the disadvantages) of the proposed investment. Messages of this kind usually get across to prospects.

Keep a three-ring binder with tab dividers for the various products that provide your commission revenue. Whenever you receive written testimonials and are given permission to use them by the writers, copy them and file them in the binder. Favorable articles about a product are reinforcement for your suggestions for the prospect's money.

You can let prospects take a ring binder home to read. Or they can go over the endorsements in your office. Either way, written endorsements immerse prospects deeper into the product, and that is a positive step.

Top security salespeople make sales because their presentations are based on facts, not fancy. They know their "story" well. They can anticipate questions and have ready answers that will satisfy the prospect.

TWO THINGS YOU CAN DO TODAY TO MAKE YOUR BUSINESS GROW!

1. Before you leave the office, log 30 people you are going to try to call tomorrow (clients/prospects) with a special idea.

2. Before you leave the office, complete a product inventory worksheet so that you are prepared for tomorrow's selling effort.

Closing: 9 Techniques That Work

"Sale closed!" That phrase brings a smile to any salesperson's face. The hard work of prospecting, presenting, and finally getting an order is over for the moment, a time of respite before beginning another sales attempt. A commission successfully earned is an inspiration to go out and seek more business.

Rarely do salespeople analyze how the close was obtained. For skilled salespeople, closes are similar to the physical reflex actions of well-trained athletes. Skilled sellers act and react to prospects' responses and objections, parrying, countering automatically, giving barely a conscious thought to following a specific procedure. Such professionals are fine tuned, thoroughly conditioned from the experience of giving thousands of sales presentations. They "know" what to do in various selling situations but most would be unable to articulate their own closing techniques.

Unskilled salespeople, those who get orders occasionally, sufficient only to survive but not thrive, consider any closes to have been pure luck! The low producers don't accept that they use skill in getting the order. Most of them do not really believe that they can "get better" and really *acquire* selling skills. They, like many of their supervisors, believe good salespeople are born, not made.

The key to sales success is in developing the skills common to sellers. Such techniques may be acquired in classes taught by accomplished sales trainers. Such skills are whetted by role-playing with coworkers. Books, training tapes, slides, and movies devoted to the art of selling all can help make salespeople better at that crucial skill, closing—*getting the order!*

Nine ways a seller of intangibles can close are discussed in this chapter. These nine are simply the most widely known, commonly used closing techniques. Others exist, and still others will someday be invented. But the punch in these nine can enable you to earn an above-average living every working year.

Close Technique 1: The Future Close

Face to face with a single prospect or a couple, the future close can be very effective, but it should be used only after you have gained substantial information from the prospect through a series of polite but probing questions. These questions must inform you not only about what the prospect hopes the money invested will do but what the prospect requires the money invested to do.

One of my favorite probing questions is phrased like this: "If I gave you an investment idea today about a low-risk, high-potential-gain situation and you made $20,000 after taxes by accepting my idea, what would you do with that lovely extra money?"

That question accomplishes several things. First, it plants the idea in the prospect's mind that the seller may possess some wonderful idea that just might make money. Second, it makes the prospect consider what luxuries or additional financial security might be attainable with profits earned from an investment.

The future close uses to advantage the answers a prospect gives. All you have to do is listen carefully to the response. Here are the steps in making a future close:

1. Get prospects to picture themselves in the future enjoying the results of an investment made under your guidance.
2. Point out to prospects their need or desire for the profit.
3. Close with a question such as, "Isn't that what you really want your money to do for you?"
4. Repeat key benefits.
5. Ask for an order.

The future close may come into better perspective for you as you read the following sales scenario. Assume that the prospect is a young businessman in his late thirties. Assume also that all the facts, benefits, and risk have been pointed out to the prospect and the seller is preparing to future close. The seller has asked what the prospect would do if the prospect made $20,000 after taxes from a low-risk, high-potential-gain stock that was being strongly recommended.

After an appropriate pause, the answer was, "I'd buy a late-model Mercedes, steel gray, with a sunroof and red leather interior." (In working the future close, it is important to let prospects describe fully and enthusiastically what they want profit dollars to buy.

70

Good stockbrokers have learned that the market is the best teacher of humility. They know to weigh each profit potential carefully while keeping a wary eye focused on the risk.

Broker: "I can just *see you* right now driving along the beach on a beautiful sunny day in your steel-gray Mercedes, with the sunroof open, saying to that beautiful lady by your side, 'Honey, did you know that I bought this car with the profit I made on 2000 shares of XYZ?' I can even see the admiration in her eyes as she leans back into the plush red, leather upholstery and says, 'Wow!' "

Prospect: (dreamily) "Umm! That would sure be great!"

Broker: "Isn't that what you really want? A luxury car paid for with stock-market profits? Profits earned from a low-risk stock?"

Prospect: "That's what I want all right."

Broker: "I truly think there is a real possibility of your getting what you want if you get 2000 XYZ shares while they are at this low point and hold them for the potential gain that our analyst foresees. With the low risk we believe exists you might want to get 3000 shares, especially considering the high dividend yield that you would be receiving while waiting for this potential gain. Which quantity do you think is right for you now, 2000 shares or 3000 shares?

Prospect: "I'll take 3000 shares. I might want a stereo tape-deck too!"

Of course, in the real world prospects don't just roll over and hand their money over to a seller. But prospects can be sold and are sold, by salespeople who use various techniques. The future close is one of those techniques. Try it out on carefully chosen prospects and watch it work for you.

A future close might be employed with a product like a tax-deferred annuity. Assume that the salesperson is talking to a married couple about moving bank savings into a tax-deferred annuity to build a bigger retirement fund.

Salesperson: "I have pointed out to you the really great advantages of putting your money to work into a tax-deferred annuity. By your remarks I can tell that you understand clearly that you will not pay any current income tax on the interest your money earns for you each year. You also know that you can withdraw part or all of your money any time you want prior to beginning to receive lifetime monthly checks. While your money is working for you, your principal is guaranteed safe and will grow fast and untaxed until you take it out later."

Mrs. Green: "I really do like the features that we can take some money out if necessary, and not pay any tax until our original capital has been withdrawn. I just hate to pay the government taxes every year on the interest our money earns."

Salesperson: "That is an attractive feature. The real plus is that in 16 years when you are ready to retire, at the current rate of interest your money will be approximately four times what it is today. That's a big enough sum to let you draw a large monthly check each month for the rest of your lives!"

Mrs. Green: "That sounds pretty good. I like the thought of large monthly checks coming in forever."

Salesperson: "I can just see the two of you in sunny Florida in your beautiful condominium enjoying the good life. I can picture Mrs. Green going out to the mailbox the first of each month and coming back to the apartment with an envelope saying, 'Honey, our check has arrived from XYZ Life.' Isn't that what you both really want? A happy carefree retirement in a warm climate, with a check each month

Top security salespeople who develop business through lectures have learned: "Nothing can be said after 40 minutes that means anything."

TWO THINGS YOU CAN DO TODAY TO MAKE YOUR BUSINESS GROW!

1. *Call every client with a losing position. Discuss the situation. Add on, if favorable; transfer to something else, if not. You must talk to "losers" or you will lose them.*

2. *Ask 10 clients for 3 referrals to be placed on your mailing list for 4 weeks (no charge).*

72

Good security salespeople realize that success comes from hard work involving (1) good record-keeping; (2) daily prospecting; (3) order-asking conversations; and (4) increased product knowledge. "Prepare yourself the night before for the coming day and you will do business—bigger and better."

TWO THINGS YOU CAN DO TODAY TO MAKE YOUR BUSINESS GROW!

1. *Set aside a two-hour period every week (same time) to scan ValueLine, Wall Street Transcript, Barrons. You may get an idea that will enthuse you.*

2. *Visit your local library. Skim a book listed under "Sales." to sell more, you constantly have to work on improving your selling skills.*

the rest of your life. Money that you cannot outlive! Many people aren't worried about dying, but they *do* worry about living too long and not having enough money to get along on in this inflationary world."

Mr. Green: "*That is our goal:* retirement with an assured income to supplement our Social Security and pension benefit."

Salesperson: "Since there is *no initial sales cost* to buy this tax-deferred annuity, you might want to put $40,000 of the $50,000 you have, which is now earning you taxable interest, to work right away, earning untaxed interest at a high rate until you are ready to take it out. Or maybe you want to put it all in right now while the interest rate paid you is high. Which amount would be your choice, $40,000 or $50,000?"

In the foregoing scenario the seller tries to get the couple dreaming, picturing themselves in their ideal retirement spot, enjoying the results of the earnings on their money placed in the tax-deferred annuity.

The scenarios and variations are limitless. Carefully choose prospects who can enter into imagining a future benefit; they are the most suited for a future close. Once having decided to close this way, make a strong effort to get them into a mood to dream.

Close Technique 2:
The Comparison Close

People are conditioned all their lives to compare things in order to determine values. Sellers of intangible investments should use this natural trait to help make sales.

The *comparison close* is quite simple in concept and in execution. Here are its key points:

1. State the facts and benefits of two different investment alternatives.

2. Weigh the risk versus the reward potential in each for the prospect.

3. Close with a question that gives the prospect a *choice between two positives where the choice of either results in an order.*

Let's suppose you are a broker trying to get a prospect to buy shares of common stock. The conversation might go like this:

Broker: "Our Research Department has come up with two excellent stock ideas that might make money for you."

Prospect: "What are they?"

Broker: "One is a high-technology company selling at about $25. They have a new product that should revolutionize the industry. The earnings could double in the next two years, and we believe the shares could go from 25 to possibly 50 or higher. The risk always exists that the product may not function as well or sell as well as expected. The dividend yield is only 2 percent. It's what we call high risk, high potential. Right for aggressive investors."

Prospect: "That sounds interesting to me. What's the other stock they like?"

Broker: "The other company is a special situation. The shares are selling 25 percent below book value, now about $20 per share. The current yield is 8 percent from a well-covered dividend, and we think the earnings will rise substantially because they have a big backlog of orders and because of the improving economy. It's also stock in the kind of corporation that is often referred to as a "takeover" candidate. Only 5 million shares are outstanding. This appears to be a low-risk, high-potential-gain situation that also provides good current income. Many conservative clients like this type of stock. The risk is that the economy may slacken and their backlog of orders get reduced due to cancellations."

Prospect: "That sounds good also. Which do you like better of the two?"

Broker: "You know your situation, your makeup, and how much risk you can take, as well as how you handle losses. Comparing the two, the high-technology company has greater gain potential *if* the investing public becomes enamoured of their product and the potential for great growth. It also has greater risk. The dividend is low, and so is the book value. The second company should hold its value better in a slowing economy. It

Top security salespeople merchandise one product or idea each month in quantity to clients and prospects. They learn the product or idea thoroughly and then present it with enthusiasm, confidence, and sincerity.

TWO THINGS YOU CAN DO TODAY TO MAKE YOUR BUSINESS GROW!

1. *Schedule 2 to 4 appointments for Saturday morning at your office.*

2. *Pray for rain on Saturday so that appointments will not cancel out to do more entertaining things.*

offers good upside gain potential, and the high dividend should be a help in slowing any price drop due to a general market decline. Based on your knowledge of yourself, which do *you* think is best for you right now? The high-potential, high-risk technology company, or the low-risk, high-gain-potential, high-yield special situation? They both look good right now."

Prospect: "I like the special situation stock."

Broker: "Do you want me to try to buy you 1000 shares at 20 or 800? Which quantity do you think is right for you now?"

Prospect: "Get me 800 shares for now."

When you are building for a comparison close, provide a *choice between different degrees of risk* and between different estimated gain potentials. Although you might think the more conservative alternative is more frequently chosen with the comparison close, that's not necessarily the case. The ultimate choice depends on the state of the market (bull markets create a speculative impulse in even the most conservative investor) and the prospect's personal attitude toward risk.

The attraction of the comparison close is that you present a choice to prospects and let them determine the degree of risk they want to assume.

Close Technique 3: The Small

The small-matter close is a simple close. The seller focuses the prospect's attention on some small matter, easy for the prospect to understand and use as a basis for choosing the investment. The small-matter close differs from the comparison close in that only a single investment selection is presented. The prospect is still offered a choice, but the choice centers on some not too significant detail of the sale. The key to the small-matter close is to divert the prospect's attention from the big decision of whether or not to purchase by focusing the decision process on the handling of some little matter.

To make this close effective in a high percentage of attempts, assume an attitude that conveys the message, "I know you are going to say yes. You know you are going to say yes. What we must resolve is this small matter concerning the delivery." The prospect will pick up on your confident attitude about the worthiness of the recommendation, and the emotions of fear and doubt will be dispelled, attention placed where *you* want it.

The small-matter close involves these steps:

1. Focusing the prospect's attention on some simple part of the transaction
2. Presenting the prospect with a choice of ways to handle the simple detail
3. Formulating a question the answer to which provides an order

Assume the following situation. The broker is trying to get a middle-aged prospect to buy 1000 shares of a low-risk, high-quality common stock that provides a high income from a well-covered dividend. The facts and benefits have been presented and reiterated so that the prospect clearly understands all aspects of this proposal.

Broker: "I am sure, like you are, that your investments should be in low-risk, high-quality, high-income stocks like American Telephone, stocks that offer gain potential and some prospect of increased income. Buying 1000 shares now while the market price is low seems prudent for a conservative investor like you."

Prospect: "I am conservative, all right. Safety and high income now, and more in the future is what I need."

Broker: "What you need to do is decide how you would want that 1000 shares registered. Would you want them in your name? Or would you prefer to register them in joint name with your wife?"

Prospect: "I hadn't really thought about that. You better make it joint like our other stocks. Otherwise she [wink!] might really get angry at me."

Broker: "Okay, would you want us to keep the stock here or send it to you?"

Prospect: "Send it to me and I'll put it in the box with my other certificates."

Broker: "I'll do that, and I'm really glad you chose the high-quality, high-income recommendations. At this point, investing conservatively is the right approach for you."

There are a number of other small-matter closing questions you can use. The main point is to have them prepared ahead of

There are three basic requirements for success in selling securities—Intelligence, product knowledge and persistence. Any one of them can make you successful as long as it is persistence!

TWO THINGS YOU CAN DO TODAY TO MAKE YOUR BUSINESS GROW!

1. *Set up a file of approved prospecting letters—for tax shelters, muni bonds, tax-deferred annuities, DWR individual account management, referral, unit trusts, U.S. government securities.*

2. *Test one letter today by mailing to at least 10 prospects and following up with a phone call. Log the results when you know them.*

time and use them! Keep prospect's attention away from the big decision—to buy or not to buy—by having them concentrate on settling some small matter, and you'll be on your way to more closes.

Close Technique 4: The Balancing Close

Many times when a salesperson is in hot pursuit of a prospect, the prospect manages to wriggle away from the pressure being applied by employing a time-tested defensive weapon: "I'd like to think it over." Typically, when sellers hear this oft-uttered phrase, they ease up and back off. Sellers tend to fear that if they continue to apply pressure, the "I'd like to think it over" will turn into a definite, resounding "no!" The salesperson all too often thinks, "I'll ease off and call next week!"

The prospect escapes for the moment and may devise a way to prevent the salesperson from making contact again. Of course the possibility exists that "I would like to think it over" is the simple truth; the prospect may just want more time. But more often than not, "I would like to think it over" is a device to put off the seller for the moment *and* for good.

The *balancing close* (often called the Ben Franklin close) is meant for those times when you hear those words of postponement, "I want to think it over." The balancing close can help you convert a "I-want-to-think-it-over" postponement into a sale right now. Here are the key points of the technique:

1. State any reasons the prospect has given for wanting to delay making the investment.

2. List several reasons that warrant the prospect's making a decision immediately.

3. Carefully restate the facts and benefits of the proposed investment.

4. Close with a question like the following: "Which is more likely to make you money [or save a cost], buying now while the price is low and attractive, or delaying and possibly missing out on this opportunity?"

The balancing close is a very difficult close to master. Even the most skilled sellers find it tough to change an "I want to think it over" into an immediate sale. Although it is tough to effectuate a close in this situation, don't stop trying! Think of the balancing close as simply another tool to use when the occasion arises. The more tools you have and the more practiced you become at selling skills, the higher your income will be.

Assume that a broker is trying to get a prospect to purchase 500 shares of a new issue of an A+ electric utility. The shares yield 10 percent at the offering price of $18. The buyer of the new issue shares will not have to pay a direct commission as the cost is borne by the share seller. Tune in on the conversation.

Broker: "This is an excellent opportunity for you to buy A+-rated (and that's the highest possible rating Standard and Poor gives!) ZYX shares and not pay any direct commission. The dividend has been raised every year for the past 10 years, and future prospects for more increases look good. Considering the fact that your annual yield will be 10 percent, plus a capital-gain potential, you ought to be considering not 500 shares but 1000 shares."

Prospect: "That does sound good, but I want to think it over. The market looks weak and interest rates may move higher."

Broker: "I understand how you feel in wanting to think it over before investing your money. Before you do, let's review your reasons for wanting to take more time. First, the market looks weak now and, second, the possibility of higher interest rates concerns you. Against the concerns let's look at the reasons for buying right now. First, you can avoid paying a direct commission. Second, you are buying shares near the lowest price of the past 10 years. Third, interest rates could go down, forcing your shares up in price. And fourth, the market always fluctuates; it can be weak one day and strong the next. Determining the future won't be any easier later on.

"The important considerations are that you are buying high quality at a low price and you do not have to pay a commission directly. When you balance your reasons for delaying against the opportunity available right now, you might want me to try to get you more than 500 shares at the commission-free price of $20.

"You might think it over until next week, and then decide to buy and have to pay a commission, plus possibly a higher price per share. Which really makes better sense, buying now and avoiding commission costs or trying to guess what may happen to the market or interest rates next week and having to pay the sales cost and maybe a higher price for the shares as well."

Prospect: "Okay, get me 500 shares at 18, but no commission better be charged!"

No guarantee of success comes with a balancing close (nor with any close, for that matter), but the balancing close does give you a second chance to go after an order that is slipping at least temporarily out of reach with "I want to think it over."

Practice, practice, and more practice is what it takes to increase your selling skills. Just knowing and being able to differentiate between the types of closes improves selling skills. Try them time after time with different prospects. You will quickly realize the benefits of knowing closing techniques.

When you hear the sentence "I want to think it over," picture a scale in your mind and imagine yourself placing two reasons for postponing the purchase on one side of the scale and three or more "buy now" reasons on the other side of the scale. Naturally, this creates an imbalance favoring "buy now." And that is exactly what you want to do, to try to create more closes from reluctant buyers!

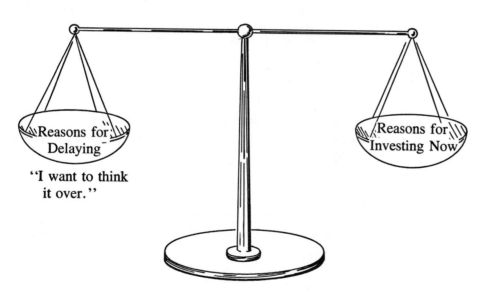

"I want to think it over."

The *authority close* is perhaps the easiest close to understand and implement. It is a powerful close and one that is often appropriate to use. It works particularly well with first-time buyers.

The perceptive salesperson is cued to use the authority

Close Technique 5:
The Authority Close

close when the prospect makes positive remarks about the proposed investment but, after being presented all the facts and benefits in a well-thought-out, logical sequence, fails to buy. When *asked* for the order, the prospect utters remarks like "That sounds pretty good" or "Gee, I didn't know that" or "That's great!" Every word the prospect says is positive, except that the words giving an order don't come forth.

In my opinion, based on years of experience, prospects fail to accept the proposal and place the order in the situations because *nobody orders them to buy!* These prospects require an authority figure to issue instructions to make the money commitment. Lacking that instruction, prospects of this type go unsold time after time, even though they always appear to be on the verge of granting an order. This is truly a frustrating situation for the unskilled salesperson who doesn't know the authority close.

Many people wealthy enough to be investing money now were raised in strict environments. They may have been told by parents exactly what to do at every point in their lives. They may have gone to military schools or other closely controlled educational institutions where they did as told. Other prospective investors will have served many years in military service, carrying out instructions issued by authority figures. People who have life experiences like these tend, as investors, to act only when told what to do in a very authoritarian manner that carries with it confidence and the assumption that the order will be carried out as directed.

As with all other closes the prospect's behavior and responses to your presentation will alert you to use the authority close. Here are the salient points in making an authority close:

1. Point out all the key facts and valuable benefits.
2. Make an authoritative statement. Do not ask a question as you would in most other types of closes.

Fortunately, there are many powerful authoritative statements that produce orders from prospects who don't say no but don't freely commit to an order, either. My favorites, ones that have worked time after time, are the following.

FOR MUTUAL-FUND SALES

"Endorse this form and your dividends, as well as capital gains, will be reinvested for you automatically without any sales charge!" This statement, clearly and forcefully presented along with the document properly completed except for the signature, has a high degree of success in obtaining the order.

FOR STOCK OR BOND PURCHASES

"Make out a check to ZYX company for [state the amount] and I will see that you get sent your certificate as soon as possible." This positive statement authoritatively issued, with the focus and reassurance on the delivery rather than the purchase, often wins the order.

FOR TAX-DEFERRED ANNUITIES

"Make out a check for [state the amount] to ZYX Insurance Company and we can put your money to work right away earning you high interest, untaxed currently, and all without risking even one dollar of your principal." This instructive close re-emphasizes the key sales points and reassures the prospect while the order is being demanded.

FOR TAX SHELTERS

"Make out a check for [state the amount] to ZYX Company and you will get [again, state the amount] in tax deductions this year, plus having your money work for you in [state the type of shelter, such as real estate or oil]." This strong statement focuses attention on the tax benefit as well as a possible future benefit from the dollars at work in the investment. Such statements are particularly effective in November and December when people are extremely tax-conscious.

To work really effectively, you must execute the authority close with an air of complete certainty that the prospect will acquiesce. The prospect must perceive that you *assume* asked-for action will be accomplished, and right now!

Close Technique 6:

The Positive-Alternate Close

Among the most ancient of all closes and common to sellers of all types of goods, tangible or intangible, the *positive-alternate close* is highly effective. It will be one of the strongest tools in your collection of selling techniques. The positive-alternate close works well with old clients as well as new. And surprise! It can be used repeatedly, year-in, year-out, with the same client!

Here are the steps in the positive-alternate close:

1. Present all the pertinent facts and benefits to the prospect.

2. Present the prospect a choice of two courses of action (two positive alternates), each of which results in an order for you.

3. Close with a question that asks the prospect to choose between the two positive alternates.

One great weakness that seems to afflict a large number of sellers of intangibles is the reluctance to ask for a large order. Many salespeople with excellent product knowledge and the ability to make fine presentations fail to earn sums commensurate with their talent solely because they are timid in requesting "size" orders. They are strong in presenting the facts and benefits and proficient at responding to technical questions. Yet they fail miserably because they ask for small orders. I can't count the times I have listened to stock brokers making a presentation in a very persuasive, coherent manner to a prospect, only to conclude with, "Why don't you buy 100 shares?" The distressing thing is that often the prospect says yes. If that same prospect had been asked for an order for 500, 1000, or more, the answer might well still have been yes!

The other upsetting aspect of the closing question, "Why don't you buy 100 shares?" is that the prospect might say no. The positive-alternate close makes it easy to ask for a large order and also makes it easy for the prospect to give an order, be it large, medium, or small. Instead of the potentially losing proposition inherent in buy/no buy choices, the positive alternate close presents the prospect with a choice of buying "*some*" or "*some more!*"

The positive-alternate close focuses the prospect's attention on investing a large amount of money or a smaller amount, rather than on investing or not investing. Here are some sample positive-alternate closes:

FOR UNIT TRUSTS

"Which would be best for you right now, 20 units of this high-yield unit trust free from federal taxation, or 15?"

FOR STOCK SHARES

"How many shares can you afford of this low-risk, high-potential stock? One thousand? Eight hundred? You tell me." It is much easier to work down from 1000 shares than it is to work up from 100 shares. Furthermore, many prospects are flattered that you consider them financially able to buy a large amount, and they respond with larger orders. Prospects often feel, too, that brokers wouldn't ask for a large order if they really don't believe a recommendation was solidly based. There is a message for you in that fact: *Don't sell something if you don't really believe in it!* If you believe in your product, ask for big orders, even if you are talking to a small potential buyer.

Give a prospect the choice always between two positives, and you will be on your way to higher earnings.

I witnessed a slight variation of the choice between two positive alternates in the office of Bill W., a top-producing broker. I overheard a conversation between Bill and a client whom Bill was trying to persuade to buy 1000 shares of a high-quality growth stock, then priced about $250 per share. You read it right: $250 per share! Bill was attempting to persuade this client to put a quarter of a million dollars into this stock! Tune in on the conversation:

Bill: "I have been following this stock for years. Technically it appears poised for a break-out above the $250-per-share level. The fundamentals look great, earnings per share are growing at 20 percent a year, dividends have been increasing each year, and a stock split is expected. The volume of trading is high and increasing. If the stock does what our fundamental research analyst and I believe, it might well sell for $400 per share this time next year. With 1000 shares you might make $150,000 as a long-term capital gain. However, if our Technical Department is right, it might have a quick run-up, to $300, in the next 30 days, and I might advise you to get out with a quick $50,000 short-term gain."

Client: "Go ahead, buy me 1000 shares!"

Bill just presented that prospect with the choice of a possible $50,000 short-term gain or a possible $150,000 long-term gain. He got the order! So will you if you use the positive alternate close.

Close Technique 7: The Sense-of-Loss Close

Sellers of intangibles invariably find themselves particularly effective with two or three closes. Trial and error and personality factors will just naturally lead the individual salesperson to believe in and regularly use the two or three closing styles effective on the greatest number of prospects. The *sense-of-loss close* is probably the most universally accepted of all closes as well as the *most powerful* close for any seller of intangibles to use on any prospect.

This particular close is easy to learn and remember, and is repeatedly effective, in various forms, with the same client. The features that characterize the sense-of-loss close are as follows:

1. Carefully outline all the facts, risks, and reward potential to the prospect.
2. Impress on the prospect the benefit of acting right away.
3. Point out to the prospect a *possible loss* that a delay might cause.
4. Close with a question.

The sense-of-loss close requires you to build the urgency of acting now into your presentation. Allow your voice to rise and fall (avoid a monotone presentation) and make your enthusiasm for the proposal obvious even to the most phlegmatic prospect. A time for action must be absolutely specified (usually next day or next week). The potential loss to the prospect for not acting by the specified time must be highlighted and accentuated, and of course truthfully presented.

This close is adaptable to the sale of common stocks, new-issue securities of all types, bonds, tax shelters, tax-deferred annuities, commodities, options, and other financial products. Here are some examples of sense-of-loss closing questions for various investment products. Assume that all the facts and benefits have been made clear to the prospect.

Broker: "Tomorrow we're underwriting a new issue of common stock of Pacific Gas and Electric. The shares will be priced at $22 each. The yield from the current dividend is 11.3 percent. It is an excellent high-income stock with good capital-gain potential as well. The risk at this level looks low compared to the long-term profit possibility. It just fits in with your conservative nature and portfolio. A really exciting feature is that buyers tomorrow, at the $22 price, *will not have to pay any direct commission.*"

Prospect: "No commission?"

Broker: "You heard me right. The company pays all commission costs. There will be only a *limited number of shares available* of this high-quality issue and I will try to get you up to 500 or 1000 shares. I have to know today what quantity you want me to try to get for you. If you want more than 1000 shares I will do my best to get my manager to try to increase our allotment. The *sooner you let me know* the better chance we have of getting part or all of what you might want."

Prospect: "That sounds pretty good."

Broker: "Not only does it sound good, it *is* a good investment. *No commission directly paid by you.* High income and high quality. I don't want you to miss out on this opportunity and later have to pay a commission and maybe a higher price per share. While we have shares available you ought to reserve some. How many do you want? One thousand? Eight hundred? *I have to know today if you are to save commission costs.*"

When you have special values to offer such as limited shares of a new issue of common stock at a fixed price, or a limited number of new-issue bonds at an attractive yield, you will find the sense-of-loss close effective with cold prospects as well as existing clients.

The sense-of-loss close is one of the great devices available when you're opening a new account. One of the best (and nicest) clients I had was obtained through a cold call and a sense-of-loss close. Here's the story:

My firm was underwriting a new issue of stock, Culligan,

Inc., a manufacturer of water softeners. The price was set at $12.50 per share. A thousand shares (commission free to the buyer) was available, so I turned to the yellow pages (a marvelously helpful prospecting manual, by the way) and looked under water softeners. There were eight listings.

I tried calling the first three but was unable to get through secretaries who were properly defending their bosses from unwanted solicitations. (Secretaries who do their job well screen callers by asking, "Who's calling please?" "Does he know you?" and "What do you wish to talk with him about?" After receiving answers to these questions, the secretary most frequently takes the caller's number and lets the boss determine whether or not to return the call. Most often the decision is not to return the call and get exposed to a sales pitch.) By the time I made the fourth phone call, my anger and frustration were at a high point, and that caused me to take a different tack to try to get through to the prospect. On that fourth call I learned the following sales technique, one that you, too, can master if you have nerve!

The conversation went like this. Remember my emotional state: angry and frustrated, and I sounded it!

Secretary:	"XYZ Water Pump Company."
LeRoy Gross:	"Let me speak to the president. Rightaway please!
Secretary:	"Who's calling please?"
LeRoy Gross:	"You tell him that LeRoy Gross [no firm name given] is on the phone, and that I *want to speak to him right now! Not later!*" [All this was said in an icy cold, angry manner.]
Secretary:	"Just a minute, please. [She wanted to get away from this nasty caller! I then heard her on an intercom.] There's a Mr. Gross on the phone. He sounds angry and upset. I believe you better talk to him."
Mr. B.:	"This is Mr. B."
LeRoy Gross:	"This is LeRoy Gross. I am with XYZ Firm and I had to talk to you right away. My firm is underwriting a new issue of Culligan, Inc., at $12.50 per share. The issue is coming out tomorrow. People who buy shares on the offering will not have to pay any direct commission. Before I sold shares to people in this area *I wanted the opinion of an expert like you!* Someone familiar with the company and its products. Since you distribute the product locally I thought you might give me your impressions."

At this point what emotions do you believe were being experienced by Mr. B.?

If you said "flattered" you were right. He was flattered that a representative of an NYSE member firm was *seeking his opinion about a common stock.*

Secondly, he was *relieved* that it wasn't an angry, upset customer on the phone, as he had been led to believe by his secretary.

Mr. B. proceeded to tell me in no uncertain terms what he thought about Culligan, Inc. He also told me he wouldn't buy it (what a mistake that later proved to be), and neither, in his opinion, should anyone else.

Those informational gems deflated me pretty well, but in the course of the conversation the following exchange took place:

Mr. B.: "By the way, what's the market doing?"

LeRoy Gross: "Up about 3 points."

Mr. B.: "What do you know about Mississippi River Corporation?"

I wasn't about to say "nothing"! I hurriedly looked it up in my trusty desk-top Standard and Poor stock guide.

LeRoy Gross: "It looks like an income stock to me. It pays $1 in dividends annually. Last price is 16."

Mr. B.: "I have been watching that stock for a few months and I like it. If you can get me 300 at 16 I'll take 'em."

A bona fide order from a local company president! I hung up after getting the necessary information concerning bank references, social security number, and so on, and then got an okay from the manager to execute the order. That first order led to subsequent orders and the eventual transfer of $500,000 worth of securities from another firm, and annual commission income of approximately $10,000 per year! All that came from a cold call to a total stranger with the intent of using the sense-of-loss close (buy Culligan tomorrow and avoid direct commission costs).

Hopefully you too will find the sense-of-loss close one of your most powerful sales-generating devices. And also hopefully you will have learned a neat method for getting through to a decision maker in the following way:

1. Create a sense of urgency in your voice and manner.
2. Sound confident, as though there is no doubt that you will be immediately put through to the person you want to reach.
3. Create the impression that you know the prospect by giving only your name without identifying your firm or business.
4. Sound angry, dissatisfied, and upset.

Remember, if you don't get through you don't make sales!

The *involvement close* is a very special close that is used only in face-to-face selling situations. It is a planned close that is brought into play only when all oral arguments and visual displays have failed to produce the desired order.

Like several other closing techniques, this specialized close requires a high degree of nerve (it's certainly not for timid sellers), and it has to be carefully rehearsed so that when it is put to actual use it is perceived in the correct light.

The typical involvement close situation arises when the prospect's signature is needed to consummate an order. Many purchases of intangible products necessitate the signing of at least one document before the seller can register a bona fide order. Here are some fairly common financial products where no commission can be earned unless the prospect signs a required paper:

TAX SHELTERS

The prospect must sign an agreement attesting to some specified minimum income or net worth.

OPTION AGREEMENT

In order to be permitted to buy and sell listed option contracts, a fairly standard form must be signed attesting as to experience, income, net worth, and age.

MARGIN AGREEMENT

In order to borrow monies/or securities through a securities firm (margin) to increase leverage, a standardized form must be completed giving the firm the power to liquidate the client's position, if need be, to protect the lender firm.

TAX-DEFERRED ANNUITY

This particular investment has an insurance company contract that the client has to sign in order to get the benefit of money earning current interest untaxed until later withdrawn.

INSURANCE POLICIES

An application must always be signed before any policy can be issued.

MUTUAL FUNDS

In order to reinvest dividends and/or capital gains, a signature is needed. To buy shares under a letter of intention at a reduced sales cost a signed agreement is necessary.

COMMODITY TRADING

In order to gain the leverage inherent in commodity transactions, a form must be signed authorizing the account liquidation if necessary, to protect the commodity firm's capital.

INVESTMENT ADVISOR SERVICES

Prospects who wish others to choose investments discretionarily must sign an authorization permitting the activity.

Many prospects facing an enthusiastic salesperson who logically, efficiently builds an excellent case for a particular product still balk when it comes to the big decision of putting their mark on the dotted line.

After all objections have been overcome by the careful presentation of facts and benefits, after all questions have been answered and an order asked for several different times in different ways, all with no beneficial result, the time has come to use the involvement close.

Here are the steps in the involvement close:

1. Place the partially completed document with the prospect's name, address, and social security number already typed in, in full view, facing the prospect all during the sales presentation. Make the signature slot highly visible by placing a large red check mark by the space where the endorsement is needed.
2. Hand the form to the prospect to check the spelling and other information before signing.
3. Hand the prospect a pen and carefully indicate the signature line.
4. Make a closing statement: "This will help get your money to work for you as soon as possible."

The skilled seller of intangibles fully understands the prospect's fears about signing documents that become positive proof of their money commitment. Most agreements are scary things. They have been drafted by attorneys who are primarily looking out for and protecting the vendor's interest. The cry of old *caveat emptor* (let the buyer beware) still rings alarm bells in all prospects' minds when they are asked to sign a legal document. Fear exists that the document is an entrapment device, full of fine print and incomprehensible clauses that could turn out to be financially harmful if the seller's verbal picture turns out *not* to come true.

This one-on-one situation often becomes an insurmountable problem for the untrained seller. When all the ammunition has been fired and still no signature obtained, the involvement close can be used.

Let's assume that our hero, Joe Salesman, is down to the wire with John Prospect. Joe is trying his best to get John to sign a tax-deferred annuity contract. All the main sales points and features have been repeated and reviewed.

The scene is the prospect's office. The tax-deferred annuity form was all filled out, except for the signature, prior to the meeting, and it was placed on John's desk all during the presentation to serve as a silent salesman. Every time John looked down at the document, he could read his name. The subtle suggestion that he was an owner emanated from the document.

Joe, being a good face-to-face salesman, reiterates the key sales points. All the time he keeps his eyes focused on those of John Prospect. (Eyes that don't wander but radiate honesty and sincerity are one of the most helpful characteristics in convincing a prospect to buy.)

Joe: "What seems to appeal to you, and thousands like you, is the complete avoidance of income taxes (state or federal) on the money your money earns while it is growing.

John: "I like that. In fact, I love it! But even more I like the fact I can get all or part of my money anytime, just about like money in the bank."

Joe: "Yes, that is important and reassuring, but just as important is the guarantee that *you cannot lose even a single principal dollar*—very different from buying stocks, commodities, or even bonds. Since you don't have to pay any initial sales cost and you can earn a high rate of interest free of current income taxes, why don't you just transfer $40,000 from your savings account now? Just *okay* this form and I can get your money to work right away."

The foregoing situation is frequent in one form or another. The prospect says all the right things, agrees with you, understands the product, but simply freezes when it comes to the signing. When you reach this point *try to gently force the signature* by removing your eyes from the prospect's face, and *stare at the form*, right at the spot where the signature is needed. Like a magnet, the prospect's eyes will be drawn to the signature spot. Seeing the name already typed or printed on the document makes it less threatening and carries with it the sense of ownership. With both sets of eyes on the signature the message is quite clear. Frequently this little extra pressure is enough to gain the endorsement.

However, if that doesn't work the next step is to involve the prospect in the action. Take a fountain pen (a good investment if you don't have one) from your pocket. Take off the cap and hand the pen to the prospect. Say something like this: "Okay this, and your money can start earning you 10 percent in annual untaxed current income without risking a single dollar!" The handing of the pen and its acceptance by the prospect is a powerful closing action, and many times, after all else has failed that will do the trick.

However, selling, like true love, seems never to run smooth. If the handing of the pen, cap removed, does not immediately cause the prospect to bend over and sign, then get up your nerve and snatch the pen back from the prospect. This action of suddenly taking away a pen that has been offered in a friendly but businesslike manner will normally create an instant flare-up of anger. After all, who likes being graciously handed something and then having it abruptly removed?

After having snatched the pen away, simply make a half-turn away from the prospect, shake the pen as if to start the ink flowing, and turn back to the prospect again, handing the pen back with this statement: "I have been having trouble with this pen all day! Try it now please."

I know you won't believe it until you done it yourself, but this really works. When a fountain pen is snatched away and then reoffered after having been vigorously shaken to make the ink flow, the natural action is for the person now holding the pen (the prospect) to test it to see if it works. The natural way to do that is to make a mark with it. The piece of paper most handy is the document with the red check-marked space for a signature. The normal test is to write one's name!

John Prospect: "This works fine now."

Joe Salesman: "You really made a smart decision by putting your money to work to earn you high current untaxed interest, and without ever risking a single dollar of your principal."

After gaining a signature with the involvement close, cement the sale by telling the prospect how smart a decision giving the order is. It really pays big dividends to have a prospect leave feeling good about having made an intelligent decision and remembering your last few words as to why the decision is smart. (The "why" is simply a reiteration of the key sales points and benefits.)

Hopefully, the prospect will tell the next several friends about this wonderful, intelligent decision. The natural inclination of investors is to bring others into the fold, hopefully to share the future reward.

The involvement close (so named because the salesmen actually involves the prospect into the closing procedure) can convert sales that seem doomed to slip away. It can also create some immediate referrals through the prospect's relating to others his actions.

When you cannot call to mind any of the eight different closes discussed in the preceding pages, use the ultimate close: *Ask for an order!* This close certainly does simplify the selling process when memory or technique fails. Ask for an order!

Don't expect prospects to be so overwhelmed by your presentation of facts, features, and benefits that they will buy from you without having you directly, clearly *ask for an order!*

Close Technique 9:

The Ultimate Close

Immunizing Against Stock-Broker Diseases

I have had the privilege of helping to train thousands of salespeople for their work in the securities industry. Additionally, I have had the chance to closely observe many thousands of other account executives at work in their natural habitat, the branch office. Of the thousands who enter the securities selling field with high hopes of success, a great number fail during the first 12 months of actual action on the firing line. The dropout rate in the securities industry is estimated at 25 percent during the first year. Another large percentage fall by the wayside in year two, and attrition continues, although to a lesser degree, each successive year.

PHONE SHOCK
One of the great causes of failure is the contracting of a broker's deadly disease that I call *phone shock*. This disease can be readily observed by focusing a trained eye on the activities of brokers as they perform their daily tasks. Many brokers who start out their career actively calling strangers and soliciting orders or appointments meet so much rejection that their egos become badly deflated. They dread making the prescribed number of "cold" calls (their own or a manager's quota), and they begin to rely heavily on direct mail. They fervently hope that what they send out will waft back to them in orders generated by the prospects being convinced merely by reading the wonderful written material enclosed.

Such brokers seem to have developed a fear that the phone

Successful security salespeople owe much of their success to treating every account as if it were their only account. Practice this and watch your production grow!

TWO THINGS YOU CAN DO TODAY TO MAKE YOUR BUSINESS GROW!

1. **Call 5 presidents of local corporations whose stocks are publicly traded. Ask to meet with them (try to get the account!) to discuss your conducting a special focus seminar on their *stock and its potential* to their employees.**

2. **Try to persuade 2 department store managers to cosponsor you as lecturer in their store on 18 ways to save on taxes. (Set up a quarterly appearance if possible.)**

will electrocute them if they pick it up to make an out-going call. They live each day in hope that some acquaintance will call them and place a fantastic unsolicited order.

In order to seem to be working hard, both to the manager and to themselves, they surround themselves with mountains of paper and envelopes and mailing lists. They always look industrious as they are addressing and stuffing envelopes, recording information on prospect cards, and getting additional supplies of printed materials. They busy themselves with the careful reading (page by page, slowly) of prospectuses, research material, *Barron's, the Wall Street Journal,* and any kind of other financial material.

Brokers who have contracted phone shock will do anything rather than force themselves to call strangers to seek orders or appointments. Many brokers suffering from phone shock become enthusiastic about technical analysis. The world of bar and point and figure charts and their daily maintenance absorbs them. These brokers kid themselves (and others, if they can) that they are making a tremendous effort in trying to select timely, "right" investment ideas, and that once their research is complete (somehow, it never is complete) they will use the phone to aggressively recommend the chosen beauty.

The only known cure for phone shock is the recognition and acceptance of its presence (a manager or an interested friend or relative may be able to point it out—tactfully) and the implementation of a daily discipline for the completion of some minimum number of order asking, appointment requesting phone calls.

CURING PHONE SHOCK

If you recognize a case of phone shock and yet can't regularly force yourself into the daily discipline of making out-going calls, sit down with your manager and perhaps ask the manager be more of a taskmaster. Prepare daily call sheets detailing the names and phone numbers of the prospects you solicit, and turn them in to your manager or sales manager. (The taskmaster should occasionally spot check a few prospects to get a feel for the prospects' reaction.)

The extra burden of the daily supervision of a failing account executive is not a chore managers love, and many let salespeople who need this type of push—who are not self starters or motivated enough on their own to go out and seek business—fail.

The realization must eventually dawn on phone shocked salespeople that if they are to make it up the ladder of success, it has to be as a result of out-going, order-asking calls, whether made by phone or face to face. Hiding under the mantle of paperwork and reading is a plot that just won't work for any length of time; and to behave thus certainly will not bring the desired degree of success.

100-Shares Syndrome

The other disease that afflicts brokers is the *100-share syndrome.* This disease is transmittable. I have visited offices where everyone had it! It is insidious, and it saps the seller's strength and enthusiasm.

The 100-share syndrome is often employed as a closing technique. It may frequently follow an excellent presentation of facts and benefits. Check the following scenario and you will spot the disease:

Joe Salesman: "Hi, John! This is Joe Salesman. I'm calling you this morning to tell you about a stock just recommended by our drug analyst. I have read the

Good security salespeople follow up leads and inquiries promptly. They know the easiest time to sell something is when the prospect is already interested. The inquiry indicates a "warm" prospect—the faster the follow-up, the better the chance of making the sale.

TWO THINGS YOU CAN DO TODAY TO MAKE YOUR BUSINESS GROW!

1. *Ask for 3 referrals from each client for whom you executed a sell/buy order yesterday.*

2. *Send out 10 research one-pagers of your favorite stock with a handwritten note: "Call me right away about." Enclose with each two return cards that can spark a request for more information.*

Top security salespeople know that a sale will be closed quicker by presenting the recommendation in person than over the telephone.

report carefully and it looks like a terrific value right now. The shares are priced at $28. The yield is 5 percent from a dividend that has been raised every single year for 15 consecutive years."

John Prospect: "That sounds pretty good."

Joe Salesman: "What's even better is that the earnings have gone up every single year for 15 consecutive years, and the stock is selling at the lowest price times earnings in its history."

John Prospect: "What has been the price range for this past year?"

Joe Salesman: "The shares have sold above $35 each and every year for the last 10 years at some time during the year, and the past 12 months have been between 27 to 38. By the way, it has the highest quality rating by Standard and Poor: A+."

John Prospect: "How about sending me the report?"

Joe Salesman: "I will do that, *but how about buying 100 shares today?*"

Many times, a salesperson will make a good presentation about a well-chosen common stock and wind up with a weak closing question: "How about buying 100 shares?" Of course, any order-asking attempt is better than none, but what if the prospect says yes? An order for 200, 300, 500, 1000, or more might have been obtained, only to be lost because of the 100-share syndrome. Skilled brokers know to ask for large orders. It is always easier to work downward from a 1000-share request than it is to move upward from a 100-share, a small order to request!

CURING THE 100-SHARES SYNDROME

The cure for this disease lies in monitoring your phone calls with a cassette tape or asking a colleague or your manager to monitor your phone calls. Once you become conscious of the presence of the 100-share syndrome, you are on your way to licking it. The cure lies in forcing yourself to ask for large orders (remember the alternate close?).

Top security salespeople reach the top and stay on top because they adhere to the three primary rules for success in our business: (1) prospect; (2) prospect; (3) prospect!

TWO THINGS YOU CAN DO TODAY TO MAKE YOUR BUSINESS GROW!

1. *Contact the president of a community college or business college in your area and see if you can persuade him or her to let you conduct a series of night classes on investing, for adults.*

2. *Contact the president of the business and professional women's club. Meet her (get the account!) and see if you can speak at a breakfast meeting.*

Making Research Reports Produce Orders from Prospects

As I write, there are over 44,000 registered representatives of New York Stock Exchange Member Firms. To this army add thousands of National Association of Security Dealers (NASD) licensed salespeople who work for over-the-counter firms.

One of the prime commission-generating products for this large selling group is common stock. Shares of common stock are bought and sold annually at a total value that exceeded 7 billion in 1979. An awesome amount to be sure and each seller of intangibles struggles to get a share of the luscious commission pie associated with $7 billion in share sales by telling the merits of current stock favorites to friends, relatives, and other prospects. Most stock solicitations are made by phone for many valid reasons, including the opportunity for dialogue, the sense of urgency that can be generated by the seller, the ease of contact, and the potential for making a large number of contacts.

Despite the attractions of making stock sales by phone, many brokers use mailings of research reports, either to back up verbal presentations or to try to initiate interest in prospects.

In my opinion, *much of the mailing is a waste of money, time, and effort.*

The average target for mailings of stock reports is inundated with unsolicited mail of all types, including investment ideas. Affluent prospects deal with the influx of "buy-me" mail by "round filing" it (tossing it in the wastebasket) after a quick glance.

Despite the low return (in terms of orders obtained) of direct mail, brokers collectively pour millions of dollars into it, hoping for a positive result. Many individual account executives find it easier to lick envelopes, stuff them with research material, and mail them (at company expense) than to go through the pain of calling or seeing people and risking rejection.

Plan the Research-Report Mailing

Uncontrolled, unplanned mailing of research reports is a drag on profits for the firm and a time-eater for the salesperson, yet its use continues to grow year after year. The mail *can* be an effective tool to open accounts and create orders for common stock, however. The trick is to plan mail strategy. When you zero in on a stock recommended by your research department as one you would like to build a strong position in for your clients, go through the following steps:

1. Prepare a story book for use in selling prospects face to face. Learn the information cold.
2. Order a supply of the reports (generally not over 200). See that the reports are original-print copies rather than photo copies.
3. Select two response cards to enclose with the report.
4. See that your name, address, and phone number are clearly marked on each report. Use a rubber stamp, a label, or attach your business card.
5. Personalize each copy with a handwritten note, preferrably block-printed in red ink.

After completing these preparations, you have set the stage to get get maximum mileage out of the mailing.

Alert: When you select the research report for the mailing, pick a one-page write-up. People normally do not read multi-page reports with any degree of enthusiasm or dedication. They most often want a capsule that is easy to digest rather than a heavy outpouring of technical data.

Personalizing each report with a handwritten message is a laborious task, but highly productive. It gets a much higher degree of readership than mailings that haven't a personal inclusion. Take great care with the personalized note. Any statement that can be considered inflammatory, nonfactual, or misleading may later come back to haunt you—in the form of a lawsuit.

The note I favor, time-tested and trouble-free, simply says, "Dear Joe: Call me right away, as soon as you have read this." I then sign it and write out my phone number.

That simple message, "Call me right away after you have read this," is good enough to make the recipient read the report, or at least look at it and think twice before discarding it. And many times that message accomplishes the goal: a call from the prospect to the broker. If you follow the personalized report up with a phone call a few days later, the imprinted message tends

MAKING RESEARCH REPORTS PRODUCE ORDERS

Henry Ford said it, and he wasn't even a stockbroker! "Thinking is the hardest part of work, which is probably the reason so few engage in it."

to encourage the prospect to grant you an appointment or even give you an order.

The New York stock Exchange frowns on the underlining of research reports, so that practice should be avoided. (The NYSE naturally believe that, left to their own inclinations, salespeople might be tempted to underline only the good aspects, failing to give equal attention to any negative parts.)

Target the Mailing

To get better results from a nonclient list, include in the mailing potential investors likely to be familiar with the spotlighted company or its products, either as suppliers to the company or as distributors or consumers of its products. Let's assume, for example, that the stock in the report is for a drug company with interests in proprietary and ethical drugs. Candidates for the mailing include:

1. All doctors (listed in the Yellow Pages)
2. All wholesale druggists
3. All pharmacists
4. All drugstore owners and managers

If the chosen stock is a photo industry stock, like Eastman Kodak or Polaroid, the nonclient mailing list should include all listings in the Yellow Pages that start with the word "Photo." The listings can run from under 50 into the thousands, depending on the geographic area of solicitation. It is always much easier to sell prospects on the stock of a company they are familiar with because of some regular contact with the company's employees, products, or services.

The positive results of a mailing of a research report are more influenced by the personalization and follow-up phone call than by what is actually contained in the report itself. *Don't mail more than you will actually follow up by phone.* That good rule makes for more effective results.

Never mail a report to a business, even though it's one with a connection to the featured company. Take the time to call the company and find out the correct name of the manager, the president, and/or key officer(s), and address the report to their attention.

Finally, let research reports remind you to pinpoint prospects who are not already in your prospect file.

Every good security salesperson could become a star if he or she only understood that the job is not to devote the bulk of time to trying to peer into the dim future but to do the daily work that can be clearly seen.

Using the Mail Effectively

As I mentioned in the preceding chapter, millions of dollars each year are spent on direct mailings by insurance salespeople, stock brokers, commodity agents, and other sellers of intangible investment products. And shockingly, most of this money goes down the drain because the salesperson who is the main beneficiary has no follow-up phone plan or undertakes a scattered, haphazard mailing of untimely or out-of-date material.

Dollars by the millions are also wasted on individualized letter writing both to existing clients and to prospects. As shocking as the money wasted in mailings is the fact that a great many college graduates escaped from their alma maters unable to construct even the simplest business letter. I have witnessed great numbers of salespeople agonizing over writing a letter, devoting hours to writing, editing, rewriting, in order to suggest a minor portfolio change or to answer a request for particular information.

Precious selling hours have been and are currently being wasted on the preparation of rather simple messages to be sent to relatively few people. You can stop this waste of time and money supply by learning the basic strategy in making the mail work for you.

Here is a typical scenario, one that is played and replayed almost daily in every sizable sales office.

Jill Saleswoman has to furnish an opinion on three stocks at a prospect's request, or perhaps she wants to compose a letter to a prospect who has just moved into an expensive house.

During prime selling time, Jill sits at her desk thoughtfully gazing out into space, pencil in hand, hand posed over a yellow pad. She jots down a couple of sentences, pauses, scratches out a couple of words, and writes another sentence. The phone rings, and Jill talks to a client for ten minutes. Hangs up the phone, picks up yellow pad, stares at it again. Makes a few more corrections. The manager calls Jill in to discuss a problem. Thirty minutes later, Jill returns to her desk. The phone rings. She talks to another client. A colleague comes over to talk about supper and Saturday night plans. Two other brokers involve Jill in a conversation about gold and interest rates. Time for lunch. The three go out for lunch. Service is slow, and they don't get back for an hour and a half. Two phone calls to return.

After those are completed the yellow pad is again picked up, stared at, and a few more scarcely legible notes made. Finally, at day's end, the note is handed to a secretary to type. Obviously, the letter won't be typed today. Besides, the secretary is overloaded, and the typing of the letter takes its place behind the others she has to do. At the end of day two, the secretary gets to Jill's letter but can't read the chicken-scratchings. She tries to locate Jill, who is out on a sales call. Note is held over until day three. Day three finds Jill screaming, "Where's my letter?"

Pointing to some hieroglyphics, the secretary snaps, "I can't read your lousy writing. What is this supposed to mean?"

Jill can't decipher it herself, makes a guess, and tosses out a few extra sentences for the secretary to remember to add. A typed copy is available on day four. Jill doesn't like the way it sounds, so she corrects the draft. This really hacks the secretary, who now has to redo it. She drags her feet, puts the letter at the bottom of the pile, and finally gets a corrected copy for Jill's signature by the next day.

The manager, whose duty it is to review all correspondence, gets a carbon copy to initial before the original goes out. He reads it and yells "Hey, this isn't right!" Jill is called in and shown the

Good security salespeople know that in the stock market the meek do not inherit the earth. Are you asking for three referrals each day?

TWO THINGS YOU CAN DO TODAY TO MAKE YOUR BUSINESS GROW!

1. *Call Boy Scout and Girl Scout leaders. Arrange to have a troop and parents visit your office one night to learn about the fascinating world of investments. Free coffee and cookies . . . and you might get some good accounts.*

2. *Clip two write-ups of business promotions from the newspaper. Send clippings and note. Follow up with phone call a week later.*

How much money could we all make if we only understood that no rule for success is more important than giving clients what they really want, not what we think they ought to want.

error. The manager also corrects some of the English, and a new draft is given to the secretary to type. The secretary is fed up with Jill by this time, and she waits another day before completing what should have been a simple business letter.

Scenes like this are quite common and extremely frustrating to all parties: the salesperson, the secretary, the manager, and the prospect, who did not get answered promptly.

The way to use selling time for real selling, take care of the normal out-going correspondence, and still use the mail to prospect is to develop what I call the *ticket-factory concept.*

I believe sellers of intangibles should think of themselves as "factories" whose purpose is to manufacture executed tickets each day. In order to maximize output, any good factory tries to automate as much as possible. Salespeople should also try to automate letter writing and mail prospecting. One way to do this is to create letters covering every key product you sell and applying to every recurring problem you dealt with in your client relationships.

Establish a sample letter file containing typed samples of letters covering every conceivable situation. Give each letter a number. Note which enclosures go with each letter. And be sure to avoid problems by having your manager approve each letter before you use it.

Once these steps are completed, have each letter typed on the typewriter your secretary uses. Most of the letters then will need only a typed-in name and address to make them personal. others may call for the insertion of special information on appropriate lines. All of them can be printed in quantity (100 to 500, depending on estimated use) at a local print shop. When a letter has to go out, all that is required is to type in the name (and blanks as/if required) with the same typewriter. The type style will then match the printed letter, although its darkness may vary depending on the state of the typewriter ribbon.

If you are featuring a certain product, such as a tax shelter or a tax-deferred annuity, you can simply instruct a secretary to "Send letter 4 to these 10 people," and give the secretary the prospect cards for names and addresses. The secretary then notes on the cards, *Letter 4, 11/12/80"* and then types on the names and encloses the designated material. All this takes place without any hassle or wasted time on the secretary's part, or, for that matter, on yours.

You will be able to review your prospect cards and easily determine what had been sent and when. Follow-up phone calls to each prospect in the mailing should be logged for a week after mailing.

A lot more sales are likely with this organized approach to direct mail, for you will virtually have automated one process for bringing a lot of orders into your factory to execute. The intent is to create a steady stream of prospects making incoming calls as a result of the regular mail solicitations they receive.

Each letter going out must be hand signed (*no printed signatures*, PLEASE). The envelope should also carry a handwritten message in red ink along the lines of the following:

1. Free SEMINAR TICKETS ENCLOSED
2. CONFIDENTIAL
3. PERSONAL
4. TAX-SAVING IDEAS
5. EARN 14% [or what currently is attractively available in high-yield investments]

Each letter must also have a handwritten postscript, (P.S.), again, preferably in red, the attention-getting color. The P.S. should be a message similar to this:

P.S.
Call me right away (555-6000) after carefully reading the enclosed.
LeRoy Gross

People are funny creatures. On the whole, almost everyone reads a short P.S. *before* reading the body of the letter. The P.S. does the real work of the letter because it calls for a specific, immediate action based on apparently urgent information.

Some branch offices have a computer typewriter with a memory unit that can store thousands of names and sample

Good security salespeople understand that history teaches that life is competition. *Compete with your own sales records, or those of other brokers, and you will spur yourself on to higher goals.*

letters. This piece of equipment is worth many times its cost in terms of the time and money it saves and the accuracy it provides.

If the branch cannot afford to lease a unit, you might want to consider chipping in with several colleagues to split the monthly charge for leasing a new unit or perhaps a lower-cost used machine. (The cost qualifies as a tax deduction!)

With the help of the computer, a regular mail contact program can be efficiently operated, and that will help to make the automated ticket factory a reality.

Direct mail does not always have to go through the U.S. Postal system!

Direct Mail Minus the Postal System

Here are some sales-building ideas for getting prospecting material into the hands of prospects at a low cost per piece:

1. Look into getting the newspaper delivery boy or girl to deliver a prospecting piece (complete with return card) with each paper. This method of distribution costs a fraction of the mailing costs. The benefits are in shortening the distribution time lines and the possibility of effecting geographic concentration in affluent areas.

2. Look into hiring a teenager to distribute the selected material under each door of a high-rise apartment or condominium. The benefits here are the same as those in item 1. Just be sure to choose a high-tariff building.

Send mail in bulk to zip code areas whenever possible; doing so avoids the expense of first-class mail. *It is better to make more contacts than to spend more of the mail money on postage per each.*

Here are some tips that will be helpful in building the master set of letters or in writing any letter:

1. Make sure the prospect's name is spelled correctly. Why alienate a potential client by failing to take the time to learn how to spell both first and last names?

2. Make sure that any title is correct. Addressing a vice president as "assistant vice president" is just asking to have the content of your letter ignored.

3. Create a headline, an attention grabbing opening statement, if you want the body of the letter to be read.

4. Be careful in your word choice. High-falutin' language can be a sales killer rather than a sales maker. The simpler you can make your words, the better understood your message will be.

5. Try to keep letters to one page. Long-winded, preachy letters don't sell as well as briefer messages.

6. End the letter by asking for an order or an appointment or an immediate phone call from the prospect.

Often, top security salespeople reach the top because they have learned to sell the interview before selling the product!

TWO THINGS YOU CAN DO TODAY TO MAKE YOUR BUSINESS GROW!

1. *Call prospects and clients until you have lined up a personal appointment for every day next week.*

2. *Call 10 strangers and ask them to buy a quality, high-yield, tax-free bond available from inventory or blue list.*

USING THE MAIL EFFECTIVELY

Cold Calling Successfully

The phone is the single greatest asset for any seller of intangibles, yet many salespeople never learn how to use it effectively. Thousands of potentially good salespeople fail in their profession because of their lack of skill in handling that perplexing plastic piece of electronic equipment.

Selling to prospects by phone is much different from, and more difficult than, selling to established clients by phone. Let's focus on the process of making cold calls to total strangers.

When you call strangers it is important to keep in mind that prospects can only judge by what they hear. Except by the still-rare use of a picture phone, prospects cannot see your natural, beautiful appearance; the immaculate clothes; the positive, reassuring manner. Nor can they view any exhibits, charts, or statistical data that normally might be used as evidence in a face-to-face meeting.

The recipient of a cold call can make judgments based only on your voice and tone inflection, the clarity of your logic, and the facts you outline. Prospects quickly form an impression of the caller. Normally, sellers making a first cold call to a prospect have about 20 seconds to make themselves and their products attractive enough for the prospect to be interested in hearing more. Those first few seconds on the phone are vital, and they should be carefully rehearsed so that you know how to grab and hold the prospect's attention.

In making *absolute cold calls* (neither a referring source nor a direct mail warm-up), paying attention to several key points can help you gain a higher degree of productivity from the effort you expend. They include the following:

1. *Pronounce the prospect's name correctly.* People love to hear the sound of their names, but *only* if correctly pronounced. This is especially true of individuals who have surnames that are difficult to pronounce. If you are unsure how to pronounce the prospect's name correctly, *ask!* Make every effort to learn the correct pronunciation *before* the sales call. You can usually accomplish this by asking the secretary or receptionist who answers the phone to say the prospect's name.

2. *Introduce yourself distinctly.* Be sure to pronounce your *own* name clearly and distinctly, without racing through it or mumbling, in your effort to get to your sales pitch.

3. *Use the prospect's name again.* When you make your opening statement, repeat the prospect's name. Whenever possible, if permission has been granted, get on a first-name basis. This reduces tension and breaks a social barrier.

4. *State a valid reason for calling.* Too many sellers barge into the cold-calling fray without thinking of plausible reasons for interrupting the prospect at work (daytime) or at home (usually night-time). Without a valid reason for calling, the conversation limps along or the prospect severely shortens it. The lack of validity in the call causes a low score, in terms of orders or appointments obtained, whereas presenting the prospect with reasons for why you are calling now creates an atmosphere of credibility.

5. *Make the conversation two-way.* To be successful in cold calling, it is important for you to involve the prospect in the conversation. You can normally accomplish this by asking the prospect questions, zeroing in on what the prospect needs or wants. A one-way, uninterrupted sales pitch is not only boring to both parties but is generally unproductive. Being a good question-asker is a key part of becoming a good sales-producer.

6. *Try to exude confidence, enthusiasm, product knowledge, and warmth.* Of the six key points for cold calling, far and away the most important is the selection of a *valid reason* for calling. Before you pick up the phone to dial a stranger, you *must* carefully select one or more good reasons for intruding on that person's time and privacy. Otherwise, your batting average will be low enough to discourage you completely, perhaps to the point of leaving the business of selling intangibles.

Many salespeople have the mistaken impression that the number of calls they complete is the only goal and measure of cold calling. They stress the quantity (which *is* important) but give too little emphasis to the quality of the call.

Top security salesmen understand full well that the future is that time when they wish they had done what they aren't doing now!

TWO THINGS YOU CAN DO TODAY TO MAKE YOUR BUSINESS GROW!

1. **Visit a nearby small town and call on at least 10 people, leaving your card and literature. Have them complete valuable services request form, preferably in your presence.**

2. **Try to complete 2 data sheets for free portfolio valuations.**

Faulty technique—no valid reason. Below is an example of a phone approach used (most ineffectually) by thousands of salespeople in the securities industry. It is an approach I have observed and absolutely deplore, because it proceeds in a bland and innocuous style and has been a primary cause of the low productivity or even failure of its practitioners.

Assume that Joe Salesman has reached John Prospect.

Joe Salesman: "Mr. Prospect, my name is Joe Salesman with QRX Company, a member firm of the New York Stock Exchange. I am calling you today to introduce myself and my firm. I would like to compete for some of your business and have an opportunity to meet you and tell you about all the fine services and products my firm has to offer. Could I meet with you this afternoon or tomorrow morning?"

John Prospect: "Sorry, but I'm tied up, and besides I already have a broker. I'm not interested in any other. Thanks for calling."

On the surface, the contents of the call certainly seem all right. An appointment is requested after the introduction has taken place; the tone is pleasant. *But there is no punch, no specific product offered, no urgency implied. There is no valid reason for the call,* at least valid and plausible from the prospect's point of view. And in order to get past the initial hurdle of a cold call, the prospect's viewpoint is the only one that matters!

Despite my negative assessment of this approach, some small degree of success may be had with it, simply because the user is making some contact with a prospect. An occasional prospect may be looking for a broker. This is where the quanity of calls can sometimes make up for their lack of quality. Some prospects will arrange the asked-for appointment or they will volunteer information or ask questions that could lead to an account and an order. But prospects *that* ripe are rare.

Superior technique—the valid-reason approach. When you apply skill in selecting a valid reason for the call, the number of accounts opened per 100 cold calls made can zoom, often astronomically.

Listen in on a different approach—a *valid-reason approach.*

Again assume that our mythical Joe Salesman has gotten through to John Prospect:

Joe Salesman: "Mr. Prospect, this is Joe Salesman with XYZ Firm. You don't know me, but I am calling you today for a very special reason."

John Prospect: "What is it?"

Joe Salesman: "Mr. Prospect [repeating the name], my firm is underwriting a new issue of common stock of Pacific Gas and Electric. The new shares are coming out tomorrow at $22 per share [specific product and specific time]. *Buyers tomorrow will not have to pay any commission cost whatsoever!* All costs will be paid by the seller. The shares yield 11.3 percent and are rated at the highest possible rating by Standard and Poor. Normally, these free-of-buyer-commission shares are offered and taken by our existing clients. However, *my manager has allocated me some shares for new accounts*, and that is why I am calling you today [valid reason for calling, one that is plausible to the prospect].

John Prospect: "What did you say the price and yield were?"

Joe Salesman: "The price *tomorrow* will be $22 per share. The yield will be 11.3 percent from a dividend that has never been reduced in over 100 years. If you are interested in high quality and high income and in avoiding direct commission cost to you, I will try to get you up to 500 or 1000 shares. [Place a scarcity value, if possible, to help stimulate the prospect's desire.] If I can get shares for you at that special price, how many would you be interested in?"

I have trained thousands of salespeople to use this phone approach effectively, and with a much higher degree of success than they have achieved with any other phone contact.

The key points to remember in constructing a valid-reasons phone approach are these:

1. Offer a specific product, preferably a high-quality, well-known name.

That which makes the difference between one man and another—between the weak and powerful—the great and insignificant—is effort.

2. State a specific time within which an answer is needed.

3. Present a specific value strong enough to induce the prospect to agree to the order or the appointment.

4. If possible, present a product that has the appeal of scarcity.

Here are some examples of valid reasons sellers of intangibles can use in their approaches to strangers:

***What to Use
as Valid Reasons***

1. *New issues of common stocks or bonds.* As in the Pacific Gas & Electric illustration, there is something magnetic about the words "new issue" that attracts buy orders from strangers. The feeling is that they are getting in on the ground floor, and at a price that is the same to all buyers, large or small. The absence of a direct commission is another inspiration to buy.

2. *New issues of unit trust with a specific yield.* A powerful valid reason for a call, with size *always limited* by the issuer these have a scarcity value easy to get across. New issues also carry an urgent message: "Act now or miss out on the opportunity." That message is one of the most powerful to open up a prospect in cold calling by phone.

3. *Common stock.* Many top brokers select a common stock with *special news* that might affect the next day's (or week's) market price. The news might be a research wire or report that the firm would like to communicate to investors as rapidly as possible so that an informed decision can be made. Or it might be some other important item like an oil discovery or merger announcement.

4. *Invitation to a "free lunch."* Sandwich and drink lecture lunches held at the office at noon for a select few

prominent people (for scarcity value) is an excellent valid reason for calling. Most people find it difficult to be rude and hang up abruptly after having been invited to lunch.

5. *Invitation to special evening seminar.* A talk featuring ways to save on income taxes is an excellent valid reason for calling: "You do want to save on income taxes don't you?" Can you imagine anyone saying "no" to that question?

Questions to Make Progress When Cold Calling by Phone

Asking questions of a prospect is a powerful way to extract information that might be helpful in determining what products to emphasize or what the potential size order may be. Here is a list of questions that have been effective in getting prospects to talk and disclose information about themselves and what they want or need. You will, no doubt, think of others that will be effective, too:

1. Can you use high, tax-free income?"
2. "Do you feel that investing in low-risk, high-potential-profit stocks fits in with your investment objectives?"
3. "Would you like to earn high interest, pay no current federal or state income tax, yet not risk losing any money?"
4. "What was the best investment you ever made?"
5. "Do you still have it [the "best" investment]?" Or "Why did you sell it?"
6. "What is your tax bracket?"
7. "Would you like to save on income taxes this year?"
8. "Would you like to have brand new Standard and Poor sheets on every stock you own?"
9. "Would you like me to get a research opinion for every stock you now own that worries you?"
10. "Would you like to have all your bonds reviewed as to quality ratings, current prices, and current yield?"
11. "Would you like a free copy of our weekly market letter each week for the next three weeks?"
12. "Would you like to have all your life insurance policies professionally reviewed and evaluated as to current worth, costs, and coverage?"
13. "Would you like to be on our select mailing list of people who are notified when new issues of common stocks and bonds are available for purchase without direct commission?"
14. "Would you like some information on how to create a tax shelter for current income?"
15. "Are you satisfied with how your money is working for you? In stock? In fixed income?"

Good security salespeople who produce consistently and earn high incomes year after year have learned that hard work, not brilliance, is truly the secret of success!

TWO THINGS YOU CAN DO TODAY TO MAKE YOUR BUSINESS GROW!

1. Be resistant to the word "no." More sales are "not made" because the salesperson gives up than for any other reason.

2. See that you survive at least 20 no's today. See that every phone call incoming or outgoing, is an order-asking call. If you do that, you will get some yeses. Most salespeople miss their potential simply because they don't daily ask for enough orders.

16. "What service do you wish you were getting from your broker that you're not getting?"

17. "What do you think a good broker should do for you?"

18. "What do you think a good insurance person should do for you?"

19. "Do you believe what you are doing with your assets is good enough considering our current inflation rate?"

The objective in asking questions is to get answers that provide clues as to what and how that prospect can be sold. Be sure to listen intently to the prospect's replies so that you can be deciding what is most suitable based on the comments.

Benefits of Cold Calling

Cold calls are very beneficial whether you are a new or an experienced seller of intangibles. One of the big benefits is that they force you to keep up to date on the products you are offering, on world events, and on economic happenings. News communication today is almost instant and can quickly cause a change in price of bonds, stocks, commodities, options, mutual funds, and even interest rates on tax-deferred annuities. If you cold call, you must stay current with such changes, and the changes give you valid reasons.

Another benefit in making cold calls is that they help you to hone your selling skills. The constant practice of trying to overcome objections and of learning to respond quickly to a prospect's questions, anticipated or not, develops sales toughness and expertise. Making cold calls keeps you alert, like a well-trained boxer.

The third benefit from consistently making cold calls is the financial reward obtained as a result of new client business.

Excuses for Cold-Call "Failures"

Despite the benefits that can be gotten from a disciplined, daily cold-call routine, many sellers of intangibles don't and won't make them. Here are some of the reasons they give for not cold calling strangers:

1. *"Tried it and failed.* I just wasn't getting anywhere with prospects." Translation: the ones who use this excuse never mastered the cold-call selling skill.

2. *"Don't like my own self-image."* Many salespeople feel it undignified to call strangers. They feel somewhat like peddlers and believe that cold calling is beneath them. Translation: ones who use this excuse have a misconception about what it means to be a professional salesperson.

3. *"Afraid of rejection."* Many salespeople are super-sensitive, and their egos are easily bruised and damaged. They can't tolerate hearing the word "no," and the occasional rudeness they encounter devastates them to the extent that they cannot get their nerve up to continue to cold call.

In actual practice, cold calls make a lot of sense and dollars for the salesperson who understands and believes in the selling game. It is necessary only to harden yourself against a certain number of failures that are certain to happen and to be cheered on by your successes.

Out of 100 cold phone calls, a good seller might open two or three accounts plus line up four or five appointments. That would be a good result! It would also mean that 90 percent or so of the calls met failure. Selling is often said to be partially a numbers game. To a great extent that is true. But the development of selling skill makes it easier to turn the numbers to your advantage.

How to be Successful at Cold Calling

Success in cold calling lies principally in three characteristics:

1. *Sticktuity.* The dogged determination to complete a prescribed number of calls each working day is essential.

2. *Product knowledge.* In-depth knowledge of aproduct helps develop confidence and breed enthusiasm, important qualities that can be transmitted to a prospect.

3. *Enhancement of selling skills.* The constant learning and practice of selling skills makes for a higher percentage of closes.

Reasons for Failure at Cold Calling

Special factors that cause failure in cold calling, even in those who doggedly complete a quota of daily calls, are these:

114

What a terrific stockbroker Dr. Joyce Brothers could be! Just listen to some of her philosophy, "I know what I want. I am not afraid to ask: I'll try asking for 10 things. If I am refused on 9, I'll simply dwell on the delight about the one yes."

TWO THINGS YOU CAN DO TODAY TO MAKE YOUR BUSINESS GROW!

1. **Place a high value on your time for selling.** *Don't fritter the day's prime selling hours away reading the WSJ, the broad tape, Business Week, company research reports, prospectuses, or posting trades and cross references.*

2. *Ask at least 20 different clients and prospects for an order today on a quality product.*

---

1. *Lack of enthusiasm.* Presenting a product in a monotone or a phlegmatic manner almost insures a turn-down.

2. *Lack of confidence.* Salespeople with only a flimsy knowledge of their products are quickly detected by prospects. Displaying a lack of knowledge of the facts and details of the product lowers the seller's confidence level and forces the prospect to reject the offer.

3. *Lack of product belief.* Many salespeople know their product but don't really believe in it or its value to a prospect. Therefore, they can only make half-hearted attempts to sell it. Here is another LeRoy maxim: *You have to believe—truly and strongly—in what you are selling if you are to do consistent good work in cold calling by phone. Your belief comes through the phone with great clarity; so does your lack of conviction.*

Cold Calling: 3 Objectives

A telephone call to a total stranger—the cold call—can be exhilarating, challenging, and often the source of a mind-boggling financial reward. Skilled cold callers know that the first step in undertaking this prospecting method successfully is to select with great care a valid, plausible-sounding reason for making the contact. Once the seller selects a valid reason and initiates the cold call, he or she carries the objectives for the call as armor during the joust with the prospect.

Although cold calling is a numbers game in the sense that a high enough number of completed calls will get some orders even for sellers with mediocre skills, acquiring a high level of phone selling skill can substantially increase the size and number of orders eventually obtained.

A skill that can up the cold-call batting average lies in this: Keep in mind the three cold-call objectives and progress from one to another until one or more of the objectives has been accomplished.

Let's look at the objectives that you should strive for on each cold call:

Objective 1:
Get an Order

When you call a stranger, what you want is an order—an order that converts the prospect into an actual, bona fide client. You want an order that will provide commissions that pay your bills and maintain your standard of living. You want an order that will boost your morale, expand your ego, and produce the

What a terrific din there would be if we all made as much noise when things go RIGHT as we do when they go WRONG!

high that you can't match with the most powerful stimulants. So the first objective is to *ask for the order!*

Objective 2: Get an Appointment

The facts of selling life are such that a diligent, hard-working salesperson might complete 50, 100, or more order-asking calls in a single day and not get a single order! With that possibility (some might say "probability") in mind, and after being told "no" to the order-asking question, it's time to pursue the second objective.

If you fail to get an order when you ask on a first-time cold call, try to get an appointment. Try to get the prospect to agree to see you, even for just a few minutes, at the prospect's convenience. Present the prospect with a choice of alternate times.

Face-to-face meetings usually result in more substantial orders than are granted on a cold phone call. Face to face, you have a chance to make your sincerity, honesty, and product knowledge more visible to the prospect. "Belly-to-belly" selling provides you with the opportunity to use visual aids of all types, the chance to break down social barriers, to create a deeper rapport, and to discover more about the prospect's assets and investment objectives.

Many financial products cannot easily be sold over the phone. The appointment and the more personal encounter make it easier to get larger orders for products like tax shelters, tax-deferred annuities, mutual funds, insurance, and the like.

Here is another LeRoy maxim: *The appointment must be "sold" just like any other product.* Prospects must perceive some personal benefit in giving *any* salesperson time in their schedule. If you ask for just a few minutes or the opportunity simply to "drop off" some special information, the prospect is likelier to grant permission.

Objective 3: Provide a Free Service

Certainly it isn't difficult for anyone to grasp the basic objectives of cold calling strangers and asking them for an order, failing to get one, and then requesting an appointment. Certainly it isn't difficult to imagine that the great majority of cold calls will result in a turn-down for objectives 1 and 2.

What's next? Defeat? Should you just quit and go on to the next prospect? No! The next step is to try to accomplish objective 3, perhaps the most important secret to being successful at opening accounts by phone: offering a free service.

Although you must keep all three objectives in mind while you make cold calls, bring objective 3 into play only after getting turned down for an order *and* turned down for an appointment. Properly handled, the offer of a free service will be accepted more than 50 percent of the time. That batting average should satisfy almost anyone, and the success factor helps to take the boredom and potential trauma out of cold calling.

The service you proffer should be so attractive that it is extremely difficult for any prospect to reject it. If possible, the service should also help to extract financial information from the prospect in order to pinpoint specifics to use later in follow-up sales contacts.

What kind of free services can you offer strangers during a first-time phone call? Here are some good items that many investors want and that most investors find difficult to refuse—items that, if accepted, *can lead to the order or the appointment you want.*

FREE OFFERS

1. *Free* Standard and Poor sheet on every single stock the prospect owns.
2. *Free* research opinion on any "worry" stock the prospect owns, an opinion that might resolve a dilemma as to whether to sell, buy more, or simply hold on.
3. *Free* valuation of a prospect's portfolio detailing current prices and yields on all stocks and bonds held, as well as gains and losses yet unrealized.
4. *Free* bond ratings on every bond issue held. Many bonds are up-graded or down-graded each month by the various rating services. These grade changes affect bond values. Large bondholders value this service.
5. *Free* subscription to the biweekly (monthly) market letter for a four-week period.
6. *Free* invitation to lunch (sandwich and drink) and/or to attend a special timely seminar on tax-saving ideas.

Top security salespeople try to make sure they do not overlook a single potential customer or sales opportunity. They stay ahead of competition by starting work earlier and planning tomorrow's calls tonight!

TWO THINGS YOU CAN DO TODAY TO MAKE YOUR BUSINESS GROW!

1. *Test your sales pitch on your favorite stock of the month with your manager. Let him test your knowledge, point out flaws, and help make your sales points harder hitting.*

2. *Do the same with some of the tougher brokers in your office. This will serve to sharpen your sales pitches and help you in making bigger sales (remembers to always ask for minimum orders of 1000 shares).*

7. *Free* analysis of all life-insurance policies.

8. *Free* booklet on tax-saving ideas.

The best free offers are items 1 through 4, because in order to get these "something-for-nothing" offers the prospect has to disclose significant personal financial information. This information can later lead to the order you are seeking.

Examine carefully the following typical cold call scenario to see how you can use the three-objective approach in your cold-calling program.

Illustration of the 3-Objective Cold Call

John Prospect: "This is John Prospect."

Joe Salesman: "This is Joe Salesman with XYZ Firm, members of the NYSE. My firm is underwriting a new issue of common stock of American Telephone at $51 per share. It is coming out tomorrow, and the people who buy it tomorrow will not have to pay any direct commissions. The shares are rated A+ by Standard and Poor and currently yield 9.9 percent. Normally these shares are taken by our own clients, but my manager has allocated me some shares for new accounts. That is why I am calling you today [valid reason]."

John Prospect: "That sounds pretty good."

Joe Salesman: "We think it is an outstanding opportunity to buy high-quality shares and not pay direct commissions. If you would like to reserve up to 500 shares I will try to get them for you. How many would you be interested in if I could get them [objective 1: asking for the order]?"

John Prospect: "Hold on, I didn't say I was interested in buying right now. All my money is tied up in other investments."

Joe Salesman: "I can understand how you might feel reluctant to place an order with some one you have never met, even though the stock is an attractively priced, blue chip like American Telephone. Look, I am going to be in your area tomorrow and again the next day. I would like to come by and drop off a copy of the prospectus on American Telephone. Even if you decided not to take advantage of this special offering where you can save on commission, you might want to read about it and the potential we believe it offers. What time would be best for you? Late tomorrow afternoon? Early the following morning? I can only spare a few minutes [objective 2: asking for an appointment]."

John Prospect: "I'm pretty well tied up both times, and it's really not necessary for you to come by."

Joe Salesman: "You sound like a very nice guy. You haven't been rude or hung up abruptly like many people [*this statement is a winner!*]. Because you have been nice enough to listen to me, I want to do something special just for you! I would like to *send you a brand new* [pause right there to give the prospect a chance to dream momentarily of a Mercedes or Jaguar] Standard and Poor sheet on every single stock you now own [objective 3: providing a free service]." (Maybe his current broker hasn't done that for him. It sure isn't likely.)

In order to get that "free" offer what must John Prospect do? You got it! He must disclose his entire stock portfolio. With that ammunition, Joe Salesman might later get an appointment or order. If the offer is accepted, the S & Ps must be sent promptly (better yet, hand delivered!). Each S & P should have a note attached: "Our research currently recommends purchase [or sale]." The prospect should be called again, after the sheets arrive, to review each holding, or to discuss quantities of any uneven lots to round up or round down, or to discuss eliminating small, meaningless holdings.

Providing the free service frequently leads to the order or appointment that you so strongly want.

To sum up cold-calling objectives, if you don't get the order, ask for an appointment. If you don't get the appointment, give away a free something that is so good it is not likely to be refused. Free "somethings" are great account builders and make the cold calling game not only productive but enjoyable.

Any experienced advertising expert can attest to the fact

Really good producers know that no monopoly exists on good sales ideas. They "copy" ideas that work for others, gladly! They don't worry about being "unoriginal." If something works for someone else, they are willing to give it a try. How willing are you to try others' ideas?

TWO THINGS YOU CAN DO TODAY TO MAKE YOUR BUSINESS GROW!

1. Plan how to better tomorrow's sales effort.

2. Write notes—"Call me right away"—and sign your name on 10 somethings (not prospectuses) that you really believe right for investors. Mail them before you leave the office today. List the names for follow-up phone calls next week. Be sure to enclose two somethings that can be completed and returned to you. Resolve to do this every day before you leave.

that "free" is the most powerful advertising weapon ever devised. Salespeople who make legal and judicious use of the word, backed up with the delivery of available services or items, will see their appointments and orders grow.

Mining the Cold-Call Gold

Gold has been a much desired commodity for thousands of years because of its wondrous qualities of durability, malleability and ductility as well as its density and beauty. It has no peer, worldwide, for retention of value and for ease of convertibility into whatever passes for coin of the realm. Gold, however, is a very scarce commodity. The primary sources of supply are South Africa, Russia, Canada, and the United States. Nations and individuals ceaselessly hunt and dig the earth in the search for a few grains of this precious metal.

In this age of modern communications, the seller of intangibles has, as the equivalent of gold, prospects. The endless supply of unknown people comprise for sellers of intangibles a gold mine second only to the Golconda. Properly mining the gold of prospects can bring the riches of Midas to hard workers who actively work their "claims" by using all their selling skills.

Here are some key points to focus on in tapping the motherlode of prospects: the daily regimen of making cold calls to total strangers. These points, if mastered, can produce nuggets of gold as valuable as those dug out of a mine or panned from a river.

Enthusiasm Sells and Convinces

Cold telephone calls permit a prospect to judge the seller, the product, and the value of the contact based *only* on what is heard. Enthusiasm is contagious. If you are to make a success out

122

MINING THE COLD-CALL GOLD

In every selling office, salespeople can usually be divided into three groups.
1. Those who make things happen
2. Those who watch things happen
3. Those who wonder what happened
Which group are you in?

TWO THINGS YOU CAN DO TODAY TO MAKE YOUR BUSINESS GROW!

1. **Make a list of thinly traded OTC issues of local banks or insurance companies. See if your firm does or can make a market in those issues.**

2. **Contact members of the board of directors (phone or personal visit) to advise them of your interest in their stock and offer to help them buy (or sell) as their need or desire arises. Many brokers have developed substantial business following this method; you can, too! Get the directors' names from the annual reports.**

of telephone cold calling, you must force yourself to be enthusiastic.

Use inflection to convey your confidence; avoid a monotonous delivery. In order for your enthusiasm to be assessed as real, not phony, you must be offering a product that (1) you truly believe is good for the prospect and (2) presents a good value at the time of the offer. a strong belief in what you are selling is one of the most powerful gold-mining tools.

Product Knowledge Sells and Convinces

Salespeople who have in-depth knowledge of the product under discussion make more sales and make them more easily. Knowledge makes it easier to overcome objections, too. Real, rather than superficial, knowledge can be perceived by a cold-call recipient very easily; and so can lack of knowledge.

If you really want to succeed in mining the cold-call gold, you must really study and thoroughly master all the information, benefits, features, advantages, and disadvantages of any product you are trying to sell to strangers. Your presentation will gain strength because you have retained a superior store of facts. Objections will not surprise or throw you; you will simply be able to counter them by relating the proper features and key sales points.

Persistance Makes Sales

Plenty of good salespeople are knowledgeable about their product and radiate enthusiasm when discussing it; yet some of them earn very little because they lack the gumption to discipline themselves to "go to the mine" every day.

To mine the cold-call gold effectively, you must dig for prospects every day. A good way to do this is to call enough prospects (*not* clients) to get at least 20 or more "no's" from orders asked for. If you daily make enough presentations enthusiastically rendered to get you 20 "no's" from products in which you believe, inevitably some golden "yeses" will creep in—"yeses" that will brighten your life like golden bars in your very own vault.

Selecting High "Buy-Ability" Prospects Makes Sales

To mine the cold-call gold, the effort must be made to call only those prospects with the financial wherewithal to purchase the product you are offering. Nothing discourages a seller more than going through a presentation to what turns out to be an unqualified buyer. Cull and restrict your prospect list to high-income people and you will naturally strike more gold, more often. Avoid calling numbers randomly selected from the white pages. There are too many unqualified buyers to make that strategy highly effective.

In-Person Cold Calls

Cold calls made face to face rather than by phone can often produce substantial clients. Most prospects feel more at ease about dealing with someone they can see. They are more likely to disclose more about their financial circumstances.

Here are some gold-mining tips to enhance your selling skills. Whenever you leave your office to go see prospects (or clients) on a scheduled appointment, adhere to the following:

1. *Bring a story book.* Visual aids are powerful persuaders to use as evidence in convincing a prospect to buy. Use them whenever possible.

2. *Reconfirm the appointment time.* The day of the scheduled appointment (or day before, if it is an early morning appointment), call the prospect and confirm the meeting time and meeting place.

3. *Ask for referrals when you reconfirm.* When reconfirming the appointment make a statement like this "I have to be in your area about 30 minutes before I see you. Whom do you think I might call on before I meet with you?" You may get a referred preappointment lead that turns out to have much larger potential than the prospect. *Remember: If you don't ask you won't get!*

4. *Ask for referrals when you leave.* After concluding your visit with the prospect, whether or not an order has been obtained, say: "As long as I am in this area, whom do you think I should see before I go back to my office?" Many prospects who are reluctant to grant a preappointment request for a referral will grant a postappointment referral request. You may have done so well conveying your sincerity, honesty, and product knowledge during

your presentation that prospects who reject your proposal may soften the blow with one or more referrals. And those who have agreed to buy your proffered product may want to get someone else into the same "hot water" they've just stepped into. Frequently, you can obtain several good leads from a prospect simply by asking directly for them. What have you got to lose? Do it!

5. *If you leave the office to make a cold call, make several.* Even if you don't get a referral on the pre- or post-appointment request, just drop in cold on a prospect in the same area and start a conversation by any means you can, then work the conversation around to your specialty and special story-book product. *There is an unlimited supply of gold in prospecting strangers.* All you have to do is meet new people every day, show them what you have to offer, convince them that they need it, and you will do business. Don't make the common mistake of leaving your office to call on one person, completing the presentation, and then returning to the office having made only one pitch. Make the time out of the office more effective by arranging to see new prospects and your business will grow bigger.

Special Tips for Special Prospects

Here are a few more sales-building thoughts that may help you in mining the cold-call gold. Certain groups of people are excellent potential prospects for hard-working, aggressive sellers of intangibles, yet these people are often difficult to reach or just unreachable. Getting through to these choice prospects is a challenge, and often worth the extra effort.

DENTISTS

One high-earning, hot-potential group is dentists. The demand for their service is high, as is their earning and investment ability. Calls to the dentist during the typical nine-to-five workday are carefully screened by the receptionist to weed out sellers of all types. What can be done to reach the target?

I have found that many dentists get to the office prior to the first appointments (usually scheduled at 8:30 to 9:00, depending on the area of the country). They arrive early in order to do some preliminary work or simply catch up on mail, pay bills, or take care of other mundane details of a practice. An early morning phone call, at 8:15 or 8:30, frequently is answered by the dentist (as hired hands normally try to show up a minute or two before the scheduled workday begins). Once you have gotten through, you have the opportunity to sell yourself and your product. No guarantees that it always works, but it is certainly worth the small amount of early morning time that it takes to try. Besides, who else of substance would you have the opportunity of reaching at 8:15 A.M.?

DOCTORS

Doctors represent another high-earning, high-potential group of prospects for cold-call gold mining. Getting through to doctors is a very difficult task. Normally they make hospital rounds in the morning and see patients in the afternoon. As with dentists, their receptionists have been carefully coached to screen out salespeople. "Leave word" most often goes unreturned. There is no sure method that works to get through to doctors, but for those of you who want to prospect doctors within a close enough radius to meet with them if the opportunity is given, I have a nifty, gutsy way to try. (If you don't have nerve and a strong desire to reach the target skip the next few paragraphs and go to the next chapter.)

For those of you who *do* have prospecting nerve and a desire for some medical gold, here is a ploy that frequently is effective. If you want to reach the doctor, simply call the doctor's office. The secretary/receptionist will answer: "Dr. John Prospect's office." After hearing this cheery greeting, just deliver the following message and hang up before any questions can be asked: "Tell John that Joe will pick him up for lunch at 12:15 Thursday. [The call is made on Monday or Tuesday.] He can reach me if necessary at 558-6000." Read the message again. There is no request to speak to the doctor. You do *not* identify your firm or your profession. You do not leave your last name. When the message is delivered, here is what frequently takes place. The doctor starts thinking, "Was I drunk recently and made this lunch date? Who is this Joe? Is my mind not functioning? Nurse, did you have me down for lunch with a Joe at 12:15 on Thursday?"

"No, doctor!"

Finally, after ruminating and questioning his memory the doctor calls the number and asks for Joe.

You got through to the target! Now you had better take advantage of the moment. Your nerve got you this far.

Joe Salesman:	"This is Joe Salesman with ZXY, members of the NYSE, and even though we haven't met, I thought you might have lunch with me Thursday at 12:15. I was going to be in your area anyway, and you might want to hear some very new legal ways to save on income taxes."
Dr. John Prospect:	"Well, it's nice of you to ask, but really I can't make it then."
Joe Salesman:	"Look, you're human, you have to eat [said

Have you ever thought that the reason you don't get more big orders is that you don't ask for them? Many brokers rush to settle for a small or occasional order without making the extra effort to increase the size or frequency.

TWO THINGS YOU CAN DO TODAY TO MAKE YOUR BUSINESS GROW!

1. *Call three of your clients to tell them their buying power. They may place an order with you once they realize that they do not have to put additional cash into the account in order to purchase more stock.*

2. *Prospect the owner of the restaurant at which you normally eat every day. A familiar face is always hard to turn down.*

with humor]! When *do* you have lunch? I'll adjust my time and you may learn some tax-saving ideas that will be very worthwhile to you. You would like to save on income taxes, wouldn't you?" (The last question is most assuredly a "hot button.")

Dr. John Prospect: "Okay, you got me. How about picking me up at 12:45."

Joe Salesman: "Okay, I'll be there."

Certainly it doesn't work every time, but at least it gives the opportunity to reach a high-income person who might not normally respond to other tactics.

Here's what I found as a result as of the "yes's" I received to the luncheon invitation. The doctors I met were, in all cases, nice, intelligent, and conscious of having been conned into the appointment. They politely, intently listened to me pitch my product of the moment. If they liked it and bought from me, of course they let me pick up the tab. Strangely enough, if they decided not to buy, they usually grabbed the check and insisted upon paying so that they would not be obligated.

Not a bad outcome. Free lunch if you "lose," in the sense of not getting an order, or a new client at the cost of a lunch. Certainly worthwhile in either case.

LAWYERS AND CPAs

How about lawyers or CPAs? Can the same ploy be used? Certainly! If you can't get through any other way, and you are sure your target is a genuine prospect for your products, try the method outlined for doctors.

All About Secretaries

Whether you are using the phone or the face-to-face approach, most of the time you will find your pathway blocked by secretaries—secretaries whose duty it is to defend their bosses from solicitations.

Secretaries for the most part are wonderful people who can help you in your desire to get through to prospects. You should never lie to or mislead a secretary. You should do your dead level best to make her like you and to get her to understand your product and the good it might do for her boss. Make a secretary your ally and not only will she help you get through to her boss, often she will help sell her boss.

Secretaries are also frequently capital pools themselves. They may have money available for investment. They may know family members that are investment minded. Their husbands may be affluent.

Yes, make every effort to treat secretaries with the utmost respect and it will pay off for you as it frequently did for me. Learn the secretary's name. Pronounce it correctly and record it for future use.

One of the best clients I ever had was secretary to the owner of a textile mill. To get to him I had to go through her. She was an extremely smart woman who knew as much about her boss's business as he did himself. I told her that I wanted to talk to her boss about a deeply undervalued textile stock uncovered by our research department. She asked me questions about it, intelligent ones, and then I walked her through my story book on the stock. It turned out that she had $500,000 in securities and cash, and was actually a bigger, more active investor than her boss! She had built up an inheritance through prudent, careful investing. She bought my idea herself and then sold it for me to her boss and a dozen other family members and friends. Yes, secretaries can be tremendous allies for cold callers who seek prospecting gold.

Phone-call expertise in gaining orders and appointments can be sharply improved if you never talk more than 30 seconds without giving the other party a "chime-in" opportunity by asking a question.

TWO THINGS YOU CAN DO TODAY TO MAKE YOUR BUSINESS GROW!

1. *Learn all the features about your money-market fund: no load, high yield, ready cash, daily dividends, free check-writing, daily compounding.*

2. *Tell the "money" story to 10 prospects today. (My bet is that you will open 1 or more accounts per 10 approaches.) The money later will come out into a commission product.*

Making Low-Cost/No-Cost Seminars Produce Big Bucks

Holding public seminars as a means of obtaining prospects is gaining increasing favor with all types of firms that sell financial products. Firms like this forum-prospecting method because it provides a relatively cheap way to reach high-potential prospects in a manner that is meant to be significant and meaningful.

However, the proper promotion, set-up, and delivery of sales-producing seminar is very difficult. One of its great proponents is Alan C. Snyder, President of Dean Witter Reynolds Insurance, who has given hundreds of effective seminars on a variety of financial topics. So have I. Our hard-won expertise is condensed in this discussion. We have used all the information related here to close sales totaling in the millions. Our success was not instant; success developed through application of good techniques characterized by hard work and good planning.

Even if you feel unsure of your ability to make effective presentations in public, try to force yourself to do it. You will improve with practice and if you follow our system, you will be positively reinforced with substantial sales.

Learn to Speak Effectively in Public

Public-speaking courses, given at night at community colleges or YMCAs, can help make your delivery better. Look for one and take it.

Toastmasters is an excellent nationwide organization to help improve speaking skills. Join your local chapter! You will also find Toastmasters members a fine group to prospect, as they usually include the up-and-coming people in the community.

Basics for the Presentation

In preparing your presentations, take into consideration the following suggestions:

1. *Prepare an attention-getting opening statement.* Example: "In every group of 100 people in the United States today reaching the age 65, 87 of the 100 are trying to survive, attempting to get along on less than $5,000 a year *from all sources* including Social Security!"

2. *Cite a negative example.* Illustration: "Don't do as thousands of people are doing, letting their money earn low bank savings rates fully taxable at their highest brackets."

3. *Cite a positive example.* Illustration: "Do as many intelligent investors are now doing placing their money [name specific products]."

4. *Prepare an order-creating closing statement.* Example: "Everyone in this room tonight should plan to take some of their money and put it to work in [name a product that you've highlighted in your presentation]."

As you rehearse your presentation to make it more effective, try to avoid the following common problems:

1. *Speaking too fast.* Racing through a presentation destroys a great part of its value. Allow time for emphasis and pauses as well as time for the audience to think and absorb what you are saying. If you want to imprint your message on their minds, slower is better!

Ninety percent or more of a broker's business is done over the telephone, yet most account executives don't realize the 90% of their problems are caused by the wrong tone of voice!

Good security salespeople make their clients understand that the AE isn't telling them what to do—but only helping the prospect arrive at an intelligent decision. How many prospects did you help make good decisions today?

TWO THINGS YOU CAN DO TODAY TO MAKE YOUR BUSINESS GROW!

1. **Keep your own troubles, problems, and complaints to yourself.**

2. **Be cheerful, look cheerful! Nobody really wants to do business with a pessimist who has a hang-dog, beaten appearance and outlook. Look carefully at yourself in the mirror before you come to work. Clothes may not "make the man" but they can sure influence your mood and others who see you.**

2. *Poor enunciation.* Be sure of the correct pronunciation of any different words you intend to use. Be scrupulous about enunciating clearly so that the audience can easily understand exactly what you say and not confuse words with similar-sounding words.

3. *Weak ending.* Don't let your voice die at the end of a sentence. Many speakers trail off and swallow sentence-ending words. That makes any listener strain to hear, and it destroys the impact of your remarks.

4. *Hesitation sounds.* Noises like "er," "um," and "uh" are destructive. They actually kill the effectiveness of even the best material. Substituting pauses for these unself-confident-sounding syllables will greatly improve the impression you make on the audience. To help rid yourself of the "uh" syndrome, simply tape-record your presentation. Listen to it with pad and pencil in hand, and mark down the number of times you hear "uh" and "er" and "um." This scoring procedure will make you conscious of the habit. Once you become conscious of it, you will be on your way to eliminating the unattractive, unself-confident sounds from your pattern of speech.

Setting Up, Delivering, and Following Up Public Seminars

Public seminars have become a most effective stage from which sellers of intangibles can sell themselves, their firms, and specific products. Many of the best producers in the country developed their clientele primarily through effective and frequent seminar presentations. What holds true for them can become true for you.

Building a business and regularly providing a steady stream of new accounts through a seminar program is not an easy task, nor is the method effective for every seller of intangibles. However, for ambitious people who want to reach a high income level and who are willing to pay the price of hard work, the seminar approach can be one of the *most rewarding and consistent* of all prospecting methods.

This chapter is devoted to helping you learn the skills involved in conducting seminars and avoid the common mistakes.

Collecting existing clients or new prospects together in a forum environment gives you, as the sponsor, a great opportunity to make large sales and to sell yourself to a degree impossible by other means.

Existing clients are an excellent target market for more business. You should not be surprised that explaining new products and services or providing an investment overview strengthens your relationship with them. What more efficient, yet personal, way could there be to inform and sell? *You are controlling the presentation.* The content can be tailored to the most appropriate group in attendance in order to maximize results. New business can be gotten from the "bring-a-friend"

Good security salespeople wanting to do better understand that they are not getting the maximum income out of the talents they have—to improve. They study what they have done and force themselves to do more!

TWO THINGS YOU CAN DO TODAY TO MAKE YOUR BUSINESS GROW!

1. *Make a list of all the affluent (real or suspected) you personally know but never have asked for an order.*

2. *Call them and ask for an order! (You can bet they are investing through someone. It might as well be you.)*

opener. New business may come from reviving an otherwise dead account. New business may develop when good clients discover you provide a service they didn't know you sold. Seminars are one professional approach for new business that maximizes your time.

Prospects are the primary source from which new business will come. The seminar gives you an opportunity to explain something of interest to potential investors in an unthreatening environment. You whet prospects' appetites with an invitation describing the benefits that the new knowledge will provide.

Listen to Alan Snyder, President of Dean Witter Reynolds Insurance: "The seminar is the tour through the kitchen. You serve the meal at the close. The new client/prospect gets exposure to timely investment ideas that might greatly benefit him." Happily, outside experts with third-party power can be used when necessary or available (e.g., financial-product wholesalers, tax-shelter or insurance specialists).

Low-Cost Ways to Beef Up Seminar Attendance

Diligent, thoughtful salespeople seek various "sponsors" to get a group together. The attendees at sponsored seminars are just as good and valuable prospects as those obtained at high expense by direct mail or newspaper ads.

Typical of sponsored seminars are talks given to civic club groups such as Rotary, Lions, Kiwanis, Optimists, and like organizations. When given the opportunity to speak before groups like the above, don't make hard-sell specific recommendations but try to intrigue the audience with new concepts such as tax-deferred annuities, tax shelters, and trading strategies.

Usually, the time allotted for such talks is only 25 to 30 minutes. Make every effort to finish in time to allow for a few questions. Inform everyone that you have made material available to pick up on a special table. The material should have your card attached and a return card of some type that can be sent in to obtain more information. Remember to check the return card so that it is not mailed back to the home office. *Put your name and branch on it!* Where possible, try to obtain the membership list of the sponsoring group for a later mailing.

Public corporations can frequently be persuaded to let you give a seminar on "their" stock to the stock-holding employees. Seminars of this type can be most productive, and you can suggest one, two, or three sessions.

Prospect for corporate seminars by calling local corporation presidents, treasurers, or key officers to explain what you would like to do. In trying to sell them on sponsoring your seminar, you might wind up with an account. A contact made under such circumstances makes phone prospecting easier. Close with a brief description of several new products and services being offered "now" through your firm.

Finding Sponsors

Many types of sponsored seminars are available to put you in front of an audience *without your having to spend any (or many) funds.* These low-cost or no-cost seminars are every bit as valuable in producing prospects as the high-cost ones. The following list shows you possibilities for speaking engagements.

PUBLIC LIBRARIES

Frequently, public libraries will furnish a room and advertising for an investment seminar. If the talk and attendance are good, you can probably arrange to hold a seminar quarterly.

Good security salespeople quickly learn that the greatest good-will builder (and referral getter) is to take more than their share of the blame for any loss and less than their share of the credit for any gain. Maybe you can take a cue from what the good and the great do!

TWO THINGS YOU CAN DO TODAY TO MAKE YOUR BUSINESS GROW!

1. **Call nonclient CPAs until you can entice one to have lunch with you today.**

2. **Topic: His view of of tax shelters from his vantage point of return preparation—which to avoid, which have been most rewarding, which he might have a future interest in for his client. Build good-will with him and you create a referral center.**

Top stockbrokers have two common characteristics. First, they are convinced beyond a doubt of the upside potential in specially chosen stock. Second, their very conviction gives them the power to persuade others.

TWO THINGS YOU CAN DO TODAY TO MAKE YOUR BUSINESS GROW!

1. **Focus on a single stock for the day and ask 50 different people—prospects or clients—to buy some. Incoming or outgoing calls? Ask for an order on each.**
2. **Try to get 20 or more executed buy orders on your focus stock today.**

CIVIC CLUBS

The "emergency speaker" letter (see Exhibit section for sample) is a very effective tool in lining up talks to groups. Calling the presidents of civic clubs and offering to conduct a program is also effective. (Get the list of presidents from your local Chamber of Commerce.)

DEPARTMENT STORES

Because they are always interested in building traffic in their stores, store managers are good prospects to whom you should try to sell the "sponsor" concept. One or two managers often will become your clients too! Notification of the seminar can be put into their customers' statements (no extra mailing cost for them or you) or the stores' newspaper ads. Offer to pay half the cost and handle the reservation requests.

PUBLICLY HELD CORPORATIONS

Seminars based on preretirement counseling for retiring employees frequently can get you into a corporation and its executives. One-session seminars based on an analysis of the company's stock versus the market may also kindle interest.

SPECIAL-INTEREST GROUPS AND ORGANIZATIONS

Accountants' societies or the medical and legal societies all need program speakers at their monthly meetings. Some sellers of intangibles regularly address the partners of major accounting firms, dispensing product information to them so that they can anticipate their clients' questions. Contacting these groups can sometimes put you in front of the wealthy, powerful people who represent the best prospects. Insurance, and tax shelters as part of an overall financial program including stocks and bonds, are good presentations for such groups. Small-business groups naturally respond to using pretax dollars to fund business insurance.

YMCAs/YMHAs/YWCAs

Frequently, "Y" associations sponsor classes on investments. Try to get yourself appointed as the instructor for a quarterly course. Many of the attendees will sooner or later make investments or buy insurance.

COMMUNITY COLLEGES/BUSINESS COLLEGES

Teaching institutions often use, and pay, experienced people to teach an investment course to students, who pay for the privilege. Imagine your getting paid to prospect! It does happen, and it could happen to you if you contact your local educational institutions.

CONDOMINIUM ASSOCIATIONS

Many retirement communities have club rooms and seek out speakers to entertain and teach retirees. The associations usually furnish the facilities, equipment, and refreshments,

Top security salesmen understand that having a high IQ is a great asset but not nearly as effective and powerful as having a high "I will."

TWO THINGS YOU CAN DO TODAY TO MAKE YOUR BUSINESS GROW!

1. *Pick a local OTC stock priced under $10 per share with good EPS prospects. Learn the facts about it; build a story book on it.*

2. *Try to "give away" 1000 or more shares each week "free." How? By approaching prospects who have existing portfolios and showing them how, by agreeing to sell some of their shares, they might generate enough premium income to fully pay for some of the OTC shares—all accomplished without drawing on their savings or checking accounts.*

Good security salespeople soon find out that the way to get ahead is to do more than is necessary for clients, and keep on doing it!

TWO THINGS YOU CAN DO TODAY TO MAKE YOUR BUSINESS GROW!

1. **Take a nice low-commission-producer client to lunch—he or she will love the special attention.**

2. **Let the person know that you will pay close attention to the account no matter how small. Also, let that person know that referrals really help you. Many of the best "bird dogs" are small investors!**

without cost to you. This market is especially big in Florida and California.

THE TOPICS

The Critical Choices

The selection of a topic for a seminar is most crucial if your promotional material is to draw the attendance that you desire. In recent market environments, subjects such as "Estate Planning," "Ways to Save on Income Taxes," and "Learn How You Can Earn a Guaranteed Lifetime Income" have normally produced the largest turn-outs. Often, lectures on specific products are too narrowly focused to draw well.

Three-session courses on learning about all facets of investing, but heavily slanted toward high-income investing, have consistently attracted attendees.

Whatever your topic selection, refresh your knowledge on the subject material so that you will increase your confidence. In presenting the material, you will want to present the image of the *helpful professional.* Your role will be to *sell yourself* to the group as a knowledgeable person, rather than to educate the group to a great degree.

DATE SELECTION

Once you have selected your topic, you must choose a date for your seminar. You should consider checking for upcoming sporting, political, TV, or local events that might detract from the potential attendance at your lecture. Be aware of major religious, state, and national holidays. Night seminars usually draw best on Tuesdays, Wednesdays, or Thursdays. Middle or late

December is usually a poor time for seminars; people are too busy with the holidays.

TIME

After carefully selecting the date, choose a time that will allow potential prospects to arrive at your site after work and dinner. For some areas of the country, where many people commute, 8:00 P.M. is ideal. In other areas, 7:30 P.M. is the most suitable time. In retirement areas, such as Florida, people will come to lectures at 10:30 A.M., especially if coffee and juice are offered, and 4:00 P.M., so that they can be through in time for supper.

Consider offering two lecture times in your promotion. One might be a morning time for retired people and the other an evening time for workers, as well as retired people. One of the most successful account executives in the country ($750,000 gross) works in a major city and developed his business solely through same-day lectures using the morning and evening times.

Lunchtime seminars can be a super-effective means of developing prospects. The best time is 12:30 P.M. to 1:30 P.M. on Thursdays. The procedure is to call local business people, doctors, accountants, and lawyers to inform them that they are invited to a special seminar from 12:30 P.M. to 1:30 P.M. on a specific Thursday. Tell them that only a limited number of people can attend, as the seminar will be held in the conference room of your office. Say that sandwiches and coffee will be served. If they "can't make it," tell them that you are repeating the seminar on the following Thursday. Make every effort to try to pin them down into accepting for that day. This process gives you Monday, Tuesday, and Wednesday to make prospecting calls offering a "free lunch" and an interesting topic. If no one accepts or shows up, you have lost nothing. If two or three attend, you have a great chance to convert them into accounts. Lunchtime seminars make calling easier and provide a lot of prospect contact.

Most people have to eat lunch and, if they can eat "free" and learn something interesting about tax savings, they may be inclined to attend, or at least to request the information. You also might draw prospects who would not go out at night to attend an investment seminar.

THE SITE

The site for your public lecture is one of the most critical choices; it will significantly affect your attendance. One key item is the availability of free parking. Local, well-known motels or restaurants solve the parking problem. Other popular lecture sites are schools, country clubs, and libraries. Choose a site, if possible, that is popular, perhaps a landmark, so that instructions for getting there are easy to follow.

Ben Feldman, the number-1 salesman for New York Life every year for over 20 consecutive years, is a great believer in goal setting—with time limits—and within reach if every effort is made. He says, Salespeople who have no place to go aren't going anywhere!

You may be fortunate enough to have large and accessible office facilities that can accommodate from 10 to 30 people. Whenever an office can be used as the lecture site, "classes" are more effective because the surroundings are businesslike. Seminars in branches also make it easy to arrange future appointments: the prospect has already "been there."

DIRECT MAIL

You have several choices available to attract prospects to an investment seminar. The most popular, and generally most successful, is direct mail. Direct mail requires extensive thought, work, and preparation. Take these points into consideration.

How to Draw Attendance at Unsponsored Seminars

1. You and the branch manager must determine the number of pieces to be mailed, due to the expense involved.

2. Select the area to be mailed carefully. You want to select affluent prospects for whom the lecture site will be easily accessible.

3. Assemble the names on cards or lists, and prepare mailing labels.

4. Decide with the manager whether to mail first class or bulk mail, by zip code area or addressed to "resident." By mailing bulk, you can realize substantial savings, reaching more people with the allocated dollars. An additional benefit to "occupant" mail is that such mail is *not* forwarded to people who have moved, so that new tenants, who would not have been on the address list, receive the "occupant" mail.

Sometimes, purchased lists are workable. However, they

usually cover too broad a geographic area to be effective for an individual branch. These are best left to national lead programs, particularly when the lists are of magazine subscribers, tax-shelter purchasers, and stock owners.

NEWSPAPER ADVERTISING

Another way to publicize seminars is to place an ad in the local newspaper. Results in garnering attendees vary widely, and local experience with seminar ads is your best guide to whether to use this medium. Sometimes, direct mail combined with an ad is highly effective. The choice depends on costs and prior experience in your area.

PHONE CONTACT

The third method for drawing attendance is to use the phone extensively to try to interest people in coming to the seminar. This way is a recommended *supplement* to any lecture, for it accomplishes two purposes. The primary goal is to try to build attendance. The secondary goal is to make contact with potential prospects for future appointments or for the sale of one of your products, *whether or not they attend the seminar.* Phone campaigns are particularly effective with existing clients. After you make the initial contact, follow up with the invitation detailing time and place.

TELEVISION

In a few areas, UHF television stations have pull power at low cost, and this route may be effective in gathering people to a lecture. The branch manager, in conjunction with the advertising department, can assess the efficacy of this approach.

ALLOW ENOUGH LEAD TIME

Once you have chosen your promotional medium, be sure to allow adequate response time. If you promote too far in advance of the seminar, the number of attendees usually drops. The same holds true if you promote too close to the seminar date. Judging from experience, direct mail with an enclosed response card should be mailed approximately two to three weeks prior to the lecture. This allows time for the normally slow U.S. mail system both to deliver and to allow the return card to be received.

Newspaper ads should be run ten days to two weeks prior

Voltaire would have been a great security salesman if he lived up to his credo: "Work keeps at bay three great evils: (1) boredom, (2) vice (!!); (3) need.

TWO THINGS YOU CAN DO TODAY TO MAKE YOUR BUSINESS GROW!

1. *Volunteer your services as a solicitor for a local charity fund-raising campaigns such as Red Cross, the Cancer Fund, the Heart Fund. This is an excellent way to meet new affluent prospects and do a civic good deed at the same time!*

2. *Tell 5 (or more) charity givers how to increase donations, get bigger tax deductions, yet not reduce their current checking or savings accounts. (Write OTM calls against owned stock and donate the premiums!)*

to the lecture, to allow coupon returns to be received and confirmed. One problem that can destroy a well-planned seminar is the failure to allow sufficient time for the direct mail pieces to be approved, printed, and received at your branch. Check this particular lead time through your manager when you are planning your seminar. Allowing time for delays is smart business practice.

Once a coupon response is received, immediately send a written confirmation on your note pad *relating the time, date, and place of the seminar.* Additionally, contact each responder by phone a day or two before the seminar to reconfirm attendance.

Confirm Reponses

Important: *This phone contact should be made by you, not by your sales assistant!* In talking to the prospective attendee, you have an opportunity to build rapport and, possibly, provide investment help or even obtain an appointment prior to the seminar. Frequently, seminar attendance can be "built" by informing each attendee that he or she is allowed to bring one or more friends. By encouraging others to attend the seminar, attendees frequently lock themselves into coming, when they might otherwise simply change their minds and fail to attend. Encourage husbands and wives to come as a unit. If they are both exposed to the same information and to your personality as the lecturer, it is usually easier to get a closing appointment.

If a three-session seminar is being conducted, *confirm each session* by mail and phone to try to keep and increase attendance.

The people who answer the telephone at your branch office must have a reference sheet with all details of the time, date, and place of your lecture so that they can properly handle phone requests. Neglecting this detail can scale down the attendance that you have spent money and hard work to try to obtain.

Rehearse Your Seminar

The best speakers in the world freely admit to being on edge before delivering a talk. When giving a presentation to a public group, you should normally expect a case of butterflies. Here are several key points that will help you to deliver a good talk despite the inherent tension:

1. *Rehearse your presentation* with your spouse, manager, or colleagues. Doing so will help you sharpen up your talk and give you more self-confidence.
2. *Make an outline of your talk* on 3 × 5 cards or printed sheets.
3. *Write your notes legibly* so that when you refer to them, they are easy to read.
4. *Time the length of your talk* and allow about 15 minutes at the end for questions. Try to limit your talk to 45 minutes to an hour.
5. *Be conscious of audience comfort.* The seats may not be comfortable for the audience, or the room may be too hot or cold. Many people need a rest break along the way. It is better to leave them wanting more information than to give them too much.

You must remember that your *main objective is to sell yourself.* Try to create an image of trust. Do not be all knowing, but try instead to project the picture of a diligent, informative broker who will make every effort to help lessen the client's investment risk and increase the client's income.

Finally, *tape-record the actual lecture,* as well as a rehearsal, to serve as a guide to the parts you did well on and to help you correct those areas in which you were weak.

Visual Aids

People learn by what they hear *and* what they see. If they can hear and see, they tend to understand more easily. Selecting and using visual aids can measurably improve the impact of an investment presentation. Many types of visual aids can help improve your talk, ranging from flip charts, blackboards, 35 mm slides, and overhead projections to video-tapes.

EASEL PADS

Use large easel pads only for small groups, where everyone in the group is close enough to read the material on the pad easily. *Don't write on the pad as you make your presentation.* The tendancy to write fast and illegibly is normal, but by doing so you will destroy the effectiveness of the thought. Besides, your back would be toward the audience, and you would find yourself talking to the pad rather than to the prospect. The one excep-

How big a producer Elmer Letterman could have been in our industry by practicing his credo: "when the outlook isn't good, try the uplook!

TWO THINGS YOU CAN DO TODAY TO MAKE YOUR BUSINESS GROW!

1. *Set a specific $ commission goal for today. Work to beat it before 1:00 New York time!*
2. *Get one new account today: cold phone call, in-person cold call, or asked-for referral. Just concentrate each day on getting those new account(s)! Your business will really grow!*

tion is if you have asked the audience to tell you their goals or otherwise contribute information.

Prepare easel-pad visuals in advance so that you have simply to turn the pages and expand upon the points shown on the pad. Print large letters and use inks of different colors to focus the audience's attention. Once you have made several easel-pad presentations, you will be equipped to give others more easily, since the work of building the presentation has already been completed.

BLACKBOARDS

Generally, blackboards are not effective visual aids, even for small groups. Visibility can be bad due to the poor physical state of the board, the quality of chalk, the size of the board, and the lighting in the room. Using a blackboard requires much erasing and rewriting. As with easels, writing legibly and rapidly is a rare talent most people lack. Using the blackboard puts your back to the audience, and you end up talking to the board.

Blackboards can best be used to list your name and perhaps one or two main themes or points that remain constantly in view throughout the presentation.

35 mm SLIDES

Many speakers like to use 35-mm slide presentations. These clearly visible aids are very helpful to the audience. If you use slides, you can almost forego your notes and instead take your cues from the slides, expanding your talk from the key points in the slides.

One disadvantage of slide presentations is that the lights must be dimmed. The semidarkness may cause nodding heads, which may disconcert you, and your lecture will, unfortunately, fail to influence the sleepers. Another disadvantage of slides is the possibility of equipment failure or that the screen will be too small for the audience to view the slides well. Despite the potential disadvantages, however, the positive features of color, high visibility, and readability make 35 mm slides a most attractive visual aid at seminars.

Be sure to number your slides so that you or an assistant may easily and carefully place them in the carousel. Out-of-order slides can seriously affect the quality of your presentation, and the audience may miss key sales points.

Many lecturers maintain slide sets already mounted in their own carousels so they need simply place the carousel on the projector. Their talk is in order and ready for the beginning of the show, with no frantic, last-minute scrambling. Keep in mind that not all slides will fit in any carousel. Most Kodak carousels do fit the different Kodak projectors.

OVERHEAD TRANSPARENCIES

Overhead transparencies are very effective visual tools for adding power to a presentation. They can be shown in a more brightly lit room than can be used for 35-mm presentations. You can write on a prepared transparency in colored pencil to highlight a particular point; that involves the audience more deeply in the subject.

As with 35-mm presentations, the possible failure of equipment can cause a problem. A large screen is necessary for good visibility. Once a set of transparencies is made, they can be used for many presentations before they deteriorate from warping or scratches.

Do not type material on overhead transparencies. Typed copy is very difficult to read from a distance. Careful, large lettering (color is helpful) by a professional graphic artist is most effective. *Don't try to save money on slide preparation.* If the visuals are poorly done, the audience's impression of the speaker suffers.

A word of caution: when you are preparing visuals with easel pads, 35-mm slides, or transparencies, don't try to crowd too much information on one panel. It is better to have more slides or panels than to crowd a slide or picture.

VIDEO-TAPE

For small groups, video-tape provides a consistency of presentation and the inherent magic of television, both of which can greatly aid the seminar. Two *caveats:* without multiple screens, video-tape is usable only for small groups. You must introduce the video presentation and then follow it up with a strong summation.

Top security salespeople know the importance of looking good and looking conservative. They clearly understand that they never get a second chance to make a good first impression!

TWO THINGS YOU CAN DO TODAY TO MAKE YOUR BUSINESS GROW!

1. **See if there is an AARP (Association of Retired People) chapter in your area.**

2. **Try to line up meetings with the chapter president (get his account) and arrange an opportunity for you to make a tax-savings or estate-planning lecture to the group.**

Giving the Seminar: Final Preparations

1. Arrive at the site at least one hour before the seminar.

2. Have with you the list of reservations, your outline, and a kit of hand-out materials to give to each attendee. If the meeting is at a hotel, restaurant, or any other place where a marquee directs attendees to the proper room, see that the name and meeting directions are correctly displayed.

3. Your own portable meeting sign (Blank Company Seminar) is a valuable seminar aid for any site that does not have a marquee.

4. See that a check-in table is set up near the entrance and is run by your spouse, a friend, or a sales assistant. Each registrant should be given the hand-out material and instructions to fill out an information request and turn the form in at the end of the seminar.

5. Check with the manager of the facility to see that water is available, to find out at what time coffee or refreshments are to be served, and to confirm that all facility-provided equipment is in place and functioning.

The Meeting Room

The selection of a meeting room can often play a major role in determining the effectiveness of the seminar. When you have the opportunity to choose a room (local branch seminars or library seminars typically do not offer the luxury of choosing a setting), consider the following checklist:

1. Is the room large enough to comfortably hold the number of people who have reservations?

2. Are there enough chairs available to seat the expected attendees?

3. Is there a podium for the speaker?

4. Is the heating or air conditioning so noisy as to cause distraction? Is the temperature properly set? Cooler is better. Do you know where the heating or air conditioning controls are?

5. Is it a partitioned room? If so, will other parts contain a noisy gathering at the time of your lecture?

6. Is there a table for water pitchers and glasses and for coffee if it is to be served later?

7. Do you know where the light switches are located? Do you or an assistant know how to control the lights properly?

8. Can you arrange the chairs so that each has a clear view of the speaker and any visuals to be shown?

9. Can the most distant person easily hear you, or will you need a microphone? (Microphone use is encouraged to save the speaker's voice and to make it easy for everyone to hear.)

10. Are there sufficient ashtrays available?

Equipment Checklist

Nothing can frustrate a speaker more than to have an equipment failure during a presentation. Despite all precautions, sometimes equipment conks out or never gets delivered to the room. In such cases, you must fall back on your own resources and rely on your rehearsal and your notes to carry through the seminar.

A little preparation and planning can help avoid the catastrophe of equipment failure. The checklist that follows will avoid problems that have plagued and embarrassed speakers in the past (including me!)

1. Bring an extra bulb if you are using a 35 mm slide projector or overhead projector.

2. Make sure you or a trusted helper know how to operate the equipment properly.

3. Retest the projector and the order of your slides.

4. Bring an extension cord long enough to reach the appropriate outlet.

5. Arrange for a large screen.

6. Learn how to raise the screen if it is a portable one.

7. Make arrangements for a microphone. Make sure it works properly.

8. Either arrange for a projectionist for any 16 mm sound film you intend to show, or make certain that you or a helper know how to thread and run the machine.

9. Preset the video machine to start in the right place. Avoid those agonizing minutes waiting for it to start.

Encourage early attendees to seat themselves at the front of the room. On their own, people will generally sit toward the rear. If attendance is small, to have everybody clustered at the back is discouraging. Here are more hints that will help you to run a better seminar:

1. *Don't start on time.* Parking may be a problem for many people, and late arrivals may spoil the early part of your talk by creating some disturbance as they check in and get to their seats.

2. *Don't start too late.* Starting much after the scheduled time tends to irritate the punctual arrivals. Plan on starting 5 to 10 minutes after the scheduled time.

3. *Arrange for someone to tape your presentation* for later review.

4. *Try to relax the audience with your opening remarks.* Use humor if you can, but nothing ribald that might convey the wrong impression. The best humor pokes fun at the speaker.

5. *Encourage questions at the end of your talk,* as well as during your talk, to involve your audience. If you ask frequently for questions, you tend to liven the lecture with audience participation. Your answers become more meaningful because you assume the role of a teacher or a learned person.

6. *Don't be afraid to say, "I don't know, but I will get the answer for you."* This lends credibility to you as a person.

7. *Sum up the key points of your presentation* and create an open forum for questions. (If a second session is to be given, remind the audience of the time.)

8. *Coffee after a seminar is a great help in keeping people in your presence* and giving them a chance to ask individual questions. This gives you a chance to get appointments.

Seminar Follow-Up Procedures

You may do everything right in planning for and executing your seminar, but if you don't use good follow-up procedures, the effects of your lecture and all your effort may go for naught. The following guidelines can show you how to maximize post-seminar appointments and obtain clients:

1. *Send a letter the day after your seminar* thanking the prospect for attending. Personalize your response by mentioning some of the questions you feel you answered especially effectively. Enclose a portfolio review form or an information request card.

2. *Call each attendee within 48 hours.* The impression you gave attendees is most vivid in the first few days after the talk. As time passes, your image and what you discussed rapidly fades from their memory, as well as any impulses

they may have had to invest with you. When you call, seek a critique of your talk. Exude friendliness and try to pinpoint any investment interest. You must seek an appointment to discuss investment matters that bother them, points not covered in your lecture, or points not made clear to them.

3. *Send a letter to those people who confirmed their attendance but did not show.* Invite them to your next seminar. Seek a personal appointment. Don't write them off too quickly; as they responded once before.

4. *Send a second letter within two weeks* and keep attendees on a regular mailing list for six months. Remember, most prospects become clients only after the fifth or sixth contact. Don't give up unless there is an obvious insurmountable personality conflict or unless they just aren't suitable prospects for any of your products.

5. *Call again after the second letter* and seek an appointment. Tell about a specific feature in a particular product. Sometimes you may open the account with a very small order and then get a personal appointment to review a client's entire financial situation.

Increasing Your Sales Power and Income: 3 Magic Words

All sellers of risk investments (stocks, options, commodities, bonds, mutual funds) recommend situations that sometimes produce capital losses for clients, rather than the hoped-for, sought-after capital gains. Sometimes these losses are merely due to general market declines that carry the specific investment to a lower-than-purchase price. Sometimes the losses are due to some specific change in the fundamental aspect of the investment.

Whatever the reason for the decline in value, the investor is less happy with losses than with profits. As long as the loss goes unrealized, the investor can hope that the investment value will increase back to or above the original purchase level. Many times losses in investment value are transitory and of short duration; and other times they worsen and the investment value appears permanently impaired.

Dealing with an investor who is holding a loss is not the easiest of jobs, especially if the position was entered into at the salesperson's recommendation. Many times sellers change their opinions about the future prospects of an investment they once thought superb. When you find yourself in this situation, contact the investors and tell them exactly why you no longer like your previous choice. Most investors understand risk and appreciate your staying in touch, keeping them informed. Countless clients are "lost" or move on to other salespeople simply because when a client suffers a loss, the salesperson is so uncomfortable that he or she fails to call the client or keep the client properly informed as to what's happening with the investment.

Like most humans, salespeople hate to face the music and

admit the error of their ways. Their first bad judgment was in the original recommendation. The second is that, instead of calling clients who have the loss, they often neglect them, thereby making these clients a rather easy target for other salespeople. Occasionally, a seller will compound the problem by offering false hopes of recovery rather than advising acceptance of the loss.

How should you handle a client enmeshed in a losing situation, particularly one that you originally recommended?

First, be honest and straightforward. Call the client and say that in your opinion the value of the investment has changed, and say why the situation is different. Salespeople with integrity make the same effort to get a client to accept a loss and move the money to a more attractive investment as they expended to get the client to invest originally.

Many clients, however, will not sell anything at a loss. They don't want to give up the hope of making money on a particular investment, or perhaps they want to get even before they get out. The "getevenitis" disease has probably wrought more destruction on investment portfolios than anything else. Rather than recovering to an original entry price, many investments plunge sickeningly to even deeper losses. Investors are also reluctant to accept and realize losses because the very act of doing so proves that their first judgment was wrong. Buying high and selling low is certainly not the way to build assets!

Investors who accept losses can no longer prattle to their loved ones, "Honey, it's only a paper loss. Just wait. It will come back." Investors who realize losses must admit their folly to the IRS, when they file that itemized tax return. For all those reasons and more, investors as a whole are reluctant to take losses, even when they feel that to do so is the right course of action.

Sometimes you will prevail with an investor, gain the order to liquidate the losing position, and then hear the investor say, "Send me the proceeds." That phrase signals the eventual termination of your relationship with this particular client.

When you suggest that the client close at a loss a transaction you originally recommended and invest the proceeds in another position you are currently recommending, a real act of faith has to take place. That act of faith can more easily be effected if you make use of some transitional words that I call "magic selling words."

The words that I consider to have magical power in the sense that they make for a more easy acceptance of a loss are these: *"Transfer your assets."* The words by themselves, however, have little force. You must prepare the ground for these magic words.

"Buy" is a pressure word. If you understand that, you will see that sales are easier to make when the word "buy" is avoided. "Sell" is also a pressure word, and "sell at a loss" is even worse—depressing, sometimes terrifying, phrase. If those words are avoided and more appealing words substituted, you have a greatly improved chance to consummate additional sales.

To show you how to ease into the magic selling words, "Transfer your assets," look at the dialogue that follows. Assume a broker is talking to a client (or prospect) who owns 500 XYZ bought at $30 and now priced at $20. The broker wants the client to sell 500 XYZ at $20, accepting the loss, due to a changed outlook for XYZ's business. Upon completion of the sale, the broker would like to have the client buy 500 PDQ at $20. PDQ is a company whose prospects appear much brighter in the eyes of the salesman.

Joe Salesman: "John, I have been reviewing your portfolio of securities, particularly your common-stock holdings. What you have invested in XYZ is your assets. I assume that what you want from your assets is the *best chance to grow in value* from the current level, combined with the *least risk of loss.* Isn't that what you are really after?"

John Prospect: "Sure, that's what I want. More gain possibility and less risk. I have found getting that happy combination not so easy. Look at my XYZ, for instance."

Joe Salesman: "I have been looking at your XYZ [valid reason for the call], and that's why I'm calling you today. At the time you bought XYZ, earnings were increasing, and prospects looked great. However, unexpected contract cancellations and cost overruns turned an expected increase into a loss [reason for suggesting the transfer].
The near-term future prospects look rather bleak at this time. I called you when the price declined from 30 to 25, but you decided to wait for a possible up-turn closer to your purchase price."

John Prospect: "I was hoping to get out of XYZ at a price closer to even."

Joe Salesman: "I know how you feel. [Empathy] Often I have done the same thing. With XYZ now about 20 it appears to me that you would have a better chance to accomplish what you say you want [client's objective mentioned again], a better chance for your assets to grow in value from the current level combined with a lesser chance of loss. You can meet that goal if you simply *transfer your assets* [the magic words] from 500 XYZ into 500 shares of PDQ. PDQ has none of the current problems affecting XYZ, and the earnings prospects are bright. [The close] They are both approximately the same price. If you make the transfer now you won't have to put up any additional money."

John Prospect: "Well, if you think I will be better off, and since I don't need to put any additional money to make the transfer, go ahead and do it [the order given]."

Read the scenario carefully again and note these crucial elements:

1. The word "sell" was never used.
2. The word "buy" was never used.

Avoiding those two pressure words whenever possible makes sales easier to come by. The two separate transactions (moving out of the loss and moving into a new position) are made to flow together by the magic words "transfer your assets." The prospect thought he was making a single decision, switching one investment into another. He was not being asked to think in terms of selling XYZ and collecting the proceeds, then having to think of many different ways to reinvest the proceeds. Joe Salesman simplified the process and made it easier for John Prospect to make the move by focusing John's attention on the following key sales points:

1. Increasing the gain potential of his assets.
2. Decreasing the risk of loss possibility.
3. Avoiding the investing of additional funds to make the transfer.

Sales hint. (Whenever possible make the purchase amount the same as or lower than the sales proceeds.) If necessary, as additional sales power you can bring the tax deductibility of the loss to the prospect's attention.

In 1973 I was asked to conduct a special sales meeting in my firm's Birmingham, Alabama, branch. Ths branch had 16 experienced salesmen. Their mood at the time was one of

Top security salespeople have learned that if they want more money to keep track of, they'd better keep track of their selling time.

TWO THINGS YOU CAN DO TODAY TO MAKE YOUR BUSINESS GROW!

1. *Send an interest-rate fact sheet (various rates of interest available on many different products from TDAs, U.S. notes, bonds, to municipals) to different CPAs or attorneys.*

2. *Call each and tell them to look for it in the mail and let you know if they would like to have this information on a regular basis. (You are almost certain to get some referrals or accounts.)*

Security salespeople who manage to produce at a high level through bull and bear markets explain that their TRIUMPH is due to their adherence to the first 3 letters in the word.

TWO THINGS YOU CAN DO TODAY TO MAKE YOUR BUSINESS GROW!

1. *Make up 100 kits: outside envelope, current research material; TDA, muni bond info, 2 response cards, and portfolio review form along with return envelope.*
2. *Distribute the kits to prosperous-looking individuals at their place of business. Code all the return cards so you can quantify the results.*

despair, due to a sharply declining stock and bond market. The regional manager brought me in to motivate, stimulate, and energize the loss-stricken account executives.

I presented my sales techniques and ideas with remarkable clarity in an exhilarating manner. The presentation certainly counted as one of my best. An A+ rendition. (Bashful I am not!)

When I told the assembled group of the power that lay in my magic words, "Transfer your assets," and how those words might produce sales the very next day and forever after, there was a general wave of enthusiasm. However, one man in the back of the room obviously did not share the group's delight over my suggested phrase. He stood up and, in a deep Alabama drawl, said, "LeRoy, that's nonsense!"

Calmly, trying to keep him from destroying the meeting's effectiveness, I said, "Jimmie, I have found this phrase to work wonders in all of the other 49 states. Tell me, why do you think it won't work here in Alabama?"

Jimmie replied, "I'll tell you why it won't work here in Birmingham. It's because I have financially killed every investor in and around Birmingham who had any significant amount of money. I sold my clients real-estate investment trusts that came out at $20 per share and later went to $1 per share! And I sold them others that did even worse! I have had the unique ability to select the worst performing stocks recommended by our Research Department."

He continued, "I happen to be one of the best amateur golfers in the state of Alabama, and I can't get a foursome to play golf with me any more. I have really *destroyed* people. Following me, my former friends have lost their kids' education money, seen their retirement plans disappear. When it comes to stocks I've just been snake bit. *Your magic words* won't work on my clients!"

"Jimmie," I said, "that is a mighty sad tale, but I believe my words will work even with your clients and their sadly worsened financial condition."

Jimmie said, "You meet me in the office tomorrow morning at 9:00, and I will show you my account book. I'll prove to you that your phrase won't even make them budge."

Who could resist a challenge like that? I agreed to meet Jimmie the next morning. At 9:00 A.M. I was sitting at his desk, leafing through the ledger pages where his clients' trades and positions were itemized. As I poured over the pages, tears came to my eyes. He really *had* financially damaged everyone. The best looking of his stock positions was down 50 percent in value!

Jimmie looked at the expression on my face. "I told you I was snake bit. Now do you believe me?"

"I believe you have had bad luck, bad advice, or bad judgment, Jimmie. I also believe that my magic words will work here in Alabama, just as they have elsewhere."

"Okay, let me call this guy. He used to be my buddy. Played golf with me every Saturday and Sunday, but now he doesn't want to talk to me. He owns 1000 XYZ bought at 20, and now 9."

"Call him, Jimmie, and give the story on PDQ. Tell him to *transfer his assets* from one to the other and why you think he should."

"All right, I'll give it a try, but you sit right here, 'cause I just feel uneasy about talking to him, considering all he's lost."

Here's a recap of the conversation between Jimmie and his erstwhile friend and client, good buddy Joe:

Joe: "Hello."

Jimmie: "Joe, this is Jimmie. How ya doing? I am sittin' here with a vice president from Noo Yawk. He likes a stock, PDQ, and he's done looked at the thousand XYZ you got that's giving you a pain. He says you better transfer your a— out of that one, into this one right now!"

Every security salesperson should understand that every one wants to make money and keep money. The way to get them to listen is to:
a) talk about benefits, and
b) tell how to avoid loss.

Top security salespeople who get hit occasionally with a case of bear-market blues have learned that the best way to lift their morale and forget their own problems *is to* help clients and prospects solve their problems.

TWO THINGS YOU CAN DO TODAY TO MAKE YOUR BUSINESS GROW!

1. *Carefully review each client's statement position balance. Note odd-lot positions and call to round up or sell off. Check long positions versus your followed list and call client to transfer weak holds and sells to the strong buys.*

2. *Ask your clients for their current most favored stock; they might be so enthused in telling you that they will themselves talk themselves into buying more! (Also, they might disclose large "other" positions held with another firm. I'll bet you can figure out what to do about that!)*

Joe: "Well! if that's what he thinks I should do, Jimmie, go ahead and do it."

After Jimmie had written and entered the two order tickets to sell 1000 shares and to buy 1000 shares, I made the following observation: "Jimmie, you thought my magic words wouldn't work here in Alabama, but they did, just as I told you they would. You have two good orders to prove it. But Jimmie, you would have gotten the order just as easily if you had used the phrase I taught you, *'transfer your assets,'* rather than your abbreviated version."

You who sell intangibles will, I hope, forever remember Jimmie and his sad tale of woe. I hope you will also remember that you can make a lot more sales when you say "Transfer your assets" than when you use the higher pressure, two-decision phrase "Sell this. Buy that."

Using "Chair Position" to Help Make the Sale

Face-to-face selling can be the most stimulating, demanding, and challenging of the various selling techniques. Insurance salespeople, stockbrokers, sellers of commodities, and mutual fund salespeople normally close their biggest accounts at personal meetings with prospects. Face-to-face selling was, for me, the most rewarding and exhilarating of all.

There are many advantages to being "eyeball to eyeball." Observant sellers can carefully watch the facial expressions and body action of prospects. Observations can clue sellers in to alter a sales approach or try an entirely new one. The great flexibility of using visual displays, exhibits, and various third-party proofs to help convince the prospect to buy simply isn't available except in face-to-face sales encounters.

Once the face-to-face appointment has been granted, and the salesperson is in the prospect's presence, the real work of trying to obtain an order begins.

In the Prospect's Territory

When appointments are in prospects' homes or offices, it is quite likely that prospects will place a barrier between themselves and you. Such barriers are meant to place you in a position inferior to the prospect. Sometimes a barrier is there to show the prospect's power and authority. The barrier, most often, is a desk or a table. Frequently a desk is in an elevated area, the chair behind it, again to try to make you constantly aware of the prospect's power and superiority. The barrier is intended either

Successful security salespeople know that this is not a market-hours-only business. Over 90% of the highest earning brokers are successful because of efforts made before the opening and after the close, and to stay "tops" they are willing to do business on weekends and other time off as well.

TWO THINGS YOU CAN DO TODAY TO MAKE YOUR BUSINESS GROW!

1. Work hard to get up 4 appointments for Saturday morning with prospects: 9:14, 9:55, 10:35, 11:25 (people remember odd times and are more prompt).

2. Pray for rain on Saturday morning (so that no one cancels)!

to prevent a sale from taking place or to produce a sale with the most favorable terms possible—for the order-giver.

Whenever you are faced with such surroundings, ask the prospect for permission to move your chair *next to the prospect's chair.* Most often, permission will be granted, especially if you carefully explain that by sitting together at the desk or table (or on a couch), the prospect will be in a better position to see, and to interpret, the visual data in the presentation.

If necessary, take pains to show how hard it will be to see the material if you and the prospect are not seated side by side. Sell this "we" approach as your participation in helping the prospect better his or her financial situation. By breaking down the social distance created by the barrier, you can take a friendlier, less aloof attitude as both you and the prospect, shoulder to shoulder, pore over the details of the proposal. *Note: Be sure to keep yourself immaculate.* Heavy body odor or bad breath can destroy the impact of a well-presented idea.

In Your Territory

If the face-to-face appointment has been scheduled to take place in your office, arrange the chairs side by side (or use a couch if one is available) before the prospect arrives. The "together we decide" approach is a powerful closing technique.

If you are trying to sell two prospects (usually a husband and a wife) try to place your chair *between their chairs* so that all three of you can easily see the visuals while you are extolling the virtues of the proposed investment.

By placing yourself between the prospects, you divide their united resistance to your proposal. They can't kick one another under the table (at least not without alerting you!), squeeze a hand, or easily exchange a warning look. "Divide and conquer" is a good way to win a battle or a sale!

Too many offices give little thought to the chair position of client and account executive. Firms invariably plan desk layouts so that the prospect is opposite to the broker in a standard adversary pose. In my view, this layout is totally wrong, and one that leads to other problems. In the typical brokerage office, the salesperson's desk and chair face the ticker tape and the client's chair faces the broker. This not only makes the "we" approach impossible, but the running tape is constantly in the broker's sight. What a distraction! The broker's tape watching often makes prospects or clients resentful.

If the purpose of the appointment is to sell the client, arrange for a side-by-side presentation to be made in a conference room, if one is available; or arrange your private area so that you and the prospect can work closely together to shape the prospect's financial horizon without the distraction of tape happenings.

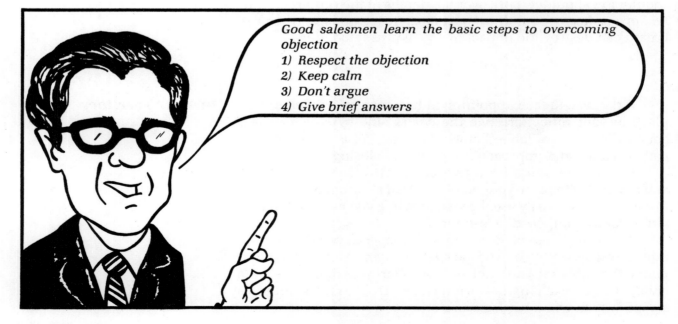

Good salesmen learn the basic steps to overcoming objection
1) Respect the objection
2) Keep calm
3) Don't argue
4) Give brief answers

USING "CHAIR POSITION" TO HELP MAKE THE SALE

Power-Packed Selling Phrases for Option Specialists

The listed-options market has blossomed into one of the biggest revenue producers for major retail securities firms. Many account executives have devoted countless hours to learning the intricacies of option activity. The complexities range from margin rules that are incredibly difficult to understand to a myriad of tax consequences that tax the mental capacity of CPAs and other experts.

The compliance surveillance ladder extends from the Securities and Exchange Commission to the major option and stock exchanges to the individual firms to the salesperson. Before consummating a single option sale, salespeople must have passed a difficult (and growing more so) examination on option rules, regulations, strategies, margins, and tax consequences. The terminology used in the option world is strange enough, and threatening enough, to discourage many would-be participants.

In addition to all the special knowledge salespeople dealing in options must have, they must also monitor carefully to ensure that any option activity undertaken by a client is "suitable" for that client. Suitability is based upon some rather stiff minimum asset guidelines that may or may not be truly useful. The threat of a suitability lawsuit by a client who has lost money engaging in option activity is a real worry for salespeople and their firms, especially since courts and juries continually seek greater protection for the consumer.

Despite all these deterrents and the substantial risks that option participants face, the business continues to grow. This growth is fostered by the attractive features that options have for those who buy them and those who sell them.

Option buyers are generally speculators willing to risk total (100 percent) loss of their investment while seeking a return that can be 2, 3, 10, or more times the amount of their investment. Even though an option buyer risks total loss, this loss potential is predeterminable, and it is fixed. Loss can never be larger than the money paid for the contract. Along with the fixed risk and large profit potential, the option buyer enjoys a high degree of leverage. Small dollar investments in option contracts can control underlying stock values measured in thousands of dollars for a finite period of time. Each contract is subject to adjustments as per the actual terms of the contract.

Despite the apparent advantages for option buyers, it has been my experience that salespeople who try to build a clientele oriented to the purchasing of option contracts will not be long-term successes. Losses incurred buying options leave the investor with bitter feelings, despite all prior warnings of the risk involved. Option buyers' trading is frequently frenzied and dictated by emotion. This makes for difficult accounts and causes an inordinate amount of the salesperson's time to be spent in tape watching and hand holding. Additionally the great majority of option buyers commit only a small part of their assets to the activity (at least that is the prudent road to follow) while committing the balance to other investment areas.

Small losses from buying options will frequently cause investors to switch the rest of their investment dollars to more "conservative" brokers, thereby transferring the commissions away from the option salesperson.

Typical sellers ("writers") of option contacts are pecentage-minded folks who seek a high annual return on the capital committed to back the option contracts they have issued. Sellers can go about seeking their high annual return by means of a variety

Top security salespeople know it's not the number of hours they work that makes them successful; it's how they use those hours! Are you using your hours to tell clients and prospects of the opportunities that exist in tax-deferred annuities and municipal bonds?

TWO THINGS YOU CAN DO TODAY TO MAKE YOUR BUSINESS GROW!

1. *Have a lunch at a nice restaurant near your office. Ask to speak to the owner/manager, compliment him on the food and service. Try to get the account.*

2. *Ask if the owner would like to distribute with the menu each noon, printed on your note pad, the latest market info: DJIA _____, 10 most actives _____, courtesy of _____. (You will have to arrange daily mimeographing and distribution.)*

Good security salespeople understand that the world is made a better place by the men and women who sell products and service—not by those who talk about selling them.

TWO THINGS YOU CAN DO TODAY TO MAKE YOUR BUSINESS GROW!

1. *Review the status of all uncorrected problems that are over 2 weeks old. Notify your manager and give him a list; have him sign and date your copy.*

2. *Call clients with the oldest problems still outstanding and let them know you are following up. Ask them for more business!*

of strategies, limited only by the sellers' imagination (and capital). They can sell contracts in a conservative or a speculative manner depending on their knowledge, attitude toward risk, the extent of their collateral to back the contracts issued. The seller's risk varies, depending on the strategy chosen.

If, dear reader, you have gained the impression that I believe writing options is a more conservative, more certain way to earn a return than buying call options, I have conveyed the wrong impression.

Buying options in many instances may be less risky and more conservative than buying stock and writing calls. Other strategies involved in writing options may involve substantially greater risk than option purchase speculations.

As a salesperson out to attract and retain clients of substantial financial means, you will find it much easier to extol the potential benefits that may evolve from issuing option contracts than it is to gain acceptance for call-buying strategies.

A prospect with $1 million in liquid, investable assets might be persuaded to risk up to $50,000 or so in an option-buying program. That same prospect might, under the ministrations of a well-versed option salesperson, commit upward of $500,000 to a regular program of issuing options. With that in mind, it makes sense to concentrate on option writing in order to get large dollar commitments.

My view in approaching wealthy prospects is to get as large a percentage of their investable assets as possible under a planned program utilizing option strategies that are in line with the prospect's investment objectives. Focusing on writing options simply makes the control of assets easier to accomplish.

The salesperson who concentrates on seeking out clients who will regularly, repeatedly, sell option contracts has an excellent handsome living year in, year out, through all the ups and downs of the stock market.

If you obtain option writing clients, you will normally do very well in commission terms for these excellent reasons:

1. *Greater capital investment.* The typical option writer puts more capital to work than the typical option buyer.

2. *Greater staying power.* The typical option writer continues the investment strategies over long-term periods usually measured in years. Compare this to the months or weeks that constitute the usual life-span of option buyers.

3. *Greater net earning likelihood.* Among the numerous option accounts I have surveyed, a far greater number showed net year-end profits from their option-selling strategy than did the accounts that were primarily option buyers.

4. *Greater client satisfaction.* In talking to thousands of Registered Representatives throughout the United States, I was informed continually that, in general, regular option writing clients were satisfied with the results of their activity. These clients evidenced their satisfaction by the sticking with the procedure. Happy client! Happy salesperson!

The big problem practicing brokers seem to encounter is in obtaining accounts of sizable wealth. After managing to learn the complexities of option margin requirements, option tax consequences, option rules, and option strategies, many brokers find it difficult to acquire and retain clients for whom options are appropriate.

The mysterious jargon used in the Option Clearing Corporation prospectus and in verbal communications makes "understanding" difficult and often makes a prospect afraid to enter the activity.

"Be prepared to listen, and listen to be prepared" is a good motto to follow on the road to becoming a top seller of securities.

Top security salespeople know it's more important to get a small order on the books than none at all.

TWO THINGS YOU CAN DO TODAY TO MAKE YOUR BUSINESS GROW!

1. *Compete! Bet a buddy that for this week you can complete more "asking for the order" calls to strangers and open more accounts than he or she can.*

2. *Send each new account opened a personal note thanking them. This note should go out the day the account is opened.*

As a broker, I learned to simplify the complex in order to make it understandable and therefore more palatable to a prospect or a client. This ability to communicate difficult concepts with ease helped build my production to a high level and to maintain the higher level.

The terms of the option world should be rephrased so that prospects can understand them enough to make a prudent financial commitment. In the rephrasing I developed *power-packed words and phrases* that investors everywhere throughout this country really understood. When these words are used in face-to-face encounters, including investment seminars, people quickly understand, and easily commit funds to, the suggested strategy.

It is important to understand that the word "option" turns off may prospects. To them "option" connotes risk. To many "option" means outright purchase, speculation in its rawest form. Call writing, an accepted term in the option world, has little meaning to many investors, including a high number of market sophisticates. To them "option" means something complex and possibly time consuming.

In trying to create interest in the writing of options I found more attentive listening ears whenever I completely avoided the use of the words "option" and "call writing" in my initial presentation.

Here is another LeRoy maxim: *Good salespeople in any field understand that the initial presentation must be well accepted, interesting, and plausible or there will be no second presentation.*

The following scenario shows how to use my power-packed selling words to interest a prospect in call writing. Read the presentation words carefully. You will discover that the words "option" and "call writing" do not appear, since they are negatives in an initial presentation intended to develop a prospect's

"Starting at a Profit"

interest. In later conversations their usage is certainly permissible, even desirable. Later, prospects feel they have been admitted to a club with secret passwords when they hear "option" and "call writing."

Assume that Joe Salesman is making an initial call on John Prospect, who is a wealthy investor. Also keep in mind that the decade 1970–1980 was a hectic, volatile, generally unrewarding decade for stock and bond investors. Assume also that the initial greeting formalities have taken place.

Joe Salesman: "Tell me honestly, John, have you been satisfied with how your money has worked for you in the stock market for the past year or three years or five years?"

John Prospect: "Truthfully Joe, I haven't been too pleased. In fact, I would have been better off just doing nothing but owning Treasury bills. Sure, I have had some winners, but they have been more than offset by my losses. I don't mind paying brokers' commissions when I am making money, but it hurts to lose capital and pay out lots of commissions too."

Joe Salesman: "I understand how you feel. The past several years have really been tough for stock investors. Blue-chip growth stocks and blue-chip basic industry stocks haven't been the money-makers people thought they would be."

John Prospect: "You're telling me! I own IBM, Sears, U.S. Steel, G.M., Exxon, and a dozen others and am sitting on substantial losses despite the fact I have held them a long time!"

Joe Salesman: "Maybe I can help you like I help other clients."

John Prospect: "How's that?"

Joe Salesman: "*How would you like, starting tomorrow morning when the market opens, to begin every stock purchase transaction at a profit [magic power selling words], a profit paid to you cash in advance, a profit that you can count immediately. usually in hundreds, sometimes in thousands of dollars?*"

John Prospect: "That sounds too good to be true. What's the catch?"

Joe Salesman: "No catch. You can do it too, just as a lot of my clients are doing. *You can start every stock purchase transaction [repetition sells] you ever make the rest of your investing life at a profit. You can buy a stock and agree to sell your just bought stock at a higher price than you paid.* For agreeing to sell high what you just bought low someone will pay you hundreds, maybe

Good security salespeople know the truth of the old axiom, "when in doubt, tell the truth!" They have learned that honesty is a most valuable tool in selling and retaining clients.

TWO THINGS YOU CAN DO TODAY TO MAKE YOUR BUSINESS GROW!

1. *Review your YTD progress with your manager—set new goals—settle "differences," if any. Ask him to gather "new ideas" from some fellow managers for you.*
2. *Treat your spouse or "love-in" to something special that is unexpected and expensive; then work hard to get an order to pay for it.*

thousands of dollars. What makes this even more attractive is that you get to use the money paid you to help pay for the stock you buy!"

John Prospect: "You mean to tell me that for just agreeing to sell at a higher price than I pay someone will give me hundreds of dollars to keep? I don't ever have to pay it back?"

Joe Salesman: "You got it right! And the agreement periods currently never extend for longer than nine months. The agreement periods are often as short as a month or two."

John Prospect (suspiciously): "What about the dividends?"

Joe Salesman: "You, as the stock owner, get to keep any and all cash dividend as well as the advance money."

John Prospect: "What does the other person get for his money?"

Joe Salesman: "He has hope that the stock will rise above the agreed price by an amount enough to return his original dollars, plus a profit. He is really a high-risk-taker willing to lose 100 percent of his money in a short time period. As long as there is a supply of these willing riskers, you ought to collect some of their money."

John Prospect: "There must be a catch in it. It sounds too good. What risk do I run?"

Joe Salesman: "There really is no real dollar loss risk to you greater than you ordinarily take in owning stock. In fact, your stock ownership risk is lessened by the cash cushion these riskers provide you."

John Prospect: "Well, let's try it on a couple of hundred XYZ. That's a company I like and wouldn't mind owning at the current price."

Read the scenario, and then reread it. If you engage in selling option strategies you will find your "closes" coming easier.

The initial sale is the key sale. That sale converts a prospect into a client. Whether the client becomes a long-term client producing a steady stream of commissions each year will depend on your knowledge and expertise at making, and getting the client to accept, suggestions to lessen risk and increase return.

My power-packed phrases and words are designed to help open accounts. (Account management techniques for retaining accounts would fill another book.) Let's examine other powerful, ear-catching words that can help you change prospects into clients.

"Three Sources of Profit"

The phrase "three sources of profit" carefully uttered in a prospect's presence awakens the natural greed instinct. You can enact the following scenario using those special words to produce orders from prospects.

Learn the phraseology. Use the words daily in your prospecting and you will make sales.

Joe Salesman: "You have told me that you have not been too pleased with the results of your stock market investments."

John Prospect: "That's right. I am dissatisfied with the return, or lack of it, on my stock portfolio."

Joe Salesman: "Starting tomorrow, how would you like to have *three sources of profit* every time you buy a common stock?"

John Prospect: "Three profit sources? What are they?"

Joe Salesman: "First, you could collect a lot of dollars—maybe hundreds, sometimes thousands—for simply agreeing to sell your just-bought stock at a higher price than you paid. This agreement money is paid to you right away, on the very next business day—money that's yours to keep forever. Your second source of profit could be the cash dividends due you as the owner of the stock. The third source of profit would be in the increase in price of the shares from what you paid, to the agreed selling price.

"By agreeing to sell at a higher price than you bought, all you are giving up is the unknown, unknowable profit possibility above the agreed price. In return, for relinquishing some of the profit potential *you collect a handsome amount of cash that you can immediately spend or reinvest, as you choose.*"

John Prospect: "That sounds pretty good."

If we only wanted to be happy it would be easy; but we want to be happier than other people, which is always most difficult, since we think them happier than they are.

Joe Salesman: "Not only does it sound good, it is good. You can do it with stocks you already own or stocks you are willing to buy."

John Prospect: "Well, why don't you look over my portfolio and see if we can't collect some of that advance cash on stock I already own."

This scenario, like others in this book, shows how a typical successful close is accomplished through using *power-packed selling words and phrases.* Don't be naive enough to believe that each time you follow a selling scenario featuring the use of magic words you will make a sale. All you can expect is to increase your batting average, get a higher percentage of "yes" answers per 100 presentations made.

If you use my words and sales techniques as recommended, your commission income will rise substantially. Don't expect perfection. As your skill in using power selling words and techniques grows, so will your confidence and your ability to close. However, you will still have strike-outs, "no sales." Failures are part of sales attempts. So don't let a few failures keep you from steadily using these time-tested selling strategies. Your successes should encourage you to make greater numbers of presentations, and the presentations will eventually build a commission income that will be your pride and joy.

Here is a phrase to be spoken face to face to an investor who is burdened with losses, and has experienced unsatisfactory results from stock trading activities: "You don't have to pick winners to make money in the stock market." Remember, an eager listener is what you want and need to obtain an order. Let's look at another scenario using these powerful words:

You Don't Have to Pick Winners to Win

Joe Salesman: "From what you tell me I know that you aren't too happy with your stock investments."

John Prospect: "Disappointed and unhappy would be putting it mildly."

Joe Salesman: "In order to make money as a stock buyer you have to pick winners, and that's hard to do consistently, even for so-called experts."

John Prospect: "You're telling me!"

Joe Salesman: "Would you like to hear how a lot of my clients are making money in stocks without having to pick winners?"

John Prospect: "I would sure like to hear about it but I am a little dubious."

Joe Salesman: "A lot of my clients, as well as many other sophisticated investors, buy stocks and agree to sell their just-bought shares at a higher price than they paid. For simply agreeing to sell high what they just bought low they get paid a handsome sum of money. Sometimes hundreds, sometimes thousands of dollars."

John Prospect: "That sounds pretty good."

Joe Salesman: "It is good. And if you were to do it, too, I can guarantee that *you will make money every single time if you have to sell your shares at the agreed price.*"

John Prospect: "That sounds terrific but supposing the stock doesn't go up to the agreed price?"

Joe Salesman: "Good point. It's possible that you might buy a stock low and collect cash for agreeing to sell it high, and the stock at the end of the agreement period is unchanged from your purchase price. If that were to happen, I guarantee that you would make money every single time.[1] In other words *you don't have to pick winners to make money.* If you just have the god-given ability to pick stocks that stand still you will do well! And if you can't pick stocks that don't move you might follow our Research Department. We have a long-term track record of being able to pick stocks that don't go up [say this with humor in your eyes and voice!]"

John Prospect: "My current broker can pick flat stocks with no apparent effort. Just look at my portfolio."

Joe Salesman: "The strategy I am suggesting for you is even better than I have told you. If you buy stocks and agree to sell them at a price higher than you

[1]The buyer's premium payment would be considered earned as a short-term capital gain upon expiration of the contract. The income would be taxable in the year of expiration, which could be a different year from the year of receipt.

Top-flight brokers constantly set goals for themselves—better than the previous year, month, week, but not so high that the goals can't be reached with extra effort. They keep score of how they are doing on commissions, new accounts, new contracts.

TWO THINGS YOU CAN DO TODAY TO MAKE YOUR BUSINESS GROW!

1. *Look at your best day in each of 3 previous months. Average them. Set a goal of having 2 or more days this month that exceed your average best.*

2. *Call spouse (or best friend) and say if you achieve your goal, you will treat to a super-deluxe dinner. Interest the person in your achieving the goal. He or she may even come up with some good prospects.*

bought at, they might decline in value. At the end of the agreement period, if your stocks are below purchase price you still might make money."

John Prospect: "That sounds sort of incredible. How can I buy a stock and see it go under my purchase price and still make money?"

Joe Salesman: "If the stock doesn't drop as much as the advance cash you collected you still could make money even though at the end of the agreement period the stock was lower in price than your original cost. The only risk[2] you run is in a stock price drop greater than the advance cash you collected. Even that risk might be reduced by strategies I will go over with you. I just want you to clearly understand (1) *that you will make money every single time that you sell a stock as per the agreement* (assuming the initial facts of buying stock and agreeing to sell at a substantially higher selling price) and (2) *that you will make money every single* time that you buy a stock, agree to sell it at a high price, and have the stock unchanged in price at the end of the agreement period. You don't have to pick winners to make money!"

John Prospect: "What are we waiting for? Let's get started!"

Carefully review the use of the word "guarantee" in the above scenario. The compliance departments of brokerage firms are leery of having security salespeople using guarantees that

---

[2] Be sure to explain that you have omitted commission and dividends for the sake of simplicity. Each person prospected for any option activity must be delivered an option clearing corporation prospectus.

might later subject the firm to a lawsuit. However "guarantee" as used exactly above is factual, not a misstatement or an overstatement. Never guarantee improperly or guarantee something that's not absolutely accurate and true.

Judiciously used, as illustrated, the guarantee is certainly factual, and it produces sales. *With equal emphasis given to the only capital loss risk (a stock price drop greater than the first premium collection)*, a large number of prospects can be converted to regular clients with an initial "testing" of the strategy.

There you have it! Power-packed words and phrases to help sellers of securities expand business through the writing of call options. Use the words and phrases and watch your business grow!

Selecting Common Stocks to Help Sell More Shares to More People More Quickly: 8 Criteria

Every salesperson who works on commission for a brokerage firm should certainly be aware of the risks inherent in investing in common stock as well as the rewards. The risk of loss through stock trading creates such great fear in many sellers of securities (as well as in their clients) that they try to build and maintain business that concentrates on low-risk investments. These anxious souls push treasury bills, short-term bonds (government, municipal, and corporate) and no-risk products like tax-deferred annuities or insurance (which don't lose value except for inflation, a risk that cannot be avoided).

In order to make a living, though, the majority of security salespeople must face the loss of clients and clients' capital because they offer investments associated with risk, such as stocks, long-term bonds, convertible bonds, and listed options. A few are hardy enough to tackle the magnified risk of commodity trading.

I learned early in my career that if I was to protect my clients and their capital in stock or stock-related investments, I had better learn to protect myself against the suggestions of research departments and syndicate departments. Those departments do the best they can to make what they believe to be appropriate recommendations, but chaff inevitably gets mixed with their wheat. Another LeRoy maxim: *Carefully screen all research and syndicate suggestions.* Often I was encouraged to merchandise inventory stocks to keep the firm from losing on a position or to earn a profit for the firm. The problem there, though, is that the firm isn't weighing the profit potential of the inventory item versus other investment alternatives for the client in respect to the client's objectives and the risk.

NYSE firms work continually to up-grade and improve research. I found it far better to make stock choices from their approved lists than to choose from other sources. Even with NYSE lists, I had to stay wary, realizing that lemons could still creep in.

During the learning process I suffered many a hard knock in the form of lost clients) when I encouraged clients to make investments I didn't believe in deeply or to purchase financial products about which my knowledge wasn't broad enough. *The broker's "book" of clients is his or her single most valuable possession.* It is a possession that can provide a high level of income year after year if it is most carefully watched over. Constant care must be exercised to control clients' risk of loss to as modest and reasonable a level as possible under even the most adverse circumstances.

It was my experience (shared by thousands of stock brokers) that every client for whom I made a lot of money stayed with me. After all, who would want to risk change during a winning streak? And I kept almost all the clients for whom I made a little money. Oh, they grumbled and mumbled about not having the current takeover candidate or the hot stock of the moment, but they stayed with me—traded with me—remained loyal to me. I found that I was able to keep most of the clients from whom I lost a little money. They too, would complain about the lack of winners, the aggravation, my commissions, and their losses, but they stayed as clients, attracted by the service I gave them, the hand-holding, and my sincere effort to make money for them.

I lost almost every client for whom I lost alot of money. They naturally became bitter about their losses and sought a different broker to get a fresh start, a new viewpoint, in an effort to regain their lost capital.

That range of experiences convinced me to choose and weigh the risk when I was dealing in common stocks. I learned to estimate the risk before suggesting a purchase. My focus was on *not losing large amounts* of client's money.

The perplexing problem lay in the initial selection of a common stock. Brokers are simply inundated with volumes of information. The large wire houses, in particular, produce so many research reports that it is beyond the ability of any broker to read and comprehend the total output. Many of the reports, although well researched and perhaps well thought out, are written in an incomprehensible manner. Some appear to be written to show off the writer's erudition rather than to inform the reader, simply and explicitly.

This is the problem you face. In addition to being deluged with your own firm's research, you are likely to be knee-deep in stock suggestions coming from a myriad of investment services, such as Value Line, Standard and Poor, other brokerage firms, *Barron's* and *Business Week*, just to name a few. On top of the blizzard of printed material, tips and rumors abound. Hot tips

Top security salespeople know that true sales skill consists of telling a prospect all that is necessary—and nothing that is not necessary.

can influence you to make hasty recommendations without having determined the real value, and without having recognized the true risk. Frustrating and aggravating are the mildest descriptions of this dilemma you face: trying to choose a stock to recommend from all of the thousands of candidates.

In order to simplify the procedure so that my selling time would be maximized, I devised a system for selecting common stocks. This system is workable in all types of markets. This system takes careful recognition of risk, and it allowed me the opportunity to *sell as much as I could, to as many as I could, as quickly as I could.* The system I devised for picking common stocks is not perfect; no system yet designed is fail-safe. But the system I designed is easy to understand, to adopt, and to use. Over time, my system has worked successfully for thousands, to whom I taught it. It can be a factor in *your* building and keeping a book of clients.

The eight points you will learn to use are meant solely to help you with the initial choice of a stock to recommend. I believe it is necessary to develop a large position in several stocks, each stock carefully chosen, rather than to maintain client portfolios dotted with dozens and dozens of different stocks accumulated willy-nilly over the years. You cannot carefully monitor portfolios laden with too many different stocks.

In my opinion, establishing large positions in a few select stocks is a better route to follow, and actually less dangerous over the course of time. There is no more satisfying, thrilling experience in a broker's life than to build a large position (50,000–1,000,000 shares) in a stock, watch it rise to a sell point, and then advise clients to sell the profitable shares and reinvest the proceeds.

In choosing a common stock to recommend, you want a selection that will enable you to sell as much as you can, as quickly as you can, to as many as you can. Compliance-department requirements must be kept in mind at all times to permit the maximizing of the sales effort. My eight criteria for stock selecting *almost assure broker freedom from compliance department restrictions.*

Stock-Selection Criteria 1:

If you are going to devote time to building a substantial stock position in your clients' portfolios, and if you are going to have clients exposed to the financial risks of stock ownership, you should have an anticipated, hoped-for, minimum profit target of at least 50 percent. This target is hopefully to be achieved in 12 to 24 months. Nothing creates referrals or retains clients and encourages client activity so much as the attainment of a large percentage gain in a holding period just long enough so that the gain qualifies for a low-taxed, long-term tax treatment. If you aim for too low a gain, you never get that profit-satisfied client who is the core of repeat business.

Aim for big wins and you aim for bigger, longer-lasting clients.

Stock-Selection Criteria 2: Choose High-Quality Issues

As you seek to establish a brokerage business in your community, concentrate on recommending high-quality issues consistently. The more "unknown" you are, the more necessary it is to stress quality. The rationale is really quite simple. Strangers find it easier to say "yes" to a purchase if the offered product is high-grade. High quality in the investment adds assurance that transcends the salesperson. By constantly stressing high quality, you build an aura—create an image—about yourself and about your firm. The quality image, mirrored by your product recommendations, makes it easier for strangers to recommend their friends and family to you as potential clients.

In addition to making it easier to get "yeses," focus on quality makes for larger orders. Big orders help propel you toward what must be your constant goal: selling as much as you can, to as many as you can, as quickly as you can.

ONLY HIGH QUALITY-RATED STOCKS

When selecting a stock to attempt to merchandise in a big way to many people, one of my essential requirements is that the stock be rated A−, A, or A+ by Standard & Poor. These ratings are based on an assessment of a company's financial strength. The quality rating has no bearing whatsoever on the direction the price may take in the future. There is great misunderstanding in the financial selling community about the S & P ratings. This misunderstanding tends to reassure the under-informed and uninitiated about the security of the current price or the potential for price recovery of a particular stock.

THE POWER OF THE A

Here are my reasons for suggesting that each stock chosen for position building be quality rated A−, A, or A+. All of us have been brainwashed since the day we entered grade school that the letter *A* is good. All *A*s on our report cards gained praise and recognition (and maybe a dollar or two). When you enthusiastically suggest a common stock rated A, the prospect receives the message, "This is a good stock." This thought makes it much easier for the prospect to buy.

Furthermore, when investors first make their entry into investing in corporate or municipal debt issues they are taught that the rating A is good, AA very good, and AAA excellent. Therefore, A linked to a common-stock recommendation makes the stock seem more acceptable, respectable, prudent, and desirable, all of which encourage the prospect to go along with your advice.

When a potential investor delays purchase, many times it is to allow time to seek the opinion of a third party. People most often sought out for stock opinions are other brokers, bankers, lawyers, and CPAs. If the stock is of recognized high quality, it is hard to knock or denigrate the recommendation. Frequently the high quality of a recommended issue brings about an affirmation from the third party. Ths agreement helps cement or create the sale.

When your living, your financial survival, depends on the commissions you earn, why jeopardize even one sale through accepting low quality? Just as many potentially good situations exist with high-quality stocks as do with lower-quality stocks. At least at the recommending stage, the high-quality stock will create the better impression.

A-rated stocks provide more restful nights for investors. When stocks fall in price either because of circumstances at the individual company or because of a general market decline, holders of high quality issues are generally less likely to panic. They are more likely to "average down" with additional purchases. High quality makes it easier for credibility to your clients to believe that the company will survive in an adverse economy and that price recovery is likely to occur, profits eventually to increase.

THE PERILS OF LOW QUALITY

Holders of low-quality issues become very uneasy in falling markets. They worry about company bankruptcy or the dearth of analysts advocating their positions. All the analysts seem to seek safety in bad markets by concentrating on recommendations for the purchase of high-quality stocks. Owners of low-quality stock very easily get panicked into selling into a steepening decline as they begin to doubt more and more seriously the company's ability to weather bad times. The flight from low-quality stocks magnifies losses. There is often a massive rush to liquidate but only a few takers. Quality stocks certainly are not immune to severe price drops in market declines, but generally they enjoy a thicker market, a market more willing to absorb quantities at fairer prices, than is the case with low-rated issues.

HIGH QUALITY HELPS WITH COMPLIANCE

A-rated stocks help restrict compliance interventions. Salespeople out to do the best selling job they can on a stock which they are thoroughly knowledgeable and convinced the issue is right for his clients and prospects at the current price for clients and prospects can better accomplish their goal by focusing on A-rated, quality stocks. Brokerage house compliance departments properly performing their job of supervision frequently limit salespeople in the accumulation of shares of a low-quality issue, but they seldom restrict the accumulation of shares in high-quality issues.

To me it does not make good sense to make the effort to learn all aspects of a common stock and start a selling effort, then, *solely because of low quality, be limited as to the number of people as to whom the issue can be sold.* Limits by watchful compliance officers may also be placed on the number of shares being bought.

The business of selling securities is tough enough without your creating unnecessary barriers to attaining sales success.

Compliance departments must do their very best to protect firms from lawsuits and also to protect their firms "capital and clients' capital. Time after time their careful watch over the accumulation of low-quality issues has proven its value. If you concentrate your selling efforts on A-rated issues, you will normally will be allowed to sell as much as you can to as many as you can—and that's what the selling game is all about.

Another significant benefit is that you will be able to sleep better at nights as a merchandiser of quality stock shares. Your own self respect is a fragile but necessary ingredient that can best be preserved through knowing you are a purveyor of quality. When clients lose money, you will suffer along with them, but your distress will be less if you have full knowledge that a profit was sought with a prudent eye toward quality. When high-quality investments lost value, their holders are less likely to litigate, by the way, than they would be with similar losses in low-rated issues. Investors who lose money on high-quality issues frequently direct their anger more toward the market than toward the broker who recommended the stock. Investors who lose on low-quality issues tend to direct their anger toward the broker, and they may seek redress through court action.

Regular cash dividends are bonuses to the investor who is seeking capital gains. It is important to recognize that many investors measure their returns on investment solely by the cash dividends paid to them as shareowners. Therefore, in selecting a stock in which the goal is to build a significant position, give careful consideration to the cash dividend: its amount, its security, and the likelihood of increase.

Stock-Selection Criterion 3: Seek Cash Dividend Income

You will find that it is much easier to sell larger quantities of a given investment vehicle to more investors if the yield approaches or exceeds the rate currently being paid for bank passbook accounts (5½ percent at the time of this writing).

By purchasing shares that pay good dividends, most investors persuade themselves of their prudence, based on the expected income. They feel the gain potential is a super added benefit. Should the stock fall in value from their purchase level, they console themselves that the dividend provides a return on their cost. The regular dividend stream makes the losing investor a more patient holder and often a fairly eager willing purchaser of more shares with only the slightest encouragement from the salesperson.

I know there are some doubting Thomases in the financial community who decry cash dividends as being meaningless to the high-bracket investor. It has been my experience that very rich investors who talk about the low value they place on cash dividends because they are in such a high tax bracket do so just to impress the listener. *Those same highly taxed grumblers will often move their money from one bank to another to gain one-quarter percent more in taxable interest!* The cash dividend *is* a plus when you are trying to get the wealthy to buy. Also, a cash dividend may act as a yield anchor in falling markets, keeping the stock from slipping as much as stocks that pay lower dividends.

In selecting a dividend-paying stock for sales focus, I look for a stock (1) that has maintained or raised its dividend in each of the previous five years and (2) for which the prospects for more of the same are forecast. Good dividend income just makes it easier for the majority of prospects to buy.

Stock-Selection Criterion 4: Focus on Low Risk

No rational investor wants to lose money. Most investors want to be able to perceive themselves as profit chasers who recognize, understand, and exert some control over risk. Given the choice between seeking a profit from a high-risk, high-potential-gain investment and a low-risk, high-potential-gain investment, they will most often choose the latter, convinced of their prudence.

As you strive to achieve sales stardom and client retention, make every effort to recommend stocks that you believe at the time are low-risk, high-potential-profit situations. By so doing you expand the number of clients and prospects for whom the proposed investment is suitable. You also expand the share quantity that each might prudently buy.

All these factors nicely dovetail with the objective of selling as much as you can to as many as you can as quickly as you can. Of course, the question arises, How do you judge whether or not a stock is a low risk at the time of purchase? A very fair question.

In order to be able to use the powerful selling words "low risk" when you try to convince a prospect to buy, some substantiation for the statement must exist. That substantiation may be available in an excerpt from the fundamental research report that the analyst wrote or from a technical projection furnished by the technical analysis section of the research department. ValueLine estimates and projections are often helpful for determining the risk potential. If none of the above are available for use in risk estimation (hardly likely, but possible) reasonable assumptions might be determined by carefully studying past high-low price history, past high-low price-to-earnings ratios, and extrapolations into the future based on year-ahead estimates of earnings.

Accenting a legitimately determined expected low-risk feature develops large sales and many substantial referrals. Isn't that what you want?

Stock-Selection Criterion 5: Pick a Company Whose Name or Product Is a Household Word

Stock brokers should try to make their task—creating commission sales—as easy as possible. The job of selling shares of stock is greatly simplified if you are recommending a company that is well and widely known.

Prospects feel less doubtful more like buying if they personally know of the company, its reputation, the quality of its products or services, and are familiar with its advertising campaigns. Under such circumstances, prospects' fears are better allayed and they are much less suspicious of the salesperson and much more likely to believe in the profit potential of the investment.

Let's assume that you have been looking at the motel industry as potentially an advisable investment area. In trying to narrow your choice to the single best candidate for purchase you have carefully reviewed the basics such as earnings per share, dividends, book value, return on invested capital, occupancy trends, projected earnings, current stock prices, and other related factors including balance-sheet statistics. Let's also assume that two companies appeared to be equal opportunities in your eyes:

Holiday Inns
La Quinta Inns

In my view it is axiomatic that Holiday Inns would be the choice. The familiarity of the name alone would make it easier to sell more to more people with less effort expended.

Too many brokers earn less than their abilities call for simply because they have not taken proper cognizance of the "comfortable shoe" feeling that owning shares of a familiar company brings to a prospective buyer.

Concentrate your sales efforts on well-known shares and watch your commissions magnify!

Nothing warms an investor's heart so much as picking a winner! Making money on a stock investment is balm to the psyche. The profit creates a glow that spreads to the immediate loved ones and extends to practically everyone coming in contact with "the winner." Investors' driving desire to win led me to focus on companies that were number 1 in their industry (the number 1 rating could be for any of several things, including total sales, total profit, return on investments, just to name a few. I found that my sales strength was greatly improved and closes more frequently made if I could enthusiastically, resoundingly tell a prospect: *This company is number 1 in its industry!*

That is a power-packed selling statement that conveys the impression to the prospect that the company is a winner because it has that coveted number 1 ranking. "Number 1 in the industry" translates in the prospect's brain into "Investment in the shares will make [the prospect] a winner!"

Selling shares of companies ranked number 1 is just an easier job to perform than selling shares of companies without that designation. As a salesperson striving for success, the more things you can do to make sales easier to obtain, the quicker and greater the degree of success.

Stock-Selection Criterion 6: Choose a Company That Is Number 1 in Its Industry

Understanding investor psychology is a factor extremely important to developing a large brokerage business. The concept of "more is better" is deeply ingrained into people everywhere, almost from birth. The inherent greed that plagues most of the human race is a driving force toward "getting more," "owning more."

A thinking salesperson seeking a stock to merchandise to clients and prospects does more than casually glance at the quoted share price. The share price as a lone statistic can dramatically determine the success or failure of a concentrated sales effort.

It has been my experience (and that of thousands of successful stockbrokers) that the best sales results are obtained from stocks in the price range of $10 to $30 per share. Investors typically would rather buy 1000 shares of a $10 stock than 100 shares of a $100 stock. The prospects for gain from earnings, dividends, and everything else might be equal but the price alone would cause more solicited prospects to choose the lower-priced shares. Crazy? Maybe. But that's the real world.

Stock-Selection Criterion 7: Pick a Low-Priced Stock (Under $30)

Some observations may help you understand and use this phenomenon as you try to zero in on a stock to merchandise widely. First, the higher the price of the shares (particularly over $30), the greater the buyer resistance, *no matter how good the outlook for the stock.* Second, if a stock is too low in price (under $10, particularly lower than $5) prospects tend to be suspicious about the company's viability. A very low price invariably causes questions to be asked, like, "Why is it so low? Are they going bankrupt?"

In my experience, the best marketing share price is a stock share priced in the teens. That is a price low enough to assuage most fears of the company's viability and yet allow for some pleasant dreaming about those shares attaining adulthood and perhaps eventually trading at $40, $50, or better.

Stock Selection Criterion 8: Choose Stock Currently Judged "Buy" by Your Firm's Research Analyst

If the sky falls down, you don't want to be crushed by the falling debris. Salespeople seeking to survive and thrive in the ever increasing competitiveness of the market-place must be constantly alert to the fact that a lack of judgment can cause fines, censure, or even being forced to leave the industry.

In the stock-brokerage community, bear markets and falling stocks are precursors to client complaints and lawsuits, most of which are based on the suitability of the recommendation for the client. "Suitability" is a catchall covering the client's needs and wants, as well as the grounds on which the recommendation was originally made.

When you choose a stock for mass merchandising and big position building, *restrict your choice solely to issues positively recommended as current buys on a fundamental basis by your firm.*

Should the stock perform badly after purchase, it's the firm's fault! it is the research department's error. It was the analyst who judged incorrectly! You can legitimately direct the customer's ire away from you toward several other sources. You and the client can jointly deplore the bad outcome and still retain a decent relationship, and perhaps the hope of recovery by means of a different analyst's suggestion.

When you are trying to sell in quantity, you want the support of your firm, and the millions the firm normally devotes to research, to back your sales presentation.

There is no more lonely feeling for brokers, carried away by a story of the moment, than to sell the story successfully in a big way to many people and then watch the stock sickeningly slide into low-priced oblivion. Terror strikes, for such salespeople are all alone. No compliance department to side with them. No research analyst to support their buying thesis. Rightfully upset clients may sue, and burden these poor brokers with the guilt stemming from clients' losses.

Avoid recommending any stock other than the ones bearing the strongest recommendations of your research department.

Sticking to that philosophy can add immeasurable strength to the sales pitch and help multiply the "yes" answers, while making you feel good about what you are recommending and why you are recommending it.

There you have it—my eight criteria for selecting common stocks. If you use my filter system, your chances of doing well will be substantially enhanced as will be your longevity in this business of selling stocks.

Suppose though, try as you might, you don't find a stock that fulfills all eight criteria. What then? I would choose a stock to focus on if as few as five of the eight criteria were present at the time of recommendation. Here are the five core qualities that *must* be present in order to merit your effort at hard selling to position quantities of shares.

1. Seek *high gain potential.*
2. Choose *high-quality issues.*
3. Seek *cash dividend income.*
4. Focus on *low risk.*
5. Choose *research-approved* stock.

Use my system for one to three years and compare the results to any year in which you didn't seek these criteria. I am confident you will feel inclined to write and thank me for helping build your sales success.

With your focus always on avoiding loss stocks, you can't help but be a winner!

The Real Key to Success: Organizing Consistent Prospecting

The road to success in selling investment products is traveled almost exclusively by those who have learned how to organize their prospecting efforts. Consistency, as well as organization, in prospecting is necessary if you are to reach and maintain a high level of earnings.

People selling investment products should strive to *be prospect-conscious every waking hour!* Prospects abound in every area of this country. Casual acquaintances and close friends alike are prospects, and you should be asking for their business. Even if the people you know do not buy, they might refer others to you.

If you are a churchgoer or a member of civic clubs, you will always find the opportunity to meet new people and let them know that you specialize in the careful handling of money. You must continually make a special effort to widen the circle of people who know your name well enough to call you in the event that investment dollars become available to them.

Outgoing would-be sales stars look for prospects whenever they eat out in fine restaurants or bars! They start conversations with the owner or manager or with prosperous-looking patrons. Always they try to steer the conversation to the ever-absorbing topic of making money.

When you go on vacation, seek prospects among fellow vacationers. Many salespeople have found their best clients to be people met on vacations. The pressure-free environment often provides more time for a prospect to think about investing.

Good security salespeople have learned time management—using more of their available time for sales effort, the only time that adds to their income. Average salespeople waste three quarters of each day! Two hours or less are actually spent selling! How do you spend your time?

TWO THINGS YOU CAN DO TODAY TO MAKE YOUR BUSINESS GROW!

1. **Treat all prospects the way they want to be treated.** *(Ask for an order!)*

2. **Treat all prospects the way you would want to be treated.** *(How could you not make sales doing that?)*

Prospects are also to be found where you spend money for goods or services. Doctors, dentists, lawyers, accountants, and other business people are all not only potential clients of yours but are centers of influence that could lead other clients to you.

Organizing for a consistent prospecting effort involves completing the following tasks:

Many salespeople do not understand how to construct a prospect file that is easy to use and explicit. Without this invaluable tool, they handicap themselves in the struggle to earn more dollars. A good prospect file should contain *no less than 1000 names, addresses, and phone numbers.* Each prospect must be carefully selected for *"buy-ability."* Initially, buy-ability is based on what prospects do, where they work, or where they live. Each detail must be legibly recorded on a heavy-weight, lined, good-sized card that will stand up to hard use. The file of cards should be prominently displayed on top of the desk to serve as a constant daily reminder that there are calls to be made. Bad markets, inclement weather, feeling disinclined—*nothing* is acceptable as an excuse for failing to make prospecting calls.

Building a Prospect File

Once established, the prospect file should grow through the daily and weekly addition of names of people met "cold," obtained through referrals, or encountered at various kinds of functions. Each quarter the file should be *purged* to remove the prospects who are obviously time-wasters or whom you have determined have little or no investment potential.

Maintaining the Prospect File

THE REAL KEY TO SUCCESS

183

Maintaining a Daily Regimen of Prospect Contacts

Each working day (no exceptions!), a number of the names in the file should be called, seen, or contacted by mail (a common "do-able" number is 20). Each must be asked for an order on a specific attractive item. (Yes, you can ask for orders by mail!)

Maintaining an Inventory of Current Direct-Mail Pieces

In order to take advantage of timely investment opportunities with prospects who can't be contacted by phone or in person, a supply of attractive mail pieces with appropriate customer inquiry cards should be constantly available in good supply. Any items mailed out should be logged on the calendar for phone follow-up a week after the mailing.

The biggest sales successes I have met and taught say the major factor in their success is the effort made in prospecting. I have yet to meet a person who prospected diligently over a long period of time and was not successful. A strong prospecting effort alone can make you successful! A skilled, trained effort simply shortens the time and heightens the financial payoff.

Daily prospecting produces results just like a daily body building or daily diet control. Consistency of effort produces winning results only if orders are always asked for from a reasonable number (20 or more) of qualified persons.

We are born with two ears and one mouth. Some security salespeople think they have to compensate for this by using the latter twice as much as the former. Top security salespeople know that many sales are made by listening!

TWO THINGS YOU CAN DO TODAY TO MAKE YOUR BUSINESS GROW!

1. **Set up a 3-ring binder with samples of all current mailing pieces available in your office, pieces that, when returned, pinpoint a prospect's interest.**

2. **Ask fellow AEs which, if any, are pulling. Call a couple of other branches to find out their mail results.**

Handling "No Sales"

One of the most frustrating moments any seller of intangibles is likely to experience comes when the prospect declines to buy when asked for an order. This rejection may send salespeople into a tailspin. Their heads reel and they ask themselves over and over again where the sales pitch failed. *Missed key points . . . omitted sales features . . . pertinent client benefits . . .* march through their brains as they try to pick up the pieces and perhaps get back on to the sales track.

A "no sale" is particularly galling to the salesperson who has taken the time to carefully qualify the prospect, arrange a face-to-face interview, align all the facts in a beautifully sequenced presentation that finally zeroes in on a particular client stated need.

Failure to obtain an order must be an accepted fact of life in selling intangibles. No matter how logical and eloquent the sales presentation, there will be many "no sales" in an average selling week. How should a "no sale" be handled?

Sellers of intangibles must learn to control their emotions much like a skilled poker player, who cannot allow his facial expressions to be a dead give-away for his holdings. When they are told "no" by a prospect to whom they have devoted a lot of their time, energy, and thought, in the preparation of written proposals, many salespeople show irritation and anger.

This anger, once the anger surfaces and the prospect or client sees it, even for an instant, is enough to destroy the possibility of a sale at a later date or of a referral. The sellers's dissatisfaction can be seen in an impatient gesture, a fleeting facial grimace, or a quickly stifled word of exasperation.

Selling skills involves learning to control your outward emotions while inside anger rages or disappointment reigns. When a closing fails, make every effort to maintain an aura of calmness and to summon up a smile as you ask to why the prospect did not buy.

Many times, there is a valid reason why a perfectly pre-qualified prospect, properly "pitched," doesn't yield and grant an order. A death, a job change, some unexpected event might have legitimately caused a change in the prospect's investment approach. That is why it is important always to ask the prospect's reasons for not committing.

1. *Listen carefully to the prospect's response.* Perhaps an opportunity to sell at a future date will arise. Try to leave such prospects with the impression that you value their having listened to your sales presentation and that you will always be willing to help them in any possible way.

2. *Impress on the prospect that service is the key point of your business.*

3. *Leave the prospect feeling that you are a "good guy" and so the prospect "owes" you a shot at any future business.*

One of my most enjoyable and memorable sales occurred through the proper handling of a "no sale."

I had just given a lecture to some employees in the aircraft industry. After the lecture, while coffee was being served, one employee began discussing with me his personal financial situation. During the fact-finding he disclosed that he had $25,000 available for investment, and would like to meet with me to investigate various investment possibilities relevant to his particular needs. We agreed to meet at my office the following Saturday morning.

Keep good records if you want to be a top producer. Be ever mindful of the old Chinese proverb: "Even a short pencil is more reliable than the longest memory."

HANDLING "NO SALES"

Good security salespeople keep a famous adage in mind when they are talking to clients: "Be sure brain is engaged before putting mouth in gear."

TWO THINGS YOU CAN DO TODAY TO MAKE YOUR BUSINESS GROW!

1. **Meet 2 salespeople who deal in high-priced residential real estate. Try to get their accounts and also try to set up a system so you get their referrals from transfers moving in.**

2. **Call the president of the local chapter of the association of college and university women. Seek her account and ask for the opportunity to present a program at one of the meetings.**

Saturday morning arrived, and my prospect showed up promptly as scheduled. Prior to the meeting I had prepared an investment proposal for putting the $25,000 into a common stock mutual fund. I positioned my chair next to the prospect and carefully explained the benefits of professional selection and management on a continuous basis. Carefully I pointed out the advantages of diversification and the powerful compounding impact over time through automatic reinvestment of dividends and capital gains.

I waxed eloquent! Never was I more explicit, precise, and understanding of a prospect's needs and desires. The presentation was capped with a graphic illustration as to what his $25,000 could amount to in 10 years if the future results duplicated or approximated the previous 10 years. The anticipated results were just short of breathtaking! How could anyone not buy after so cogent and logical a presentation?

When I asked for the order, my prospect did not buy! My mind raced, reviewing the presentation, searching for any flaws, missed facts, or benefits. None popped to the surface. My perception was that I had made an almost flawless presentation.

Keeping my smile I asked, "John, I don't really understand why you aren't putting your money to work in this fine fund. The track record is excellent, the management prudent and highly regarded. It suits your needs and objectives. Do you mind telling me your reason for not investing at this time?"

John replied: "LeRoy, in between the time we talked, after your lecture and this appointment I received a transfer notice from my company. I am going to have to move to Burbank, California, soon. Housing in California is priced much higher than in North Carolina, and I will probably need most of that $25,000 for the difference in cost of houses."

John had a very valid reason for not investing. I could not be angry at him. The job transfer had been a sudden occurrence, and he was naturally reluctant to invest in securities before meeting his housing needs for his family.

I wished John good luck in his new job and location. I informed him that I would always be as close to him as a telephone, and that should he ever have funds to invest he could call me collect. The interview was graciously terminated. No sale was effected, *no commission earned, end of story . . . almost!*

Six months after my "no sale" I got a phone call from a Joe B. He introduced himself and asked if he could meet with me. We arranged to get together on a Saturday morning in my office.

I arrived a little early for the appointment to set the stage. I arranged the chairs at my desk next to each other. I cleared up all unnecessary clutter to provide the aura of neatness and efficiency. A mutual fund graph illustration was placed on my desk for easy viewing.

Joe showed up on time and we chatted to get familiar with each other and ease the strangeness common to first meetings between salesmen and prospects.

I asked Joe, "How did you get my name?"

Joe replied, "I was working in the aircraft industry in Burbank, California, when I got notified that I was being transferred to Charlotte, North Carolina. A buddy, John D., who used to live in Charlotte, filled me in on a lot of things I needed to know about the area. He told me that if I needed a broker you were the one to call!"

I said, "That was very nice of John, to refer you to me. What is your particular investment situation that requires my help?"

Joe continued, "Well, I sold my house in Burbank and bought one here. Housing here is much less costly than in California, and I have about $25,000 left over to invest. What do you think I should do with the money?"

As you readers might already have guessed, I sold Joe B. $25,000 worth of the mutual fund that I had tried to sell to his friend John!

The selling-skill moral of this story is to handle a "no sale" with the utmost aplomb!

1. Smile.

2. See that no anger or irritation shows, even for an instant.

3. Ask why the prospect did not buy.

4. Show that you appreciate the prospect's having given you a chance to make your sales presentation.

If you adhere to these points, you will be laying the groundwork turning the "no sale" into a future "go sale"—either with this prospect or with someone this prospect refers to you.

Picking Up on "Close-Now Signals"

All salespeople seek to close orders and lock up a commission should constantly be on the watch for buying signals emanating from the prospective purchaser. Prospects being solicited either face to face or by phone often give clues that they are ready to buy. These buying clues come in two forms. One is a verbal signal and the other is a physical signal. Physical signals are helpful only if you are making a face-to-face presentation.

Sellers of securities who do most of their business over the phone have to train themselves to be good listeners in order to pick up quickly on a prospect's verbal signals informing that a close is at hand.

Verbal Signals

Unskilled salespeople who concentrate only on what they are saying and really don't absorb the prospect's remarks often miss sales that should have been closed. Listening carefully is often more productive than spewing out a constant flow of facts and figures.

The following brief scenarios depict typical vocal signals to search for in a prospect's remarks. Whenever vocal buying signals like these are received, end the flow of facts and benefits and ask for the order.

SCENARIO I

Joe Salesman: "This stock is selling below book value and yields

7 percent from a dividend that has been raised each of the last five years! That's not all. The earnings per share are in a significant up-trend and should come in 20 percent over last year—enough to warrant another dividend increase even larger than the last! You ought to buy 1000 shares."

John Prospect: "[Verbal buying signal] When would I have to pay?"

SCENARIO II

Joe Salesman: "This bond yields 8 percent free of all federal and state tax! In your tax bracket, that would be like earning more than 16 percent in a taxable investment. The bond is AA rated by Standard & Poor's, and the principal repayment comes due in 10 years, just when you expect to need your money. You ought to get 25 of these bonds while they are available."

John Prospect: "[Verbal buying signal] How long will it take to deliver the bonds?"

SCENARIO III

Joe Salesman: "This is an excellent income stock. The current yield is 9.5 percent from a dividend that has been increased each year for the past 18 consecutive years. The outlook for future raises looks good. The dividend is paid quarterly on the first day of the month."

John Prospect: "[Verbal buying signal] When does it go ex-dividend?"

Physical Signals

In face-to-face presentations, you must not only listen carefully for verbal signals that tell you the prospect is ready to buy; you must also keep your eyes focused on the prospect's face and body for physical signals that signify the close is ready to be accomplished.

Here are the most common physical signals that it's time to close:

CHANGE IN ARMS FOLDED ACROSS CHEST

The folded-arms position is a defensive position in which a prospect envelops his or her body and protects it by wrapping the arms about the self. As long as the arms remain locked

PICKING UP ON "CLOSE-NOW SIGNALS"

One step in cracking the high-earnings barrier is to realize that the first order only converts a prospect into a client. The next step is to convert the client into a steady, repeat-business client through your service and attention.

TWO THINGS YOU CAN DO TODAY TO MAKE YOUR BUSINESS GROW!

1. *Contact a load Mutual Fund that does not have a wholesale representative covering your territory. Study the fund's holdings and performance record. If you like what you see, make an effort to get at least one order for the fund's shares from an existing client or prospect.*

2. *Contact the fund (start with the president) to obtain all current literature and tell of your interest in promoting the fund's share. Ask for all leads in the area to be sent to you. Ask for the statement copies of all fund holders in your area not presently being serviced. Tell the president you would like to try to contact each holder to encourage them to make add-on purchases. You may just fall into a bonanza! (You will never know if you don't try!)*

around the body no sale will ensue. Carefully observe the prospect, who is listening to the salient features and benefits. If the prospect audibly exhales and limply drops arms to sides, that prospect has decided to buy. Ask for the order at that point! Enough facts and benefits have been presented to win the prospect's trust and gain the order.

LOOSENING OF CLENCHED FISTS

Many prospects listen intently to a presentation with fists clenched tightly, a resistant defensive posture. If, during the presentation, the prospect suddenly relaxes those fists, the decision has been made to buy. When you see those fists relax and the hands open, stop rendering features and benefits and ask for the order.

RUBBING THE CHIN

When prospects absorbed in listening to a presentation begin to rub their chins slowly, as if stroking a Van Dyke beard, that is a clear signal that the prospect is ready to buy. Upon observing the stroking motion, stop the flow of facts and ask for the order!

STROKING THE NOSE

When listening prospects begin to stroke their noses slowly with a forefinger, those prospects have carefully considered all aspects of the proposed investment and are ready to buy. The order should be asked for as soon as the buying signal is observed!

TOUCHING OR EXAMINING A DOCUMENT THAT REQUIRES A SIGNATURE

A good face-to-face seller of intangibles pitching a product that needs a customer's signature in order to produce a bona fide sale normally keeps the document in view during the entire presentation to serve as a silent reinforcement during the interview. Documents completed except for needed signatures are much less threatening to prospects for their names have already been typed in. Only the places for signatures remain blank. (Whipping out a complicated form that has to be completed after a presentation may kill a sale. The prospect wonders about the traps lying in wait in the fine print.

The filled-out document, conspicuously in view at all times, is easy for prospects to pick up and read. A prospect who does that is transmitting a clear buying signal that shouts, "If there are no real hooks in this document, I am going to buy!" When you notice this perusal of the document, ask for the order.

Being sensitive to buying signals is just one more way of increasing sales and commission income.

Acting When Potential Profits Become Losses

Every seller of securities who makes recommendations to prospects about a potential profit in a stock, convertible bond, commodity, mutual fund, warrant, or option recognizes that an unforeseen adverse factor could turn the potential money gainer into a disastrous loss.

Having obtained an order in an investment that later under-performs, many salespeople are so upset, and assume that their clients are equally disturbed, that consciously or unconsciously they avoid contacting the clients who hold the loss position. Brokers fell ashamed that their judgment of the situation or their market timing was widely off the mark. They generally do not want to face the clients or even talk to them.

The unspoken hope is that maybe time will right the situation. If not, maybe the customer, irked by the lack of contact, will drift off to another broker at some other firm, so that the broker whose judgment was wrong will never have to confront this self-created problem.

Failure to contact losing clients shuts off the commission flow. It creates ego damage through the realization that the unwillingness to admit faulty judgment is simply an act of cowardice.

Sellers of securities are certainly aware that risk exists in almost everything they sell. They must accept the fact that losses inevitably will occur and prepare themselves mentally to deal with clients whose investments are losing money.

The consistently best approach to handling clients experiencing losses is to *stay in touch! Don't let losing customers feel that they are alone.* Call, console, write, send information about the loss situations. Ignoring a loser only creates bitterness, dries up referrals, and often results in lawsuits.

Before contacting a client holding a loss, reinvestigate the situation. Be prepared to render a well-thought-out current opinion backed up by all the most recently available facts so that the client, even though hurt, will feel that the salesperson is still deeply interested in the client's welfare.

If "hold" is the opinion, be sure the client understands the potential for further risk and all the pertinent reasons for an expected price recovery.

If "sell" is the opinion, make every effort to get the client to accept the loss and seek recovery and profit through a different investment.

Often, I have found that a drop in price occurs without rhyme or reason and affords an excellent opportunity to invest additional dollars at an even more attractive price. "Averaging down" is a very appealing strategy to many investors, and with a little encouragement from the salesperson they will follow the original commitment with equal dollars. Only encourage this tactic when you truly believe the situation merits a larger total investment. Care should be taken that clients who are averaging down do not invest too large a portion of their total assets into single situation.

Losing clients must be contacted as consistently as if they were winning. *Many investors get more upset by the lack of information and contact than by the loss itself.*

Never assume that clients are so angry over losses that they do not want further contact.

Never assume that clients have no more money to invest and therefore should not be contacted.

Never assume that losing clients will be unwilling to listen to a transfer idea that might regain the losses.

The proper action to take when a client is sitting with a loss is to call or see the client. Present all the facts. Offer recovery hope through holding, purchasing more, or selling and repositioning the money.

Losses are emotionally draining. When losses are maintained too long, they cause inertia. My experience is to eradicate losing situations when they can be offset with realized capital gains. People just naturally feel better about a loss when it is ameliorated by a gain.

Where no capital gains are available for offset purposes, attempt to get the client to accept the loss before it becomes long term so that the maximum tax benefit will be available. Deductions against highest taxed income lessens the bite of the loss and frees up the client's capital for other investment opportunities. Recommendations to accept the loss should be made only when you truly believe an equal or better opportunity exists.

Prospecting: 11 Greatest Sources

Every seller of intangibles who aspires to be a big earner is constantly on the lookout for quality prospects. Unfortunately, many of these aspirers to wealth fail because they don't uncover enough prospects nor understand how prospects can be ferreted out. The failures normally have not been exposed to the prime, easily available sources of prospects in their particular communities.

Without a steady stream of different people to subject to a sales pitch, the salesperson's commission revenue often declines to a trickle. Learning where to find an endless number of qualified prospects is one trick of the trade that can be mastered by anyone willing to work the established mother lodes listed in this chapter:

Prospect Source 1:
The Daily Newspaper

Daily papers in every community are studded with names of likely prospects for you. The best names to collect and add to your prospect file are the names of people just promoted to a higher job. Usually the promotion announcement is accompanied by a photo and is planted as a news release. The free news write-up serves three basic functions: (1) it recognizes a valued employee; (2) the article possibly attracts new business; (3) the article serves as a free ad.

The following story illustrates the power of collecting these free leads.

I sat at the desk side of a successful account executive in our

Denver, Colorado, office. Gene O. was a mature (fiftyish) salesman who had spent 20 years in military service, retiring as a colonel. Gene chose Denver for his adopted home because of the climate, his love for skiing, and the growth of the area.

When he entered the brokerage business for his second career, he was faced with the challenge of learning all the rules, regulations, and various details about investment product details. In addition, he was to trying to build a clientele in a town in which he was a complete stranger. Within three years Gene was netting over $50,000 a year!

Between Gene's phone calls, we chatted about how he had gone about finding prospects. *Gene told me that he used the newspaper as his sole source of leads!* Gene daily perused the business section and clipped articles about executives who were being promoted or recognized for some particular accomplishment. Gene then taped each clipping to his stationery and sent it to the executive with a simple note saying something like this: "I thought you might like to have an extra copy of your recent write-up in the paper. Congratulations!" Then he simply signed his name.

A week later Gene would follow up with a phone call. (He almost always got through by telling the secretary this call was in reference to his letter and the newspaper article of the previous week.) Most often he was warmly greeted and thanked for his thoughtfulness. Gene carefully would work the conversation to investing and mail the prospect some interesting investment ideas. Another follow-up phone call was made, usually followed by an appointment where an order was obtained.

That prospecting process alone was sufficient (augmented by inevitable referrals) to propel Gene to a high level of earnings within 18 months. You might want to follow Gene's lead in building a prospect file.

Top-earning salespeople know:
"Beginning is the most important part of work."

Top security salespeople reach the pinnacle of success because they make the effort to see that each recommended security fits into their clients' overall picture. Make sure that your suggestions suit the clients' needs and you will reach the top!

TWO THINGS YOU CAN DO TODAY TO MAKE YOUR BUSINESS GROW!

1. *Don't speak too rapidly; slow down your speaking rate and increase your inflection. You will be better understood and make more sales. Be fact-sure, and confidence will radiate.*

2. *Don't use broker jargon, like "P/E ratio" or "break out from a long base." Concentrate on the following 3 things and you will get more sales.*

   —*profit potential (be clear about your expectation)*
   —*time frame (state the expected time to earn)*
   —*risk (point out the risk, if any)*

The simpler the language, the greater the number of orders you will get.

In 1972 I conducted a sales training program attended by Jerry H. Jerry was an aggressive young man in his twenties with an MBA and a strong desire for the finer things in life. Jerry listened and learned in class. After completing the sales training program Jerry began to sell in one of our northern New Jersey branches. At the end of his second year, using the sales ideas he had learned, he was earning at a $35,000 annual rate! Not bad, but not good enough for Jerry. Jerry began to feel a geographical restriction due to being surrounded by competing offices of his own firm. In addition Jerry had a hankering for the faster business pace of New York City as opposed to the more tranquil suburban life.

Jerry decided to change firms and go to work for an old-line respected firm that had comparatively few retail branches. He left behind his established accounts and set about the task of prospecting and building a new clientele. Within four years' time Jerry's net earnings exceeded $300,000 annually.

I asked Jerry where he obtained his prospects. Jerry told me that his main source of prospects was the Dun and Bradstreet Directory of million dollar corporations, a book that is normally available in every public library to those who can't or won't pay the annual fee for their own copies.

Jerry thinks that book is an absolute gold mine! It lists the name, address, and phone number of every corporation that has more than $1 million in revenue annually. It also gives the names of the key officers. "All I do," said Jerry, "is call these business people at their place of work and present a timely idea. I make sure to ask for an order! I get plenty of turndowns, but enough 'yeses' come through to make me one of the highest-paid people in Wall Street!"

Not bad for a young man now in his thirties! Perhaps you can take a clue from Jerry and develop a lot of high-quality prospects into clients from this exciting prospect pool.

Prospect Source 2: Dun and Bradstreet Directory of Million-Dollar Corporations

**Prospect Source 3:
Fine-Arts Patrons**

Almost every city has a little theater, an art museum, or a symphony orchestra that is supported by local people who appreciate and patronize the arts. These kind people want their children and friends to acquire culture, a love of various art forms. They generously give time and money to make art appreciation available to the general community.

Often the only recognition they receive is to have their names printed on a program at a performance or included in some publication acknowledging their contribution. These names usually include many of the wealthy people in the area and are a prime source of prospects. You only have to take the time to gather the names and look up the addresses and phone numbers for your prospect file. Making regular contact with the patrons on these lists, and asking them for orders will produce substantial commission revenues.

**Prospect Source 4:
Contributors to Charity**

Every community conducts annual charity drives. Wealthy people invariably are asked to make substantial contributions to such community fund-raising campaigns. Most charities, like United Way, the Heart Fund, or the American Cancer Society, use volunteers who offer their time and expertise. These volunteers are supplied with names, addresses, phone numbers, and the amounts of contributions in previous years.

These charity drives are a double-barreled opportunity for you. They give you a chance to do a civic good at the same time you are presenting yourself to wealthy prospects who could be substantial sources of new business and referrals. I have met many fine people who later became clients while soliciting donations to local charities. Offer your services as a solicitor for charity drives in your church, the YMCA–YWCA, Red Cross, Community Chest, or any of hundreds of charitable organizations that solicit contributions.

Another aspect of working for a charity is to offer the use of your office for a telephone contribution callathon on some Saturday or Sunday. Of course, this can only be done with your branch manager's approval. This also assumes that you have 15 or more phones available for the solicitors to use.

In addition to providing a civic good, you will find excellent prospects among the solicitors themselves. (Don't forget to arrange for free coffee and cookies, and to clean up after they leave!)

Often the solicitors will leave you with copies of lists naming last year's givers, which are an outstanding source of prospects. A little effort in the right place may pay off in obtaining the finest clients.

**Prospect Source 5:
Annual Reports**

Another great source of prospects often overlooked is the annual report. Particularly valuable are annual reports of companies located in or near your workable territory. Each of these

Successful, experienced account executives learn from others' mistakes. They know that they will never live long enough to make all the errors themselves!

reports invariably lists the names of the members of the board of directors. These people are influential, and usually affluent enough to serve as directors. They make ideal prospects. These prime prospects are used to making decisions, they are familiar with dealing in large dollar amounts, and they fully understand risk. Their grasp of investment ideas is quick. Approaching such people consistently and logically will give you a chance at big commission prospects who could become long-term clients.

I told one of the attendees at a sales course about this magnificent source of prospects. He was excited at the idea of zeroing in on this high-quality market. Perhaps some of his excitement stemmed from the fact that he was only 23 years old, and selling securities was his first full-time job.

We discussed in detail how he was to approach this particular market segment. His branch office was in Fort Lauderdale, Florida. This particular area abounds in publicly traded securities of small local banks and insurance companies.

Here are the steps I outlined for him:

1. Compile a list of all the companies headquartered in the area whose stock is publicly traded.

2. Obtain an annual report from each company.

3. Make up a prospect file consisting of the names of the members of the board of each company.

4. Systematically call or see each board member.

5. Ask each board member to make any open-market purchase of company stock through him or sell shares through him.

6. Follow the companies' stock prices on a regular basis; also become familiar with its business fundamentals.

7. Alert the OTC trading department to notify you when blocks of stock became available for purchase or sale.

In just three years' time this young man, at age 26, was netting $75,000 per year from clients obtained from this one prospecting source!

Prospect Source 6: City Directories

One of the finest sources of quality prospects easily available in every community is the city directory for the area. This wondrous book lists names and phone numbers of the residents on each street. If you do not already know them, get someone to point out the streets where the most affluent people reside. Then you can construct a prospect file with the names of people who live on those streets, and each person is mailed, called, and, preferably, seen. This source alone led me to a high annual income in less than 24 months.

Yearly updates of the directory keep a flow of new prospects available. Here is a special sales hint that you might find very valuable. If you are selling in an area where competition is strong and highly motivated, work your city directory prospecting street by street from *Z to A* rather than from A to Z. Those people living on streets beginning with the last letters of the alphabet are usually not subjected to as many sales attempts as those people who live on streets beginning with the early letters of the alphabet.

City directories are usually available in every public library. In the event your firm does not furnish one to you, just visit your library.

Prospect Source 7: Yellow Pages of the Telephone Book

The telephone directory should be one of your most valuable sources of prospects. Normally, I recommend avoiding the white pages as they contain too many unqualified prospects. The best candidates for conversion to clients are from the listings of lawyers, doctors, CPAs, dentists, and other licensed professionals. To those lists can be added the heads of the companies that advertise in the Yellow Pages.

Some of my best clients were acquired by calling a place listed in the Yellow Pages and asking to speak to the boss. One of the best approaches for securities salespeople is to examine any current research reports carefully and determine what prospects might be familiar with the researched company or its product. After compiling a list of people who might be interested, I'd call each one and offer to send a copy of the research report for them to read. If the answer was "no," I'd tell them that after they read the report they very well might concur with the analyst and want to invest in the shares. If the answer was "yes," I'd make a pitch to add to the existing position.

All in all, the Yellow Pages are as filled with gold as their color indicates.

Top security salespeople are always new-account conscious. They seek new accounts each month from referrals and from their prospecting methods. They know full well that without a continuous supply of new accounts their account base (and thus income) will shrink due to the normal attrition of customers who die, others who relocate, and others who grow disenchanted with the market.

TWO THINGS YOU CAN DO TODAY TO MAKE YOUR BUSINESS GROW!

1. *Select a quality, research-recommended stock in which to try to build a position of more than 10,000 shares in 30 days.*

2. *Build a book of information about that stock for instant reference and to furnish you with the kind of knowledge that helps kindle enthusiasm.*

ASK FOR THE ORDER!

One of the most underutilized sources of prospects in most communities is the name list compiled by organizations like Welcome Wagon or New Neighbors.

Such organizations contact new arrivals in the community, offering all types of services, merchandise discounts, friendliness, and a pat format to introduce new people to each other and to the community.

Usually each organization has a monthly luncheon featuring a guest speaker. See if you can't arrange to be the speaker one or more times during the calendar year. There are from 25 to 100 or more attendees at the typical luncheon. Many of them are potential investors or have spouses that invest. This nest of prospects is certainly one of the most lucrative to work, as the newcomers to the area normally establish new insurance and brokerage relationships. The first salesperson on the scene usually has an inside track to their business.

In addition to the monthly luncheon, for a fee the organizations supply a short biographical sketch on area newcomers. This list is usually supplied on a weekly basis to subscribers and is well worth the money.

A great starting point is to contact the hostess(es) in your area personally. Meet with them and try to win some small part of their investment business. If they do business with you, they are most likely going to tell countless numbers of newcomers your name. Successful efforts here can bring a steady stream of prospects your way.

Many firms have a large number of inactive accounts as well as a supply of old leads that never became accounts. These names many times can be contacted with a fresh idea or a different approach and converted into excellent clients. I acquired at least six large accounts from the branch dead file! Send a letter

Prospect Source 8:
Welcome Wagon

Prospect Source 9:
Inactive Firm Accounts
and Prospect Lists

to each name, *followed up by an order-asking phone call* on a specific timely investment.

Gregg C., San Antonio, Texas, less than six months out of my sales course, obtained a supply of old leads (not accounts) to work on for a municipal bond offering. One such contact resulted in an immediate order for municipal securities large enough to provide a net commission to Gregg of $1200. A subsequent order the following month yielded a net commission to Gregg of $7200! Not bad for a 24-year-old just starting up the ladder to success.

Free leads like those above are many times available just for the asking.

Prospect Source 10: Club Members

Country clubs, swim clubs, social clubs of all types exist in every community throughout this land. Their membership lists are usually easily available through an existing member, or many times they can be obtained simply by asking. Social-club members are excellent prospects for investment and for insurance business.

The more elite and exclusive the club, the more likely it is that the investment and insurance business available through the individual members is large. A direct pursuit of the members by a mail campaign with phone follow-up can reward you with substantial business plus high-quality referrals.

It is not necessary to go to the expense of joining a club solely for the potential business that exists from the members. If your ideas are good and well presented the prospects will buy whether or not you are a club member. The same applies to civic clubs. It is not necessary to join to be able to obtain business from members.

Even if you are the joiner type, just being a member does

Top security salespeople all had to strive to overcome failure. They understood that it was far better to try hard and fail than to do nothing and succeed.

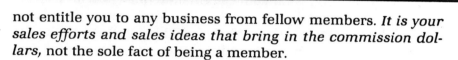

Top security salespeople learn to answer objections before they are raised. They present their sales ideas in a manner that kills off negative thoughts before they become implanted in a prospect's mind.

TWO THINGS YOU CAN DO TODAY TO MAKE YOUR BUSINESS GROW!

1. *Call your college alumni office and get a current list of local alumni to prospect.*

2. *Draw a circle on your daytimer and enter the number of prospects you asked for an order today! (It had better be a double digit!)*

not entitle you to any business from fellow members. *It is your sales efforts and sales ideas that bring in the commission dollars,* not the sole fact of being a member.

Prospect Source 11: Noncompetitive Salespeople

One of my most treasured prospect sources was any salesperson who sold products or services that did not compete directly with my own products. Salespeople, particularly commission-based salespeople, are normally outgoing, garrulous folks, who feel a kinship with their brethren who are trying to earn a living through selling. The feeling of kinship is naturally strongest toward noncompetitors.

Whenever salespeople get together, they often exchange stories about prospecting methods, closing techniques, and earnings potentials. Sharing successful ideas can benefit the participants in many ways. One great benefit I found was to exchange prospects. New, quality names to call and see are constantly needed if sales are to expand. The old saying "the more the merrier" is an absolute truism when it comes to clients and prospects.

Learn who the outstanding salespeople are in noncompetitive fields in your area. Make it a point to call them and meet them for breakfast (lower cost!) or lunch. Concentrate on the high earners in real-estate, Cadillac, Continental, or foreign car sales; yacht brokers, and the like, and you will find people who know the people you would like to have as accounts. Make a friend, be a friend to successful salespeople, and they will frequently either give or make available the names of dozens of top-drawer prospects.

General Motors annually furnishes Cadillac dealers with a list of late-model Cadillac owners in the immediate area. This list is, of course, a primary tool for the salespeople at Cadillac dealerships to use in trying to sell more cars. This list can be extremely valuable to you. Usually the people who own late-model Cadillacs are in upper income brackets and investment oriented. Make an effort to get a list copy, either from a salesperson or from a secretary you befriend.

One of the men who went through my sales course was from Minneapolis. This prospect source fired his imagination, and upon returning to his home he went to the leading Cadillac dealer and was given a demonstration ride (what else would you expect?) and an excellent sales pitch. He told the salesman that some day soon he hoped to buy a top-of-the-line model and that he would encourage clients to use stock-market profits to buy Cadillacs. Sugarplums danced in front of the car salesman's eyes about the future car sales possible through this young man. A second meeting was all that it took for my young salesman to get a copy of 2800 names and addresses of late-model Cadillac owners. This one source produced over 100 new accounts for him and started him on the road to sales success.

Ford also supplies Lincoln Continental dealers with lists of late-model Continental owners. That list's power is just as good as the Cadillac list, and every effort should be made to get it.

In my view, the noncompetitive salesperson is one of the greatest sources of quality prospects around. Carefully explore the potential for good business that these colleagues provide.

The prospect sources listed in this chapter by no means exhaust the possibilities. Many others are available to you, as a seeker of names, including purchased lists from list brokers. The main thing to understand is this: the bigger your pool of high-level prospects, the more likely it is that you can extract commissions with a consistent contact approach.

Build a good prospect file. Keep adding to it. Make order-asking contacts with the people in your file. You will be a success!

Using the Most Important Hour of the Day: 3 Sure Steps to Success

"Plan your work! Work your plan!" These perhaps trite, shopworn phrases are used by salespeople in all industries to incite cohorts to ever-higher levels of production. The message is clear, but the application is often difficult to accomplish.

Sellers of intangibles need a clear head and a clear view ahead each day if they are to succeed in their endeavors. Carrying out the following suggestions will sharply clarify the sales path for you to follow each working day. Accomplish each step at the end of the business day before you leave for home.

It is very difficult to be effective at sales if your desk is strewn with hundreds of scraps of paper, two or three weeks' collection of the *Wall Street Journal*, memos from the home office, half-eaten sandwiches, full ash trays, research reports, annual reports, and countless other "in the way" items. *Every business day before you go home, tidy up!* Put everything in its proper place and prepare your office or desk area as if the richest, most desirable client in the world was going to pay you a visit the next day. Once you form this habit, you will feel better when you leave the office and when you arrive the next morning. The decks have been cleared for action.

Many potential clients are turned off by visiting a salesperson who conveys an impression of sloppiness in handling paper. The thought enters the prospect's mind, "Maybe this person will be as careless with my investments as he [or she] is in keeping this desk orderly."

Step 1:
Clean Up Your Desk

Step 2:
Spend up to One Hour
With Yourself

Take one uninterrupted hour each day. The secretaries and receptionists should be instructed to take messages only. Take no phone calls unless a true emergency has arisen. During this one-hour period, mentally review every sales attempt you made that day. What was it you said to Mr. Smith that got him to give you that big order? What was it you said to Mrs. Jones that caused her not to buy? What might you have said differently that would have closed the sale? Were your facts incorrect or not convincing enough? Did you fail to radiate confidence and enthusiasm?

After throughfully reviewing each sales effort for that day you are now ready for step 3.

Step 3:
Write Down Tomorrow's
Sales Plan

One of the best aids in becoming sales-effective is to know exactly what you want to accomplish each day, from the minute you arrive at work. The best way to accomplish this is to write the details of the action plan the night before.

CREATE A PRODUCT WORKSHEET

With a written plan in hand at the day's beginning, you will find selling a much easier task. The plan makes for a disciplined approach rather than the typical, haphazard, "Let's see what the market is doing "before trying to contact clients and prospects" method. Insurance salespeople can easily modify the following list to insurance products.

Here is the minimum information necessary to write down on the planning night. A sample form is shown in the exhibits.

1. *Favorite growth stock.* Itemize all the meaningful statistics and select a reason for buying now.

2. *Favorite income stock.* Itemize all the meaningful statistics and select a reason for buying now.

3. *Favorite short sale.* Itemize all the meaningful statistics and the reason for selling short now. Include a target downside objective. This coolly chosen selection is necessary for that occasional prospect or client who feels bearish and asks point-blank for a short-sale recommendation. When asked to enthusiastically, confidently suggest a short sale, the average securities salesperson is usually unable to render a logical suggestion. This unreadiness often shows through, and the "impulse order" is missed. By having this information prepared the night before, you will sound smooth, professional, and prepared, able to respond to the request by saying, "I was thinking about short sales last night [true!] and here is the one that looks best to me right now."

4. *Favorite AAA-rated municipal bond.* Itemize all the

When bear markets come, as they inevitably do, good security salespeople become mindful of an old adage: "Hell is truth seen too late!"

meaningful statistics, including the dollar price to the client, plus the reason for buying now.

5. *Favorite A-rated municipal bond.* Itemize all the meaningful statistics plus the reason for buying now.

6. *Favorite convertible corporate bond.* Itemize all the meaningful statistics plus the reason for buying now.

7. *The taxable unit trust currently available.* Include the dollar price per unit, all meaningful statistics, and the reason for buying now.

8. *The federal tax-free unit trust currently available.* Include the dollar price per unit, all meaningful statistics, and the reason for buying now.

9. *The two most attractive covered call write opportunities.* Include the returns if exercised and if the stock is unchanged at the end of the time period, plus the reasons for buying now.

10. *The most attractive put option to buy.* Itemize all meaningful statistics plus the reason for buying now.

11. *The most attractive call option to buy.* Itemize all meaningful statistics and the reason for buying now.

12. *An interest-rate fact sheet.* List the various current returns on tax-deferred annuities, Treasury bills, GNMA securities, and money-market funds.

Collecting and entering the foregoing information on a product worksheet will normally take 20 to 30 minutes once the daily information resources have been identified. You may want to use a buddy system in which each participant daily digs up certain of the necessary data.

Other product information should be added as your interest dictates.

Once the product information is gathered and entered on a *single, easy-to-read worksheet, that sheet becomes a powerful tool in selling prospects and clients.* You will never again have to interrupt a phone conversation to scramble madly to find a wanted detail or information about a product.

With the completed sheet in front of you, you can always sound like a professional. It becomes easier to flow from one product to another as you talk to clients and prospects. The smooth flow makes sales come easier and enables you to feel much more confident. The transmittal of this confidence to the prospect is what makes the sale. That confidence is generated by the previous night's work.

LIST YOUR PHONE PROSPECTS

After completing the product worksheet, write down the names and phone numbers of 30 (or more) people you are going to call next day to attempt to sell one of the ideas on the sheet.

PLAN THE DIRECT MAIL

When the 30 or more names and phone numbers are listed, complete the direct mail plan. Each night before leaving the office, 10 to 20 "somethings" should be mailed to prospects to try to generate an incoming order, phone call, or information request. These 10 to 20 pieces should be accompanied by enclosed, easy-to-fill-out response cards. Each name mailed should be carefully logged for a call one week later.

When all these plans are completed, you can go home *relaxed.* You have carefully prepared yourself for the coming day. You should rest well, secure in the thought that you are

If you are ever inclined to imbibe to relieve your worries, pay heed to Thomas Edison who said, "As a cure for worrying—WORK is better than whisky."

TWO THINGS YOU CAN DO TODAY TO MAKE YOUR BUSINESS GROW!

1. *Contact one or more list brokers and purchase a tax-shelter buyer's list for your area (and any others that you and your pocketbook might want).*

2. *Sell a buddy on sharing the cost of subscribing to the ValueLine convertible service, if your office doesn't get it.*

paving the way for future success. You can face work tomorrow with full knowledge of the day's work plan, confidently pursuing orders from prospects and clients.

Each day's product worksheet and list of names to be called should be three-hole punched and filed in a binder. This retained file can then be reviewed and prior suggestions tracked and monitored. In the event of a prospect call-back months later about an earlier recommendation quickly scanning the sheet can pinpoint the product and the price you recommended it at. The client will be impressed, and that fosters sales. Retaining the sheets is also clear evidence for how hard you have worked, for your daily sales attempts are logged.

All this can usually be accomplished in a quiet hour at the end of the work day. If you do it, and apply the other selling skills and ideas outlined in this book, I am confident success will come your way—and soon!

All that remains to be done is to do it! Start today to make your million investing other people's money.

Good luck!

Appendices

Profiles of Successful Professionals

BARDHYL QUKU

FIRM: Dean Witter Reynolds Inc.

POSITION: Senior Account Executive

TITLE: Vice President, Investments

AGE: 41

Bard is an experienced, tough-minded, aggressive, outgoing salesman who has been a production leader in his firm for over a decade. Bard graduated the Reynolds Securities Training Program in 1968 and progressed to the point where in 1975, he was selected by *Financial World* as one of Wall Street's outstanding brokers.

Bard lives in Wyckoff, New Jersey and works in Dean Witter Reynolds, Inc., World Trade Center office. He is married to the lovely Gerri, and he is the father of five beautiful girls.

Here are some of Bard's comments concerning the sales ideas of LeRoy Gross. "LeRoy's sales training has been the foundation of all of my sales techniques. His approach to seminar techniques is unique and the best in the business."

Bard is open-minded and a quick learner, as well as a hard industrious worker. He zeros in on his clients' financial needs and makes a sincere, dedicated effort to help them achieve their financial goals.

Bard's career earnings (1968–1980) totaled over $1,000,000! Bard is an all-sport enthusiast with a particular love for tennis. He has instilled this tennis love in his five girls—so don't be surprised if you someday see the name "Quku" in the women's national rankings.

PERRY BACON

FIRM: E. F. Hutton   **POSITION:** Manager

TITLE: Vice President   **AGE:** 34

Perry Bacon is a young, aggressive, intelligent man who has developed into one of his companies outstanding managers. Perry began his brokerage career with Reynolds Securities in 1971.

After completing the Reynolds training program and getting exposed to LeRoy Gross's sales ideas, Perry was assigned to the Baltimore office as an account executive in his first full production year. Perry earned $40,000! An excellent achievement for a young man only 24 at the time.

Perry later transferred to the Washington D.C. office of Reynolds and became a regional syndicate manager. His quick, probing mind led him into the listed option world, and he became an institutional option specialist, raising his earnings in 1976 to $70,000!

Perry has a rapier wit, inquisitive mind, and seeming boundless energy. His intense drive led him to the challenge of opening and managing a specialized retail branch for E. F. Hutton in 1977.

Using his well honed selling skills to continue personal production while actively building a new full-scale branch office was a difficult task. In four years, Perry led his office to one of the best in the E. F. Hutton system as measured by average production per man.

Perry's net income also advanced so that he earned over $150,000 in 1979 at the ripe old age of 33!

Here is a comment on the value of LeRoy's sales training excerpted from a letter from Perry. "LeRoy has increased the product knowledge and marketing capability of thousands of account executives. Industry personnel who implement LeRoy's ideas will find those ides to be a rewarding addition to their professionalism."

Perry is married to Susan and the father of Perry III. He is avidly interested in politics, finance, and sports.

By 1981 year end, his career earnings 1971–1981 should top $1,000,000!

LINDSAY C. HERKNESS, III

FIRM: Dean Witter Reynolds, Inc.   **POSITION:** SENIOR ACCOUNT EXECUTIVE

TITLE: Vice President, Investments   **AGE:** 37

Lindsay is a bright, hard-working broker who began his career with Reynolds Securities in 1966. After completing his brokerage training, he sharpened his selling skills and merchandizing techniques by applying many of my ideas.

Lindsay was selected by *Financial World* magazine in July 1976 as one of Wall Street's top brokers. His career earnings at the end of 1979 totaled over $1.12 million. Here is one of Lindsay's comments: "I found LeRoy Gross to be one of the most highly organized, disciplined, and effective brokers in the business. He helped me a great deal."

Lindsay Herkness lived in Switzerland during his childhood and there learned to speak French before he could speak English. Later, when he became a stockbroker, he came up with the idea of giving lectures in French and English to passengers on French Line cruise ships. Some 600 of them are still his clients. "I think the lecture circuit is the most professional way for a broker to build up his business," says Herkness, who figures that 25 percent of his audience will open accounts. He now has 850 retail clients with portfolios worth $95 million. To keep up with it all, in his first six years in the business he worked seven-day weeks. Now he has two full-time assistants to do the paper work, leaving him free to watch the market and his client's portfolios, which he analyzes with the help of Dean Witter Reynolds' computerized portfolio evaluation system. A "conservative" broker, his portfolios are basically long range, with little turnover. And his office is a comfortable distance away from the boardroom.

Lindsay is single (at least at the time of this writing) and is interested in travel, racquet sports, and leading the good life.

WAYNE F. NELSON

FIRM: **Merrill, Lynch, Pierce, Fenner & Smith**   POSITION: **Account Executive**

TITLE: **Vice President**   AGE: **35**

Wayne is an articulate, handsome, likable young man who entered the securities business in 1972. After graduating from the Reynolds Securities Training Program, he was assigned to the Arlington, Virginia, office.

Using direct-mail techniques and lecture methods, he became the number-one opener of new accounts for Reynolds Securities for two consecutive years. Along his new-account growth grew his earned income. By the end of 1980, his relatively brief stay in the securities industry had earned him over $600,000!

Wayne went through sales training with me. Here are some of his observations: "LeRoy is a master salesman! He is as good at the job of selling securities as anyone in the business. He teaches by using compliments, examples, and anecdotes. There is no question but that a person would become successful in the securities business by listening to what LeRoy had to say and doing what he preached."

Wayne is now a leading producer for the Merrill Lynch office in Washington, D.C. He is married to Marti, who is soon to receive her M.D.

Sports are of great interest to Wayne, as is reading and writing. Wayne has written a book published by McGraw Hill, *How to Buy Money.*

Power-Packed Prospecting Letters That Sell

In their normal function of trying to create business, salespeople write letters to prospects and clients. Most salespeople are not trained to create sales-inducing epistles. Yet, hours, and even days, are spent composing, editing, and rewriting notes intended to arouse interest—to the point of placing an order—in the prospect.

Preparing letters that light fires and produce results is a very difficult task. To make your job easier, I have culled letter samples from my files. These letters have worked well for salespeople at many different firms, and they just might produce good results for you too. Change the copy to suit your personality and your location (but there is then a risk of lessening the impact). These time-saving letters may pay off in *big dollars* for you, as they have for others. Collect other letters used successfully by colleagues in your firm until you have built a letter library. *Remember: every letter sent must contain one or two response cards.*

Mailing Objectives and Procedures

This section of sales letters is designed to help you develop sales via direct mail. While a letter is not likely to be as effective as a telephone call, and certainly not as productive as a personal visit, direct mail has proven its effectiveness in sales building when properly conceived, executed, and then followed through.

As to conception, identify your objective for a mailing. That objective will normally fall within one of these four categories:

1. *Getting leads.* Mailing with the objective of building up a list of prospects, people interested in the market for your specific intangible product. You send a mailing to a list of good addresses, people you can safely assume are at least reasonably affluent. Your replies then become prospects for quick follow-up, just as with advertising leads. Good addresses not replying to a first mailing should receive other mailings. *Don't assume you've "worked out" a list wit a single letter, a single sales appeal.* Keep working over a good list as long as you get a satisfactory percent of responses.

2. *Following up on leads.* Mailings with the objective of "warming up" prospects. The majority of investors cannot be converted into customers with the first follow-up to a mailing or an advertisement. Since your aim is to impress these qualified prospects with your range of services and your definite interest in their personal investment situation, these lead follow-up mailings should, of course, be followed by phone calls. Request a personal interview when the potential is good.

3. *Controlled-call mailings.* A series of letters to "warm up" selected affluent prospects such as executives and other professionals, working toward a personal appointment.

4. *Inactive accounts and out-of-town customers.* Letters to remind periodically of your personal interest and that your services are available.

These sales letters cover a range of selling appeals. Only through experimentation will you ascertain the pulling power in your area. It is important to keep records of the responses to each mailing—and find a successful formula through testing.

Don't expect a high rate of return from a mailing of any letter. Direct-mail experts consider a 5 percent response to be outstanding. Your aim should be to develop a sufficient number of responses (qualified leads) so that, when properly followed up, you develop more than enough business to cover all the mailing costs. Follow up *each* letter with a phone call one week after mailing. Don't mail more than you are willing and able to follow up with phone calls.

In trying to get leads, you want to reach at least reasonably affluent people. Make up your lists from better neighborhoods in cities. Work from your city directory or cross-reference telephone directories. Mail to good suburbs. Some nearby towns or cities may not have been prospected recently. Use the Yellow Pages for professionals, accountants, doctors. Try to get lists of company personnel of concerns in your area. (Perhaps you can "obtain" their internal telephone directories.) New residents' addresses can often be obtained. Also, you might get names and addresses of members of country clubs, university graduates (members of local alumni clubs), fraternal organizations, Chambers of Commerce. And, mail to any advertising leads or other prospect names that may not have been aggressively pursued within the past year or two. Lists can also be purchased from direct-mail houses: for example, owners of two cars or people with incomes over $25,000. *The main point in mailings is to avoid waste.* Direct your mail only to addresses that should prove productive due to the profession or business position of the addressee.

With any good list of names, you should plan a campaign of at least three letters, one per week of different types. Any name worth mailing once is worth following with other mailings and phone calls for the proper registration of your interest and range of services.

To avoid any suspicion of yours being junk mail, hand address your mailings. Sometimes responses can be significantly increased when addressed with an unusual ink, such as green or red.

Letter Reproduction and Postage

Because sales letters are normally used in quantity, here is a brief description of common methods of reproducing letters using stationery with your local office letterhead. Contact local letter suppliers, who may be able to reproduce at low prices and give you local control and prompt service.

1. *Letterpress with typewriter ribbon.* Most lettershops have their own name for this generally satisfactory technique. The letter is printed from type through a cloth ribbon. The result is an extremely well-simulated letter. The cost range is reasonable for 200 twenty-line letters. The per-unit price drops dramatically as the quantity rises. If you're doing a "fill-in" (described later) on these letters, the same ribbon can be used that printed the letter to achieve a perfect match.

2. *Offset letter.* This is done from a printing plate made from a photograph of a master letter. Letterhead and text are printed in one step. Offset is frequently used for mass mailings.

3. *Multigraph letter.* This is the most common process, and the average person would find it hard to tell it was a printed letter. The multigraph process can be done with or without fill-ins and signature.

4. *"Fill-ins," addressing, and signatures.* Many sales letters are effective without any salutation. Instead, use an intriguing headline or a printed salutation as general as

"Dear Investor" (or "Dear Customer," for inactive accounts). But the appeal of some of the letters can be enhanced by personalizing with a fill-in, such as a one-line "Dear Mr. Jones."

A four-line fill-in (including address) is not necessarily prohibitive in cost. When four lines are used with a window envelope, the cost and time of separate addressing of the envelope is saved. And the personal quality of the letter is enhanced.

Ideally, all sales letters should be hand-signed to properly personalize (I do *not* recommend a rubber-stamp signature). If time does not permit hand signing, most local letter suppliers can reproduce your signature with a "slug," dropped in when your letter is printed.

Postage. Any mailings you undertake will normally have to be sent either first-class or third-class mail. First class is usually used on sales letters because undeliverable first-class mail is returned automatically. Thus you can avoid waste in future mailings to these addresses. Also, first class is required by the postal authorities for typewritten, individualized correspondence.

Third class should be considered for *mass* mailings. When booklets are used (in quantity mailings) that raise the overall weight per piece to over one ounce, use third class. The only mail acceptable for third-class bulk rates is "printed matter," not typewritten or individualized. Sales letters addressed "Dear Investor" or "Dear Sir" and reproduced by the processes described in the preceding section should qualify as "bulk printed matter."

Bulk third-class mailings require a bulk permit number, which is obtainable from your local general Post Office. Your Post Office will advise you as to how third-class mail needs to be bundled and sorted by city, state, and zip code.

Sales Letters
Index

EXHIBIT 1
New Tax-Free Bond Prospecting Letter

STATE OF _____ BONDS

(Paying interest free of all Federal and state tax to
_____ residents.)

Within the next two weeks your community will be
offering fully tax exempt municipal bonds. The interest
paid on these bonds will be <u>federal tax free</u> and for
                    residents also state tax exempt. The
yield should be attractive and the bonds will be sold in
lots of $5,000 on a commission-free basis to the purchasers.

Presently, I am taking noncommittal "indications of
interest" subject to further details and inspection of
the prospectus. Preliminary prospectuses are available.
If you are interested in placing an indication of interest
or simply having a prospectus sent to you, please call me
directly at (   )   or toll free 1-800-   . The
bonds are subject to availability, and will be allotted on
a first-come, first-served basis.

Sincerely,

AE

AE/typ

P.S. Please let me know if you have any friends or rela-
tives who might be interested in this issue. I would be
pleased to help them.

Enclosures:
1. Return envelope with your AE number
2. Return card for <u>referrals</u>

EXHIBIT 2
Municipal Bond Prospecting Letter

Dear

　　Most people have little control over their income taxes.
There isn't much you can do about tax rates on your basic
income from salaries, professional earnings, or business
profits.

　　You, as a taxpayer and investor, do have a control
capability over one segment of your income--a significant
control that can bring you legitimate and permissible tax
relief. We're speaking of your secondary income, your
investment income, the "top layer" taxable income that
rides above your regular earnings and incurs the highest
tax rates.

　　This top layer is, in effect, your most expensive in-
come--but you can control it by taking advantage of the
tax-exempt status of municipal bonds.

　　In this high-tax era, taxpayer-investors are finding
that the transfer of taxable investments into "tax-exempts"
not only reduces the cost of that top layer income but,
　　　　　　　　　　in higher income-tax brackets, generally results in an increased spendable return.

　　I am sure municipal bonds would be helpful and potentially profitable in your investment program. With this
in mind, I am enclosing our municipal bond booklet to give
you a better understanding of the tax-free income story.

　　　　　　　　　　　　　　Sincerely yours,

AE/typ

P.S. If you would like our list of A-rated municipal bonds
currently available and yielding over 8%, federal tax-free,
complete the enclosed card.

Enclosures:
1. Value services mailer
2. Return envelope
3. Muni booklet

Dear

    In answer to your recent request, we are enclosing a copy of our booklet "Tax-Free Bonds: Your Path to Lower Federal Income Taxes." You have taken your first step toward reducing your taxes. We would like to call your attention to the table on pages 8 and 9, which demonstrates the size of the tax savings you can realize through tax-exempt municipal bonds, depending on your tax bracket.

                                  participates in virtually all major new issue underwritings and secondary market offerings of municipal bonds. Some of our present offerings that may fit your investment objectives include:

Description	Coupon	Maturity	Yield to Maturity	Approximate Dollar Price
1.				
2.				
3.				
4.				

    All bonds suggested here are of investment quality and are appropriate securities for individual investment. Note that we have shown the yield to maturity for each bond. These yields will help you find the taxable equivalent value of your investment (in your income bracket) by referring to the table mentioned above.

    If you have any questions about these or any other municipal bond issues or if you would like any other kind of investment information, please call me at

                              Sincerely yours,

Enclosures:
1. Valuable services mailer
2. Return envelope
3. Muni booklet

EXHIBIT 4
Municipal Bond Prospecting Letter

Dear

    Are you interested in reducing your taxes on your investment income? Learn how you can cut your taxes and obtain current income that's all yours--tax free--through an investment in tax-exempt municipal bonds.

_____ has prepared a comprehensive tax-exempt bond guide for the individual investor which:

* Gives five advantages of investing in tax-exempt municipal bonds.
* Explains simply the investment features and details of municipal bonds.
* Clearly explains the various types of municipal bonds available to you.
* Illustrates how you can obtain a net return, equivalent to 10%, 12% or even 15% or more taxable depending upon your tax bracket.
* Shows you how to acquire and/or sell municipal bonds with ease.

    The booklet talks about safety, liquidity, and comparative investments, and it shows why so many individuals are now receiving the same tax advantages that have been enjoyed by institutions and trusts for years. High quality municipal bonds, the security of which is considered second only to U.S. Government securities, currently provide high yields. And, the interest you receive is completely free from federal income tax--and generally exempt from state taxes in the states where issued as well.

    Reduce your taxes. Act now! Get your free copy of this guide without obligation, by completing and returning the enclosed, postage-paid reply card.

                      Very truly yours,

Enclosures:
1. Valuable services mailer
2. Return envelope

EXHIBIT 5
Tax-Exempt Bonds for Customers and/or Prospecting

TAX-FREE INCOME ....Are you interested?

We're always glad to come to the aid of investors who find their tax bite too sharp for comfort. So we suggest your consideration of the advantages of <u>municipal bonds</u>!

These securities are available at historically high yields, ranging from around _____ or more--TAX-EXEMPT. This means that an investor in a 50% tax bracket can now enjoy yields equivalent to ____ to ____ or more in taxable income. Or putting it another way, if your taxable income is $25,000 or over, a municipal bond will give you considerably more after-tax income than the same amount in a savings account or another taxable security with a similar yield.

Municipal securities are usually either backed by the full faith and credit of the issuing municipality or secured by revenues produced from such basic services as water, light and power, throughways, bridges, and airports. Historically they have proven a relatively safe form of investment. And of course, they are readily marketable in the event you needed to sell to raise funds for some financial need.

If all this sounds interesting to you, I would be delighted to show you an up-to-date list of attractive municipal issues. Or you may want further information on this type of investing. In either case, just fill in and return this letter in the enclosed envelope.

Cordially,

Account Executive

Please contact me regarding current municipal bonds yielding 9-1/2% or more.

Please send me a copy of your booklet, "Tax-Exempt Bonds".

_____   _____
        Name   Address

_____
        Telephone
Enclosures:
1. Envelope with AE number
2. Valuable services form

EXHIBIT 6
Tax-Swap Prospecting Letter

Dear Investor:

I hope you had had a good 19__.

You may have achieved capital gains through one of the following:

1. Sale of stocks or bonds
2. Sale of land
3. Sale of a building
4. Sale of a business on a yearly payout

If you own municipal bonds purchased in the past few years, they probably are worth less than you paid for them because interest rates have risen. We can sell those bonds, thus creating a loss, and with the proceeds buy another bond of equal quality and yield at approximately the same price of your sale. This would reduce your tax liability on your capital gains already achieved.

Call me, or better yet, come in with your list of bonds to see how we might possibly reduce your taxes.

Sincerely yours,

P.S. Of course, if you do not own municipal bonds, we can probably accomplish the same tax advantages by swapping corporate bonds or utility common stocks.

Enclosures:
1. Valuable services mailer
2. Return envelope with AE number

EXHIBIT 7
New-Issue Prospecting Letter with Return Card

An Invitation To Be On The   "Net Price"
            Offering List

       is one of the United States' largest
underwriters of securities for American industry.

Because of this, we are able to offer to our clients an
opportunity to purchase a wide variety of stocks and bonds
at "net prices," which under certain circumstances means
that you will not have to pay a normal brokerage commission
(see the prospectus of the offering for full cost and details). Furthermore, your cost price for each share of
stock or bond will be exactly the same as it is for every
investor, large or small.

Since these offerings are frequently in demand, there
is usually a limited amount of time in which to contact
clients who may be interested in participating in such
issues.

I will be happy to place your name on my "Net Price
Offerings" List. This in no way obligates you, but enables
me to promptly contact those people who wish to be notified
of these offerings.

If you are interested, please phone me, or complete and
return the enclosed postpaid reply card today.

            Very truly yours,

            Account Executive

Please place my name on your "Net Price Offering" list.

Name_____

Address_____

City_____ State_____Zip_____

Home Phone _____Business Phone_____

_____Acct.#_____

EXHIBIT 8
New Issue Prospecting Letter

NOTICE TO INVESTORS:

ARE YOU INTERESTED IN SECURITY OFFERINGS
WITHOUT PAYING ANY DIRECT COMMISSIONS

You will be glad to know that as a client of
_____ you could, from time
to time, have an opportunity to purchase listed and un-
listed securities at "net prices." This means that you
would not pay any direct brokerage commissions on such
transactions.

How is this possible? Occasionally a company may need
new financing, or an individual may wish to sell a large
block of stock. The reasons for such sales may be numerous but generally, the size of such an offering is quite
large. Thus, the seller, to enhance marketability, is
willing to pay both his commission on the sell side and
your commission on the buy side. This enables you, the
buyer, to acquire the stock without paying any commission.

"Net price offerings" generally present a cost-saving
opportunity. For this reason, to accommodate clients who
wish to be notified of such offerings, I keep on file the
names of interested clients.

If you are interested, I will be happy to place your
name in my "net price offering" file. This in no way obligates you but enables you to take advantage of selective
"net price" opportunities that may arise in the future. I
suggest that you phone me at _____ or
complete the card enclosed, and return it to me today.

Sincerely,

Account Executive

AE/typ

Enclosure:
1. Commission-free-offering card

EXHIBIT 9
Lecture Prospecting Letter

Dear _____:

As a public service to organizations and clubs like
yours, we are establishing an EMERGENCY SPEAKER SERVICE.
In the event that your organization needs a speaker at the
last minute due to a cancellation, all you have to do is
call _____(your name)_____. We will make available
on instant notice (without charge) a speaker on investment
topics such as those listed below or on any topic concerning
investments which you feel will be of interest to your
members:

- How to earn high interest (currently untaxed) with
  guaranteed safety
- How to use listed call options to increase income
- High-yield common stocks that have increased dividends
  10 consecutive years
- Ten principles for stock investors
- Three ways to invest in federal tax-exempt securities
- Five ways to invest in U.S. government guaranteed
  securities that yield more than savings accounts

In addition to a speaker, we might make available the
use of our office facilities (limit _____ for a night
meeting of your group where you may examine a brokerage
office and how it works.

To inquire further about this service, call me at or
write to me at the above address.

                              Sincerely,

                              Account Executive

AE/typ

Enclosures:
1. Commission-free offering card
2. Valuable services mailer

EXHIBIT 10
Lecture Follow-Up Letter

Dear _____:

It was a pleasure to have you attend my seminar on
_____. I hope that
what you learned will prove to be of great benefit to you
in the future.

Service is the key factor in my business, and it will
be my pleasure to assist you. Please feel free to call
me at _____ for advice concerning
any investment or for an appointment to review your particular situation.

Cordially,

Account Executive

AE/typ

Enclosures:
1. Commission-free offering card
2. Valuable services mailer

EXHIBIT 11
Investment Class Follow-Up Letter

Dear _____:

    Do you remember the investment principles that you
learned in my investment course on _____?
Have you put them to good use or have you simply been
waiting for an attractive opportunity? If you have used
them, I am delighted.

    Please call me at _____ as I
believe you could use your knowledge and benefit by investing now in two special-situation stocks that we feel
have a good potential for capital gain as well as providing good current income from well-protected dividends.

            Sincerely,

            Account Executive

AE/typ

Enclosures:
1. Commission-free offering card
2. Valuable services mailer

EXHIBIT 12
Prospecting Letter for Attorneys

Have you had this frustrating experience?

A good client of yours passes away. His widow (so
sheltered that she had never balanced a checkbook) starts
to lean on you to take case of a host of financial matters
formerly handled by her husband.

Because no one of her requests consumes more than 30
minutes of your time, perhaps because you are on a first-
name basis, you are reluctant to present a bill. Yet after
16 such requests, you've lost a day's income.

You are justifiably resentful.

If I may have a few minutes of your time one day next
week, I can explain a simple procedure used by a growing
number of busy attorneys to stop this drain on their time
and their earnings.

The service I have in mind would give the widow part
ownership in an investment portfolio under continuous,
professional supervision. It would provide her with a
check per month, size of the check to be determined by
her. If the amount she decides upon is more than the
portfolio's investment income, there would be a reduction
in the capital account.

I'll phone you early next week to find out when I may
call upon you so that I may tell you more about this plan.

Cordially,

Enclosures:
1. Valuable services mailer
2. Return envelope with AE number

EXHIBIT 13
Prospecting Letter for Doctors

Dear Doctor:

All day long you give diagnoses....prognoses....prescriptions.

So do we.

Your work is vital to your patients. Ours is just as essential to our clients.

We have this in common, also...rarely is there a day that you can direct your intellect and concentration upon the complexities of a totally different field of endeavor. You cannot create the time to be a better than average investor. Likewise, we don't have the time--even if we had the training--to take up part-time medicine.

In general, how has your investment portfolio performed in the past ten years? Are you satisfied with the results?

Professional consultation with you may aid in improving the overall health of your present investment portfolio. Depending on your particular individual needs, we may suggest tax-exempt securities, listed call option writing, or U.S. government securities.

I will call you soon to set up an appointment to review your "financial health" and prescribe appropriate investment changes. For more information, return the enclosed.

                          Cordially,

                          Account Executive

AE/typ

Enclosures:
1. Tax-exempt return card
2. Commission-free offering card

EXHIBIT 14
New Acquaintance Letter for People "Cold-Called" on Phone or Newly Met in Person

Dear ____________________:

I enjoyed talking with you today and look forward to doing so again in the very near future.

As promised, I have enclosed the information you requested. In addition, I have enclosed a Valuable Services request form.

When you return it to us (completely filled out, please), we will give you a comprehensive valuation of your holdings plus our comments and recommendations in line with your investment objectives.

Naturally, all the information you give is confidential, and there is no charge or obligation for this service. You can also have any of our special investment booklets sent to you without charge by simply checking the appropriate box on the form.

Cordially,

Account Executive

AE/typ

Enclosures:
1. Valuable services mailer
2. Commission-free offering card

EXHIBIT 15
New Account Letter

Dear _____:

    Thank you for opening an account with me at _____.

    The most important part of my job is to keep my clients informed and to provide meaningful investment services.

    Please feel free to call me at _____ with any questions you may have regarding investments. I will be in touch with you soon.

                             Cordially,

                             Account Executive

AE/typ

Enclosures:
1. Commission-free offering card
2. Valuable services mailer
3. Return envelope with your AE number

EXHIBIT 16
Referral Request Letter

Dear _____ :

　　If you believe we have made a good effort for you, will you please list the names of others you think we can help by having their names placed on our mailing list of timely investment ideas.

　　If you are not getting some or all of the items indicated on the enclosed cards, please complete one for yourself.

　　Call me at _____ if there is any investment situation on which you would like more information. It has been a real pleasure working with you.

　　　　　　　　　　Good luck!

　　　　　　　　　　Account Executive

AE/typ

Enclosures:
1. Referral card
2. Valuable services mailer

EXHIBIT 17
Option Prospecting Letter

WOULD YOU LIKE TO HAVE MORE INCOME.....

than you now get from common stocks you own?

Of course you would, but how and at what risk? Those
are questions that might fly through your mind.

Investors just like you are discovering that they can
substantially increase their annual income from their
stocks and lessen their common stock risk at the same time.
They are doing this through an investment method known as
"covered call writing".

Some of the investors significantly improve their
annual dividend income--some simply add to their dividend
income. If you would like more information about this
investment method, including risks and rewards, call me
at _____, or return the enclosed
card to obtain detailed information and an Options Clearing
Corporation prospectus.

It will be my pleasure to assist you in this or any
other investment matter.

                                Cordially,

                                Account Executive

AE/typ

Enclosures:
1. Valuable services mailer
2. Return envelope with AE number

EXHIBIT 18
Option Prospecting Letter

INFLATION HURTS!

　　It is especially hard on those who depend on dividend income from common stocks.

　　Would you like to learn how to possibly lessen your common stock risk and substantially add to your income?

　　You might be able to do both as many other conservative investors are doing through an investment method termed "covered call writing".

　　To learn more details about risks and rewards, call me at _____ or complete the enclosed form to receive an Options Clearing Corporation prospectus and an analysis of your stocks that will show you the amount of additional income currently available to you..... amounts that may take the "hurt" out of inflation for you.

　　　　　　　　　　　　Cordially,

　　　　　　　　　　　　Account Executive

AE/typ

Enclosures:
1.　Valuable services mailer
2.　Return envelope with your AE number

EXHIBIT 19
Option Seminar Prospecting Letter

Dear

    [Brokerage firm] will hold a seminar on [date] that should be of interest to you. It will be devoted to <u>LISTED OPTIONS</u>, a subject that is attracting increased investor attention.

    Members of the [firm] staff will be on hand to discuss the potential risks and rewards of this new investment vehicle and to answer your questions. Whether you consider yourself a conservative or a speculative investor--or somewhere in between--you should find the seminar worthwhile.

    Please call [firm telephone number] to reserve your place at this listed options seminar. No obligation, of course.

                     Very truly yours,

Enclosures:
1. Reservation card
2. Valuable services mailer

EXHIBIT 20
Handling Inquiries from Local Advertising Leads
(Leads not responding to this letter should be followed up by
phone or by other letters if phoning is either impossible or
impractical due to distance.)

Dear

    Here is the information you requested. We hope you will
find it interesting and helpful.

    With our market letters and research reports,
_____ offers a valuable
service in providing investors with up-to-date information
on the securities market.

    I would be delighted to send you these reports as they
are published. No cost or obligation, of course.

    Just fill in and return to me the enclosed card, in the
post-paid envelope. I'd welcome the opportunity of being
of greater service in your personal investment situation.

            Sincerely,

            Account Executive

AE/typ

Enclosures:
1. Valuable services information request form
2. Return envelope with AE number

EXHIBIT 21
General Prospecting Acknowledgment and Enclosed Card

IF YOU WOULD LIKE TO RECEIVE SOME OF OUR TIMELY
RESEARCH LITERATURE ON HIGH YIELDING STOCKS, AND CAPITAL
GAIN OPPORTUNITIES, JUST PUT YOUR CARD IN THE ENCLOSED
PREPAID ENVELOPE AND MAIL

(OR COMPLETE OUR ENCLOSED CARD)

Enclosure Card

_____
Name

_____
Address

_____
City   State   Zip

_____
Telephone Number

EXHIBIT 22
General Prospecting Letter

ARE YOU CONSIDERING PURCHASE OR SALE OF ANY OF THESE STOCKS OR SECURITIES

( ) American Tel and Tel.
( ) ASA
( ) Burroughs
( ) Chase Manhattan Mortgage
( ) Citicorp
( ) Consolidated Edison
( ) Continental Telephone
( ) Eastern Airlines
( ) Exxon Corporation
( ) General Motors
( ) Lockheed
( ) Motorola
( ) Polaroid
( ) Sears Roebuck
( ) Syntex
( ) Texaco
( ) U.S. Steel
( ) Xerox

( ) New York City Bonds
( ) New York State Bonds

If you are considering their purchase or sale--in view of today's rapidly changing markets, wouldn't it be prudent to have a _____ opinion on them at this time?

There is no charge or obligation.

Simply fill in the coupon below, check the stock or stocks in which you are interested, and return this letter to us--you will hear from us promptly.

IF WOULD ALSO LIKE _____ POINT OF VIEW ON ANY OTHER OF YOUR STOCK HOLDINGS--PERHAPS A "WORRY STOCK" WHICH IS GIVING YOU SOME CONCERN, SIMPLY INDICATE THE NAME OF THE STOCK IN THE SPACE BELOW.

_____
(Please print name of stock)

Cordially yours,

Account Executive

_____

Evening telephone _____ Day Telephone _____

Name _____ Address_____

City_____ State_____ Zip Code_____

Investment Objectives: Income ( ) Capital gains ( )
                        Trading ( )

Enclosure:
1. Return envelope with AE name

EXHIBIT 23
General Prospecting Letter

ARE YOU COMPLETELY SATISFIED WITH YOUR BROKERS SERVICE?

   If you are not, or if you have been contemplating changing brokers, why not allow an opportunity to compete for some of your brokerage business?

   Enclosed is a booklet that briefly describes the facilities of our firm. We are especially proud of our reputation for personal service and sound research.

   If you wish to have me call you to discuss your account and special investment requirements, fill in the information below and return this letter in the envelope provided. You will hear from us promptly. Naturally, there is no obligation.

                              Cordially,

                              Account Executive

_____   _____
          Name   Address

_____
          Telephone

My Investment Objective is:

_____ Long-term capital growth   _____Income and
                                                 capital gains
_____ Income and safety of capital
                                          _____Short-term
                                                 trading

(Optional) I am concerned about the following securities in my portfolio, and request a _____evaluation on each:

1. _____   3. _____
2. _____   4. _____

Enclosures:
1. Envelope with AE number
2. Valuable Services mailer

EXHIBIT 24
General Prospecting Letter with "Mystery" Approach

_____ Research Recommends Purchase of

This Company's Shares Now For.....

* Capital Growth
* Current Income

1. This company's shares are currently selling at five times last year's earnings.

2. This company's shares currently yield 7% from a well-covered dividend.

3. This company is the largest factor in its industry.

4. This company's earnings have increased over 20% in each of the last 2 years with further increases expected.

If you would like our detailed report on this company, fill out the below form and return in the enclosed envelope.

NAME_____

ADDRESS_____ZIP_____

PHONE_____

                              Very Sincerely,

                              Account Executive

Enclosures:
1. Return envelope
2. Valuable services mailer

EXHIBIT 25
General Prospecting Letter

Dear _____:

    Investing in Gas and Electric Utilities now can be a
"powerful" way for <u>you to get checks every single month of
the year!</u> Checks that will pay for many of the bills you
get each month.

    The following suggested portfolio of three utility
stocks will currently provide a monthly income check!

Quan-tity	Company	Current Share Price	Current Annual Dividend	Monthly Payments	Annual Yield
200	Mid South Utilities			JAJO	
200	Carolina Power & Light			FMAN	
200	Southern Co.			MJSD	

Approx. cost of 200 Mid South Utilities   =
Approx. cost of 200 Carolina Power & Light =
Approx. cost of 200 Southern Co.   = _____

                                          Total =

                         Annual Income =

                        Approx. Yield =

    All of the above utilities are rated A by Standard &
Poor, all are currently selling at less than 9 times
latest 12 months reported earnings. Call me if you have
an interest in or questions about this portfolio.

                      Very sincerely,

                      Account Executive

AE/typ

Enclosure:
1. Valuable services mailer

EXHIBIT 26
General Prospecting Letter

(Staple a new one-dollar bill to the right corner of this letter.)

Date

Mr. Jack **Jones**
Butler Sales Company
200 East Ridgewood Avenue
Ridgewood, New Jersey 07450

Dear Mr. **Jones:**

Here is a TAX-FREE dollar!! Would you like more? This kind of money is hard to come by today.

I would like to show YOU <u>four</u> tax-saving ideas that other successful men are using to get dollars that are <u>TAX-FREE</u>--LEGALLY!!

It will take me only a few minutes to show these four tax-saving ideas for you. Then you can determine which will be of interest to you.

I and my associates have spent many years showing owners and executives of small businesses how to obtain more after-tax dollars and thus increase their spendable income. You may have opportunities available that have never been pointed out to you.

I will call you for an appointment within the next few days.

Yours truly,

Account Executive

AE/typ

Enclosures:
1. One-dollar bill
2. Valuable services mailer

EXHIBIT 27
New Resident "Welcome" Letter

Dear _____:

Congratulations...and welcome to your new home. I hope you enjoy it and spend many happy years at your new address.

One of the advantages of your move, which you perhaps were not aware of, is that now you are in an area serviced by our firm.

_____, a leading New York Stock Exchange member firm, is fully equipped to handle all your investment needs. For years, we have been doing business with investors in all types of securities and commodities. We are members of all major stock and commodity exchanges. And we are especially proud of our reputation for personal service and sound research.

If you own securities, it is important in this active market that you keep up on current developments, so a new brokerage relationship nearby is of the utmost importance.

On the other hand, if you are only thinking of becoming a stockholder, I'd be glad to work with you on setting up an investment program suited to your individual needs-- whether they be growth, safety of principal, income or trading.

One or more of the subjects mentioned on the enclosed card may be of interest to you. If you'll check them off or write your own questions on the blank line and return the card to me, I'd be happy to work with you, without obligation.

                              Sincerely,

                              Account Executive

AE/typ

Enclosures:
1. Return envelope with AE number
2. Valuable services mailer

EXHIBIT 28
Inactive Account Letter

YOU FORGOT YOUR CHANGE!

For you, that sentence has a double meaning. Some time back you did business with us. You got what you ordered, it's true, but you are entitled to more. We accept the responsibility to review your holdings in the light of your personal needs and wishes and market conditions in general.

Secondly, the only thing that is constant is change. The purchasing power of your dollar savings changes, economic conditions change, the world changes, the outlook for the future changes. It is quite possible that the securities you hold today are right for you. But there is also the chance that, with today's prospects for the future, some change or additional investments are needed today.

That is why we are suggesting that we review your financial program. As the first step, enclosed is a form you may use in bringing us up to date on your current situation and the information you wish at this time. Won't you please return it in the business reply envelope?

Sincerely yours,

Account Executive

AE/typ

Enclosures:
1. Return envelope with AE number
2. Valuable services mailer

EXHIBIT 29
Portfolio Review Letter
(Modify per Customer Need)

As per our telephone conversation last _____,
I am pleased to have this opportunity to submit some comments and specific recommendations. As a possible convenience to you, there is enclosed a recent valuation of
your account.

Your portfolio is invested in _____ common
stocks having a recent market value of $_____
with annual income of $_____representing a
_____% return. You have stated that your
primary objective is _____
as well as some commitment to _____.

In general, the _____ stocks presently held
in your portfolio may be considered as "_____
_____" type of securities, which provide
representation in many of the major as well as specialty
segments of the American economy. The _____%
presently derived from the account compares (favorably/
unfavorably) with that of the Dow Jones Industrial Average,
which currently yields about _____%.

With the stock market _____
and continuing to reflect unresolved questions about the
energy situation, the international monetary problem,
higher interest and inflation, it is my belief that
considerable upgrading as well as (diversification/consol-
idation) of your portfolio would be prudent investment
policy in this instance. I have, therefore, set up a
schedule of suggested sale as well as purchase recommendations that will eliminate _____ of the more liber-
ally appraised issues; (diversify/consolidate) and tend to
upgrade your portfolio; as well as significantly increase
_____, which
is your stated objective.

Although each individual holding has not been discussed
above in detail, I have examined them carefully in accor-
dance with your objectives of _____
_____, and find the remaining
holdings to be appropriately retained at the present time.
As a possible convenience, enclosed are Standard & Poor's
reports for your records.

Page 2

Thank you sincerely for submitting your investment portfolio for our analysis and review. _____ appreciates this gesture of confidence, and as you come to know us better I am sure that you will feel this trust has been well placed. I will call you next _____ so that we might set up a time when it would be convenient for you to discuss your investments in further detail.

If in the meantime you may have some questions, or if I can be of help to you in any way, please do not hesitate to give me a call. My card is herewith enclosed for your convenience.

Sincerely yours,

Account Executive

AE/typ

Enclosure

EXHIBIT 30
Referral Request Letter

It has been a pleasure doing business with you in the past. As you know, I am in a service business. Consequently, I am continually searching for new clients. I would appreciate your doing me the favor of giving me the names of a few of your friends so that I might contact them as potential clients.

If you do not wish to do this, it is perfectly all right. If you do, please understand that any dealings between us are strictly confidential. Like any other service business that wants to grow, I need new names and clients.

I have taken the liberty of leaving a few blank spaces below so that you may fill them in.

NAME_____TEL NO._____
ADDRESS_____

NAME_____TEL NO._____
ADDRESS_____

NAME_____TEL NO._____
ADDRESS_____

May I use your name as a reference? YES___ NO____

Enclosed is a self-addressed return envelope for your convenience. Thank you!

Sincerely,

Account Executive

AE/typ
Enclosures:
1. Return envelope with your AE number
2. Annuity mailer with return card

EXHIBIT 31
New Issue Prospecting Letter

Gentlemen:

I would like a preliminary prospectus on the new issue
of Public Service of New Hampshire common stock.

Please send me a free copy as soon as it's available.

NAME_____ PHONES:
ADDRESS_____   BUSINESS_____
CITY_____STATE_____   HOME_____
ZIP_____

P.S. This new offering of common stock is scheduled for release about May 16. At the $20-per-share current price
the stock yields 9.3% based on the current annual dividend.

Enclosures:
1. Return envelope marked with your AE number
2. Return card featuring net price offerings

EXHIBIT 32
General Prospecting Letter

Dear

   Every day my clients ask me many questions about the stock market. Probably the most important question is, "How do I begin...and continue...a long-range investment program?"

   As an investment broker, I always try to have the right answer to this question.

   Investing is a serious business. And it is complex and time-consuming. Proper operation of a long-term investment program must be based on specialized study, analytical ability, even access to and visits with the top officials of corporations whose securities may interest you. Few individuals have the time and inclination to do all these things.

   Isn't it ironic that most of us train and work all our lives to make money. But, almost no training is given to keeping money?

   That's why it is necessary and wise to rely upon qualified professionals, such as my firm.

   In a few days, I'll call you to make an appointment to discuss your personal investment objectives...the risks and rewards...the costs and advantages...and how we may best serve you.

                              Cordially,

Enclosures:
1. Valuable services mailer
2. Return envelope with AE number

EXHIBIT 33
Mutual Fund Prospecting Letter

Dear

    Successful investor Bernard Baruch once summed up the difficulties of common stock investing in a quotable paragraph:

> If you are ready and able to give up everything
> else--to study the whole history and background
> of the market and all the principal companies
> whose stocks are on the board, as carefully
> as a medical student studies anatomy--to spend
> all day, every day, watching the tape--if you can
> do all that, and in addition you have the cool
> nerve of a great gambler, the sixth sense of
> a kind of clair-voyant, and the courage of a
> lion, you have a Chinaman's chance.

    Quoted in 1937 in a New York newspaper, these wise words still ring true. And, many investors will read them with sympathetic understanding.

    If you haven't the time or the inclination to become a professional investor, a well-managed mutual fund might well be the answer to your investment needs.

    We are enclosing information on an interesting fund we suggest to many of our clients. This literature points out the costs and advantages, the risks and rewards of such an investment.

    If you would like to discuss this or any other invest-ment, our professional staff is at your service.

                      Cordially,

Enclosures:
1. Prospectus
2. Fund literature
3. Valuable services mailer

EXHIBIT 34
Mutual Fund Prospecting Letter

Dear Mr.

Some time ago, a magazine story by Donald Rogers shocked many of us men. Maybe you too read it. Its title: "Teach Your Wife to be a Widow."

In essence it asked this pertinent question: "If something should happen to YOU, could your wife carry on your investment program?"

Today, increasing numbers of husbands are finding that one of the answers is mutual investment funds, which provide selection, diversification of risk through hundreds of securities continuously supervised and managed by personnel trained in the profession of investing money.

We would like the opportunity of showing you why we recommend mutual funds in planning an estate; although individuals may pass out of the picture, mutual fund management continues. Investments in mutual funds are made at the regular offering prices, which include a sales commission as described in the pertinent prospectus.

We believe you owe it to your family and to yourself to explore this modern way to invest.

Return the enclosed form, and we will furnish you free information without obligation to you.

Sincerely,

Account Executive

Enclosures:
1. Valuable services mailer
2. Return envelope with AE number

EXHIBIT 35
Mutual Fund Prospecting Letter

WHO WILL ENJOY YOUR ESTATE?

You, of course, and--if yours is a normal situation--someone else. The average accumulation of investments is enjoyed by at least two persons--husband and wife, father and son, brother and sister, and so on.

Proper investment planning requires the consideration of the investment objectives, needs, and abilities of all persons in the family who should enjoy--or who may have to depend upon--the family invested estate. We believe this can best be done by analyzing the objectives of the individual investor for himself and his beneficiaries or dependents.

In analyzing the objectives of the investor, one should not overlook the importance of benefits which may be realized through tax-saving methods of accumulating funds for college education or personal retirement. Analyzing the needs of others naturally requires consideration of minimizing inheritance taxes and costs, and providing suitable continuous investment supervision over an inherited estate.

Are your accumulations proceeding on schedule, in the light of your personal objectives? Have you taken adequate steps to make sure of a continuity of income and conservation of principal at death?

Have you provided professional management and uninterrupted supervision over your invested estate, if your own supervision becomes unavailable?

You would probably be interested in information about our approach to these questions. Whether you are interested in investing now or not, the information will be of interest to you. Fill in and mail the attached card and we will provide the information promptly.

Sincerely,

Enclosures:
1. Valuable services mailer
2. Return envelope with AE number

EXHIBIT 36
Mutual Fund Prospecting Letter

Dear

Wouldn't you like to start today to enjoy tomorrow?

By "tomorrow" we mean the date when your personal plans call for utilizing your investments as sources of retirement income.

Your personal tomorrow may be deferred by hours, days, months--or decades. Regardless of when it arrives, however, or of what your specific goals may be, it is very much to your advantage to make intelligent, sound, permanent plans today. For the investments of yesterday and today can mean a substantial difference in the degree of your later comfort, security, and peace of mind.

There are definite economic problems with increasing life expectancy; retirement income can be seriously afected by inflation and changes in purchasing power. The necessity for sound investment principles in your personal planning is growing all the time. These are some of the issues I would like to discuss with you.

Suppose I contact you in a day or so to arrange an interview.

Sincerely,

Enclosures:
1. Valuable services mailer
2. Return envelope with AE number

EXHIBIT 37
Mutual Fund Prospecting Letter

Dear

It would be hard to describe a more welcome, thoughtful, or practical gift than a gift of mutual fund shares.

True, the youngster in your family would rather have a bike or a new baby doll that really cries...and that teen-age daughter might dismiss your gift of 100 shares as "creepy!"

But you would have the deep-down satisfaction of knowing that your gift will last long after the bike is outgrown, the doll broken, and the teen-age daughter transformed into an income-minded young mother.

Yes, mutual funds can be a gift that keeps on giving year after year.

Not only will a gift of mutual fund shares give you a feeling of personal satisfaction--there may also be very real tax advantages involved.

We'd like to give you the facts...how the possibilities may well balance the costs and risks. I'll call you in a few days to discuss this further.

Cordially,

Enclosures:
1. Fund return card
2. Valuable services mailer
3. Return envelope with AE number

EXHIBIT 38
Mutual Fund Prospecting Letter

Dear

    Would you like to receive checks every month in regular amounts...

        to supplement income in retirement years;
        to care for dependents or recently married children;
        to pay for school or college expenses;
        to make rent or mortgage payments even when you're
             out of town;
        to distribute trust or estate income and assets in
             an orderly manner;
        to repay loans or other obligations;
        to provide supplemental, short-term funds for travel,
             hospital bills, living expenses;
        to meet such bills as auto leasing, insurance prem-
             iums, major household improvements, other
             current expenses;
        to spend for pleasure?

    Then, learn about this new way to use an investment account to have a check every month--supplementing investment income with, if need be, the orderly use of principal.

    I'll call you in a few days to discuss how the advantages may balance the costs, how the possibilities for profit may outweigh the risks. I'd like to answer any questions you may have or to arrange an appointment at your convenience.

                       Cordially,

Enclosures:
1. Valuable services mailer
2. Return envelope with AE number

EXHIBIT 39
Retirement Planning Prospecting Letter

Dear

    Millions of senior citizens--aged 65 and over--have an average of <u>less than $500 per month of retirement income.</u> That's the magnitude of the retirement problem facing government and industry in the years ahead.

    Many employers are helping to solve this problem by providing retirement incomes for their employees and, at the same time, reaping substantial tax benefits for themselves.

    I would like to take a few minutes to discuss the risks, costs, and advantages of one popular solution which is being used by more and more corporations. No obligation, naturally.

                      Cordially,

Enclosures:
1. Valuable services mailer
2. Return envelope with AE number

EXHIBIT 40
Retirement Plan Prospecting Letter

TAX SAVINGS FOR RETIREMENT

Tax-qualified plans increase retirement savings for two reasons: (1) you pay no tax on the money you set aside; (2) you pay no tax on the capital gains, interest, or dividends your money earns during the life of your plan.

Taxation, inflation, and the medical fact that people are living longer and therefore retired longer make it essential that you begin your retirement plan now.

Most of the master plans available to individuals, professionals, and small business people are tied to a particular type of investment. However, at _____ _____ we can make available to you flexible retirement plans that enable you to invest in a variety of assets. You or your investment advisor can direct investment in stocks, bonds, mutual funds, savings accounts, annuities, or government securities, and you can change investment as economic and personal conditions change.

Send us the postage-paid card enclosed and we will send you specific information without obligation.

Cordially,

Account Executive

AE/typ

Enclosures:
1. Retirement card
2. Valuable services mailer

EXHIBIT 40 (continued)
Retirement Enclosure Card

Please send me information
without obligation on:

KEOGH retirement plan for
self-employed.

STANDARD Individual Retirement
Account for anyone--employed or
self-employed--not presently
covered by a retirement plan.

ROLLOVER Individual Retirement
Account for anyone who wants to
tax shelter a lump-sum settlement
from a profit-sharing or pension
fund of previous employer.

PROFIT-SHARING, MONEY PURCHASE
or DEFINED BENEFIT Plans for
small or professional corporations.

I have an existing retirement
plan that I would like to discuss
with you.

Name_____

Address_____

City_____

State_____Zip_____

Home Phone_____/_____

Bus. Phone_____/_____

EXHIBIT 41
U.S. Government Bond Prospecting Letter

WHAT'S BETTER THAN MONEY IN THE BANK?

United States government bonds are being bought by the billions by individual investors (like you) who want to earn more than bank interest...bonds backed by the "full faith and credit" and taxing power of our nation!

Many U.S. government bonds today yield over _____% and the income to you is free of all state and local income tax! You can always sell U.S. government bonds as they are easily, quickly convertible into cash. Sometimes when sold they bring more than the original purchase price, sometimes less. The resale value is tied to the prevailing interest rates.

U.S. government bond buyers rest worry free, knowing that their principal is absolutely guaranteed to be paid at maturity.

If you would like more information on our current list of high yielding U.S. government bonds, call me at (_____) or return the enclosed card.

                                        Most cordially,

                                        Account Executive

AE/typ

Enclosure:
1. Valuable services mailer

EXHIBIT 42
Commodity Prospecting Letter

LEARN ABOUT <u>GOLD AND SILVER</u>

at the

October "sack lunch" seminar

"Commodity trading--risks and potential rewards"

Find out whether commodity trading is for you. Today's fast-moving commodity markets present high leverage opportunities for quick large capital gains. The pitfalls and risks will be thoroughly discussed.

The seminar is

- another in a free series of stimulating noontime discussions for investing in unsettled times

- held in the conference room <u>Morristown, New Jersey</u> from <u>1:00-2:00</u>, Thursday, October 16

Free sandwiches, beverage and dessert, make your reservation (limited seating) by calling Carol Bailey at 555-1101.

Very sincerely,

Account Executive

EXHIBIT 43
Tax-Deferred Annuities Prospecting Letter

A Tax-Favored Way to Make Your Money Grow Faster

Money is not only hard to earn these days, it's also mighty hard to keep, taxes being what they are. That's why if you're in a vulnerable tax bracket--35% or more--keeping more of your money is an important consideration for you.

In your bracket, taxable interest--whether from bank savings, CDs, or bonds--is almost as much a boon to the IRS as to you.

But now there is a safe, guaranteed way to save for your long-term needs, such as retirement. It's called [your favorite product] and it's underwritten by [your favorite company]. It allows you to earn an interest of _____% guaranteed one year with no current taxes on the interest you earn.

Tax-deferred annuities offer other important benefits to you:

* Safety because your deposit is guaranteed by
  [insurance company]

* No current income taxes on your interest

* Money when you need it

* The right to receive a guaranteed retirement income
  if you wish

_____ has prepared a free special booklet to help you learn more about [product name]. To receive a free copy, simply return the enclosed card.

Enclosure:
1. Valuable services mailer
2. Annuity return card

EXHIBIT 44
Tax Shelters

Investment Opportunities in Real Estate

Today more than ever before investors are concerned with the impact that inflation and taxation is having on their earnings and net worth. Increasingly, we are finding that our clients need and are actively seeking investments which can keep pace with inflation and provide various forms of tax shelter. From time to time, Dean Witter Reynolds offers our clients a wide range of real estate limited partnerships. These investments have been evaluated by Dean Witter Reynolds and other quality real estate professionals. The benefits to our clients of real estate investments:

- Professional real estate selection & management
- Diversification (i.e., shopping centers, apartments, commercial buildings)
- Limited liability
- Opportunities for...

  - capital appreciation
  - cash flow (at least partially tax shelter)
  - excess write-offs to reduce income from other sources

If you wish to be on our select list of people to be informed of our recommended investments as they become available, please complete the form below and return it to me.

Sincerely,

Account Executive

Name_____
Address_____
Phone No._____

EXHIBIT 45
Tax Shelters

<u>OIL & GAS INVESTMENT OPPORTUNITIES</u>

. THE DEMAND FOR OIL AND GAS IS GROWING

. SUPPLIES ARE DWINDLING

. PRICES ARE RISING

This scenario coupled with generally favorable tax treatment has created enormous interest in oil and gas investments.

From time, to time, _____ offers clients the opportunity to invest in limited partnerships in oil and gas exploration. The limited liability investments have been evaluated by _____ and oil and gas professionals, The benefits to our clients oil and gas investments are:

-- <u>Direct participation</u> in the attractive economics of oil and gas exploration

-- <u>Tax deductions</u> which could be as much as 100% of the amount invested

-- <u>Cash distributions</u> which are <u>partially sheltered</u> from taxes

If you would like to be included on our list of people to be informed of our recommended investments as they become available, please complete the card below and return it to me or call me at _____.

Sincerely,

Account Executive

EXHIBIT 46
Free Services Enclosure

15 Valuable Free Services to help lessen your investment risk, increase your return, or avoid taxes: (Check the ones that interest you)

☐ Free booklet "How to Save Money on Income Taxes"

☐ Free booklet explaining how current laws permit you to postpone taxes legally and earn interest on money you would otherwise pay to the IRS

☐ Free prospectus on municipal bond investment trusts that could provide you with monthly income free of all federal income taxes

☐ Free list of major electric utilities that have raised their dividends annually for the past 18 years.

☐ Free list of municipal bonds (rated A or better) that now provide a return of up to 6½% or more, exempt from federal income taxes

> ☐ Free valuation of your portfolio showing your gains and losses as well as the current yield on each security (please enclose a list of your stocks and bonds)
>
> ☐ Free information about writing call options to possibly improve income from the stocks you now own (an Option Clearing Corporation prospectus will be sent without charge)
>
> ☐ Free list of our Research Department's recommended stocks that we believe have capital-gain potential
>
> ☐ Free consultation without obligation to review your current holdings
>> ☐ Call me for a date   Specify date _____
>
> ☐ Free information on United States government securities that provide guaranteed returns of up to 8% or more

>> ☐ Free booklet on professionally managed real-estate limited partnerships, including their risks and potential rewards through income-tax deductions and capital gains
>>
>> ☐ Free booklet explaining the risk and reward possibilities, including tax deductions, income, and capital gains, of professionally managed oil and gas limited partnerships
>>
>> ☐ Free detailed brochures explaining professional full-time portfolio management (available for portfolios of $50,000 or more)
>>
>> ☐ Free information about earning a high return that compounds daily, and a prospectus on our short-term money market fund (there are no sales charges to buy or sell)
>>
>> ☐ Please give me an opinion on the following stocks I own that worry me _____
>> _____

- -

NAME_____

ADDRESS _____

CITY _____ STATE _____ ZIP _____

HOME PHONE _____ BUSINESS PHONE _____

EXHIBIT 47
Portfolio Review Request Enclosure

Confidential Portfolio Valuation for _____

PLEASE PRINT NAME

Security holdings—List common stocks, mutual funds, unit trusts, bond holdings and other investments in the space below. If you have a close relationship with any company, please indicate.

NUMBER OF SHARES, BONDS OR UNITS	COMPLETE SECURITY DESCRIPTION	PURCHASE DATE MO/DAY/YR	COST PER SHARE	TOTAL DOLLAR COST

If more space is required, list your additional holdings on a separate sheet.

Information Held Absolutely Confidential

Please give us as much information as possible. This will allow us to provide you with a meaningful review of your security holdings. With this information we can also make recommendations consistent with your needs and investment objectives. We request this information because the type of securities that would be considered appropriate for income oriented accounts often differs from those that are considered appropriate for growth or aggressive accounts. Each of your holdings will be evaluated in terms of your personal objectives as stated in this form.

Marital Status: ☐ Single   Age: ☐ 21-30   ☐ 51-60
                 ☐ Married   ☐ 31-40   ☐ 61-65
                                     ☐ 41-50   ☐ Over 65

Occupation or profession _____ Number of dependents _____
Are you a citizen of the United States? ☐ Yes   ☐ No

FINANCIAL INFORMATION

Approximate annual income from sources other than securities _____

Approximate Federal income tax bracket (percent) _____

Net equity of home _____ Other real estate _____

Amount of Life Insurance _____ Approx. Total Net Worth (optional) _____

Cash & Savings _____ Available for investment purposes_____

INVESTMENT PREFERENCES Please mark these in order of importance (1-2-3 etc.)

____ I am most interested in high-yielding quality common stocks with potential appreciation a secondary objective.

____ I am most interested in **municipals** (quality bonds whose income is tax free)/**corporate/government** bonds. (Please indicate your preference by circling the appropriate word(s).

____ I am interested in quality investments which could provide short-term aggressive appreciation potential.

____ I am interested in quality investments which might provide for long-term capital appreciation potential and current income.

Personal-Use Forms to Organize for Selling More Effectively

The following exhibits depict forms that sellers of intangibles can use to simplify operations and thus gain more time to devote to the actual act of selling. Naturally, you may see information on each form that might not be appropriate for you. Or you may want special information included on some forms that currently doesn't appear. Adjust any or all of the forms to your needs. Let the ones shown here simply be your guide, a memory jogger, a help in constructing what you actually need to help you do a better selling job.

FORM 1
Client/Prospect Card (Front)

Prospect / Client Card

_____
Source

Name _____ Date _____

Address _____ Tel No. _____

Age _____ No. Dept. _____ Occupation _____

| | Net | Tax | Life | |
Income _____ Worth _____ Bracket _____ Insurance _____ Savings _____

Objective: Appreciation ☐   Safety of Principal ☐   Income ☐   Other ☐ _____

DATE		TYPE		PRODUCT/TOPIC DISCUSSED	FOLLOW-UP DATE		
		PER	TEL				

OUR OBJECTIVE IS MAKING MONEY FOR OUR CLIENTS

Client/Prospect Card (Back)

DATE		TYPE		PRODUCT/TOPIC DISCUSSED	FOLLOW-UP DATE		
		PER	TEL				

OUR OBJECTIVE IS MAKING MONEY FOR OUR CLIENTS

FORM 2
Stock Information Card (Front)

Stock Information Card

INVESTMENT OBJECTIVE: _____ QUALITY: _____

| | Est. EPS | | Target | | |
| Price | Yr. Ending | Est. PER | Price | Dividend | Yield |

REASONS FOR BUYING:

1.

2.

3.

4.

Business (Company) & Position In Industry: _____

TECHNICAL: Near Term _____ Long Term _____ Support _____

PAST:

Year	Hi-Lo Price	EPS	Hi-Lo PER	Div.	Common Shares
19___	_____	_____	_____	_____	_____
19___	_____	_____	_____	_____	_____
19___	_____	_____	_____	_____	_____

COMPANY: _____ SYMBOL: _____ EX: _____ ANALYST: _____ DATE: _____

Stock Information Card (Back)

Telephone Number	Name	Account Number	Shares Bought

Daily Call Sheet

PHONE CALL LOG		DATE: _____			A/E _____	
	PROSPECT	CLIENT	PHONE	CALL OBJECTIVE	CALL	RESULTS
1						
2						
3						
4						
5						
6						
7						
8						
9						
10						
11						
12						
13						
14						
15						
16						
17						
18						
19						
20						
21						
22						
23						
24						
25						

CLIENT CALLS _____ COLD CALLS _____ RETURN CALLS _____	SUPERVISORY CRITIQUE:	SELF CRITIQUE:

FORM 4
Municipal Bond Card (Front)

Municipal Bonds

Date _____

We suggest for the portfolio of _____ the following tax free municipal bonds subject to prior sale and/or change in price: *

MOODY'S RATING	S&P RATING	AMOUNT	SECURITY	GENERAL OBLIGATION	REVENUE OR OTHER	COUPON RATE	MATURITY	YIELD TO MATURITY	APPROX. PRICE	CURRENT YIELD

*Municipal bonds are exempt from federal income taxes and most are also exempt from state and local income taxes in the state of issue.

Account Executive
Office _____

IF YOU ARE INTERESTED IN ANY OF THE ABOVE BONDS WHILE AVAILABLE CALL _____ (COLLECT IF OUT OF TOWN)

Municipal Bond Card (Back)

Tax-Exempt vs. Taxable Income

Under the Revenue Act of 1978, if taxable income is:

(Taxable Yields Required to Match Tax-Exempt Yields in Various Tax Brackets)
Example: If taxable joint return income is $45,800-$60,000 (top tax rate of 49%), then a taxable yield of 13.7% is necessary to equal a 7% tax-exempt return.

Single Return	$12,900-$15,000		$15,000-$18,200		$18,200-$23,500		$23,500-$28,800		$28,800-$34,100	$34,100-$41,500		$41,500-$55,300		$55,300-$81,800		$81,800-$108,300	$108,300 & Over
Joint Return		$20,200-$24,600		$24,600-$29,900		$29,900-$35,200		$35,200-$45,800	$45,800-$60,000	$60,000-$85,500		$85,500-$109,400		$109,400-$162,400		$162,400-$215,000	$215,000 & Over
Tax Bracket → Tax-Exempt Yield ↓	26%	28%	30%	32%	34%	37%	39%	43%	44%	49%	54%	55%	59%	63%	64%	68%	70%
4.00%	5.41	5.56	5.71	5.88	6.06	6.35	6.56	7.02	7.14	7.84	8.70	8.89	9.76	10.81	11.11	12.50	13.33
4.25	5.74	5.90	6.07	6.25	6.44	6.75	6.97	7.46	7.59	8.33	9.24	9.44	10.37	11.49	11.81	13.28	14.17
4.50	6.08	6.25	6.43	6.62	6.82	7.14	7.38	7.89	8.04	8.82	9.78	10.00	10.98	12.16	12.50	14.06	15.00
4.75	6.42	6.60	6.79	6.99	7.20	7.54	7.79	8.33	8.48	9.31	10.33	10.56	11.59	12.84	13.19	14.84	15.83
4.90	6.62	6.81	7.00	7.21	7.42	7.78	8.03	8.60	8.75	9.61	10.65	10.89	11.95	13.24	13.61	15.31	16.33
5.00	6.76	6.94	7.14	7.35	7.58	7.94	8.20	8.77	8.93	9.80	10.87	11.11	12.20	13.51	13.89	15.63	16.67
5.25	7.09	7.29	7.50	7.72	7.95	8.33	8.61	9.21	9.38	10.29	11.41	11.67	12.80	14.19	14.58	16.41	17.50
5.50	7.43	7.64	7.86	8.09	8.33	8.73	9.02	9.65	9.82	10.73	11.96	12.22	13.41	14.86	15.28	17.19	18.33
5.75	7.77	7.99	8.21	8.46	8.71	9.13	9.43	10.09	10.27	11.27	12.50	12.78	14.02	15.54	15.97	17.97	19.17
5.90	7.97	8.19	8.43	8.68	8.94	9.37	9.67	10.35	10.54	11.57	12.83	13.11	14.39	15.95	16.39	18.44	19.67
6.00	8.11	8.33	8.57	8.82	9.09	9.52	9.84	10.53	10.71	11.76	13.04	13.33	14.63	16.22	16.67	18.75	20.00
6.25	8.45	8.68	8.93	9.19	9.47	9.92	10.25	10.96	11.16	12.25	13.59	13.89	15.24	16.89	17.36	19.53	20.83
6.50	8.78	9.03	9.29	9.56	9.85	10.32	10.66	11.40	11.61	12.75	14.13	14.44	15.85	17.57	18.06	20.31	21.67
6.75	9.12	9.38	9.64	9.93	10.23	10.71	11.07	11.84	12.05	13.24	14.67	15.00	16.46	18.24	18.75	21.09	22.50
6.90	9.32	9.58	9.86	10.15	10.45	10.95	11.31	12.11	12.32	13.53	15.00	15.33	16.83	18.65	19.17	21.56	23.00
7.00	9.46	9.72	10.00	10.29	10.61	11.11	11.48	12.28	12.50	13.73	15.22	15.56	17.07	18.92	19.44	21.88	23.23
7.25	9.80	10.07	10.36	10.66	10.98	11.51	11.89	12.72	12.95	14.22	15.76	16.11	17.68	19.59	20.14	22.66	24.17
7.50	10.14	10.42	10.71	11.03	11.36	11.90	12.30	13.16	13.39	14.71	16.30	16.67	18.29	20.27	20.83	23.44	25.00
7.75	10.47	10.76	11.07	11.40	11.74	12.30	12.70	13.60	13.84	15.20	16.85	17.22	18.90	20.95	21.53	24.22	25.83
7.90	10.68	10.97	11.29	11.62	11.97	12.54	12.95	13.86	14.11	15.49	17.17	17.56	19.27	21.35	21.94	24.69	26.33
8.00	10.81	11.11	11.43	11.76	12.12	12.70	13.11	14.04	14.29	15.69	17.39	17.78	19.51	21.62	22.22	25.00	26.67
8.25	11.15	11.46	11.79	12.13	12.50	13.10	13.52	14.47	14.73	16.18	17.93	18.33	20.12	22.30	22.92	25.78	27.50
8.50	11.49	11.81	12.14	12.50	12.88	13.49	13.93	14.91	15.18	16.67	18.48	18.89	20.73	22.97	23.61	26.56	28.33
8.75	11.82	12.15	12.50	12.87	13.26	13.89	14.34	15.35	15.62	17.16	19.02	19.44	21.34	23.65	24.31	27.34	29.17
8.90	12.03	12.36	12.71	13.09	13.48	14.13	14.59	15.61	15.89	17.45	19.35	19.78	21.71	24.05	24.78	27.81	29.67

(Left margin label: TAX — EXEMPT YIELDS)

The information in this report was obtained from sources considered reliable. However, neither its accuracy nor the accuracy of the calculations are guaranteed, but are believed to be correct.

FORM 5
Product Worksheet (Front)

Product Worksheet

DESK TOP PRODUCT SHEET

EARNINGS

STOCKS SYM	PRICE	RANGE 19__	19__ EST.	19__ EST.	CURRENT P/E	PROJ. P/E 77	DIV.	YLD.	SGP RATING	COMMENTS
___	___	___	___	___	___	___	___	___	___	___

PAYOUT

UNIT TRUSTS DESCRIPTION	PRICE	ACCR. INT	MONTHLY	YEARLY	CURR. RET.	A	AA	AAA	AVG. LIFE
___	___	___	___	___	___	___	___	___	___

	RATING MDY/SGP	QTY	DESCRIP	CPN.	MAT.	YTM	PRICE	CY	CR
MUNICIPAL BONDS	___								
CORPORATE BONDS	___								
CONVERTIBLE BONDS	___								

Product Worksheet (Back)

COVERED CALL WRITERS (500 SHS & 5 CALLS)			CURRENT PRICES		RETURN ON OPTION WITH COMMON AT		ANNUALIZED RETURN	DOWNSIDE BREAKEVEN		HIGH/LOW
STOCK	OPTION MONTH	EXCH.	STRIKE PR.	STOCK OPTION	PRES. PRICE	EX. PRICE		STOCK PRICE	PCT. CHANGE	STOCK

OPTION BUYS PUT.	CALL	STOCK	MONTH	OPTION STRIKE PR.	EXCH.	CUR. PRICES STOCK	OPTION	HIGH/LOW STOCK	S&P RATING

TAX-DEFERRED ANNUITIES
AMPLAN
Capitol Life (Securannuity)

Old Republic (NY only)
Q-Plan
WNPLAN (NY only)

GNMA Rates_____
  Yield to 12-Year Average Life_____
  Corporate Bond Equivalent_____
  Current Yield _____

Prime Rate _____
Inter Capitol Liquid Assets Fund: _____
  Average Yield for Past 30 Days _____
  Daily Yield_____

NAME	PHONE	COMMENT	NAME	PHONE	COMMENT

Prospects for Sale!

In the following section, you will find listed the names, addresses, and phone numbers of list sellers. These firms will sell you a list of prospects in your area (or out, if that's what you need). Many of them will guarantee list accuracy of 95 percent or higher. They usually charge a fee per 1000 names and addresses ranging from $30 to $100 or more. The price variance is due to the difficulty in obtaining the names and sometimes to the select quality of the list or its limited use.

Prospects are categorized in various ways, such as buyers of tax shelters, donators to charity, round-lot stock owners, and so on.

Most of the list brokers mentioned here will be happy to provide a catalogue of available lists, costs, and accuracy guarantees. I have used purchased lists with great effectiveness and hope that you too will find them useful. Good luck!

Consumer's Advertising and Marketing Associates Inc.
6 Old Cranberry Road
Cranbury, New Jersey 08512
609-443-1298

Dunhill International List Co., Inc.
444 Park Avenue South
New York, New York 10016
212-686-3700

Edith Roman Associates Inc.
875 Avenue of the Americas
New York, New York 10001
212-695-3836

Kleid Co.
(*Fortune* magazine)
200 Park Avenue
New York, New York 10017
212-599-4140

MDA List Management Co.
(Diners Club, *Business Week*)
527 Madison Avenue
New York, New York 10022
212-751-2580

National Business Lists Inc.
162 North Franklin Street
Chicago, Illinois 60606
N.Y. 212-689-8960
Chi. 312-236-0305

Network Lists and Data
400 Halstead Avenue
Harrison, New York 10528
In N.Y. 914-835-5353
Outside N.Y. 800-431-1598 (toll free)

Zeller-Letica Inc.
15 East 26th Street
New York, New York 10010
In N.Y. 212-685-7512
Outside N.Y. 800-221-4112 (toll free)

George Mann Associates
6 Old Cranbury Rd.
Cranbury, N.J. 08512

Direct Mail List Rates & Data
5201 Old Orchard Rd.
Skokie, Illinois 60077

12 Response Cards with Pull Power

Whenever a salesperson sends a written communication (letter or other information) to a client or prospect, that communication should be accompanied by one or two response cards that the prospect can easily complete and return for more information. When the salesperson supplies that information, the result may be an order! *Getting orders is what the game is all about!*

The following exhibits represent "good copy" enclosure cards that have worked in the real world. There is no guarantee that they will work equally well in the future. If you don't use them as is, perhaps they will at least inspire you with some ideas for creating your own cards.

RESPONSE CARD 1

Information Request Form

Members New York Stock Exchange, Inc.

TO: _____

Without obligation, I would like the following:

☐ Recommended list of stocks

☐ Advantages of mutual funds

☐ Advantages of tax-free securities

☐ Information on listed options

My investment objective is:

☐ Income   ☐ Appreciation

☐ Income & appreciation   ☐ Aggressive appreciation

☐ Latest   Research report on the following:

_____

☐ I would like an appointment on _____
                                  (DATE)

     Please call me at _____ A.M. / P.M.
                                   (TIME)

NAME (please print) _____

ADDRESS_____

CITY _____ STATE _____ ZIP _____.

PHONE NO. _____
                               (Residence)   (Business)

RESPONSE CARD 2

Dear Mr. _____

I understand the bond market is very complex, and I would like to contact a specialist.
—Please put me on your muni bond offerings bi-weekly mailing list.
—I'm conservative and don't want to take any risks.
—I'm interested in government-guaranteed securities.
—I'm interested in insured tax-free bonds.
—I'm interested in new stock or bond issues.
—I'm interested in monthly income through the new tax-free Income Trust.
—I'm interested in monthly income through the new Corporate Income Fund.
—Please contact me about tax trading.
—I would like a computerized print on my bond portfolio/stock portfolio free of charge.
—I am interested in professional investment management.

NAME _____ ADDRESS _____

PHONE _____ ZIP _____

RESPONSE CARD 3

Please send me additional information on the GUARANTEED INVESTMENT . . .

Name _____

Address _____

_____

Phone _____ **Zip** _____

RESPONSE CARD 4

Yes

Gentlemen:

Please send the information as soon as available.

I would like additional information on —

☐ **U.S.-guaranteed bonds**   ☐ **Tax-deferred Income**

☐ **Corporate bonds**   ☐ **Tax-free municipal bonds**

☐ **Municipal investment trusts**

NAME _____ **PHONE** _____

ADDRESS _____

CITY _____ **STATE** _____ **ZIP** _____

RESPONSE CARD 5

5 Ways to Increase Your Income

Single-Payment Deferred Annuities.   They currently pay up to 9½% and more in interest, and all taxes are deferred until you withdraw your money—which can be at any time and in any amount without penalty. And the principal is completely guaranteed against loss by major life insurance companies.

Municipal Bonds & Bond Funds.   The interest is free from federal income taxes, and the effective rate can be considerably higher than with traditional savings accounts. Although subject to market fluctuations, quality municipals offer safety, flexibility and marketability.

Corporate Bonds & Bond Funds.   Bonds from nationally known companies now yield over 8%. We can also introduce you to bond funds, for increased diversification, convenience and safety.

I want to know about increasing my income. Send me information on:

____ Municipal bond funds   ____ Tax-deferred annuities
____ Corporate bond funds   ____ Municipal bonds
____ Corporate bonds

Name _____

Address _____

City_____State_____Zip_____

Telephone: Business _____ Home _____

My_____branch is_____

RESPONSE CARD 6

FREE OFFER

NOW YOU CAN RECEIVE THE "TIMELY INVESTMENT OPPORTUNITIES" LETTER FROM

EVERY MONTH, "OPPORTUNITIES" UNCOVERS SPECIAL SITUATIONS OF IMMEDIATE INTEREST TO INVESTORS. IN ADDITION, IT HIGHLIGHTS AVAILABLE RESEARCH REPORTS AND OFFERS MATERIAL ON BONDS, TAX-FREE INCOME, ANNUITIES, UTILITIES AND MUCH MORE.

TO BEGIN RECEIVING YOUR COPY OF "TIMELY INVESTMENT OPPORTUNITIES" JUST COMPLETE AND MAIL THIS CARD. THE POSTAGE IS PAID.

NAME _____

ADDRESS _____

CITY_____STATE_____ZIP_____

HOME PHONE _____ BUSINESS PHONE _____

RESPONSE CARD 7

Please rush complete information about earning high income dividencs that compound daily. I would like the free prospectus detailing all pertinent information including any fees or expenses. I will read the material carefully before investing or sending money.

Some special features and benefits of a money market fund are:

—High current yield
—No sales charge to buy or sell
—Free check-writing privileges ($500 minimum)
—Daily dividends
—Daily compounding
—No withdrawal penalty
—No minimum period to earn dividends
—Simplified record keeping

Account Executive or account number if any

Name_____

Address _____

City _____ State _____ Zip _____

282

Understanding Options

A Guide Prepared by

THE CHICAGO BOARD OPTIONS EXCHANGE

For your free copy of this enlightening pamphlet and a current OCC prospectus, just call me at or fill in the information below and return it to me.

Account Executive

_____

NAME _____

ADDRESS _____

CITY _____

STATE _____ ZIP _____

PHONE _____

Tax-Free Income

Each week we publish a list of **municipal bond offerings.** I'll be glad to place your name on the mailing list if you will call met at _____ or return this card.

Account Executive

_____

Please mail tax-free offerings weekly to:

NAME _____

ADDRESS _____

CITY _____

ZIP _____

PHONE _____

RESPONSE CARD 10

Please send me reports and current opinions on the following securities:

1. _____

2. _____

3. _____

Please give me your current ideas for investment. I am interested in:

☐ Long-term growth ☐ Put & call options
☐ Income & relative safety ☐ Tax-advantaged investments
☐ Young, aggressive companies ☐ Commodities
☐ Corporate stocks & bonds ☐ Tax-deferred annuity
☐ Mutual funds ☐ Retirement programs
☐ Tax-free municipal bonds ☐ Computerized technical timing

My Account No. is _____

☐ I wish to open an Account.
☐ I would be interested in attending an investment seminar.

NAME _____ HOME PHONE _____

STREET _____ OFFICE PHONE _____

CITY_____STATE_____ZIP_____

RESPONSE CARD 11

Please return card if you would like to be added to our preferred mailing list.

NAME _____

ADDRESS _____

CITY_____STATE_____ZIP_____

BUSINESS PHONE _____ HOME PHONE _____

I am especially interested in the following:

☐ GROWTH STOCKS ☐ MUTUAL FUNDS ☐ U. S. GOVERNMENT SECURITIES
☐ INCOME STOCKS ☐ TAX-EXEMPT BONDS ☐ OPTIONS
☐ CORPORATE BONDS ☐ CURRENT INCOME

RESPONSE CARD 12

Ideas...Portfolio Analysis...Prospectus

Gentlemen:

☐ Please send me your weekly option strategy idea for the 4 weeks WITHOUT CHARGE.

☐ Please option analyze my portfolio WITHOUT CHARGE. (My list of stocks is enclosed or attached.)

☐ Please have a valuation of my portfolio of stocks and bonds prepared WITHOUT CHARGE.

☐ Please send me an Options Clearing Corporation prospectus.

NAME _____ RES. PHONE _____

ADDRESS_____BUS. PHONE_____

Lead-Getting Lecture Invitations and Reservation Cards

One of the prime prospecting methods for aggressive, outgoing, upward-striving salespeople is presenting lectures to groups. Group selling enables you to reach many prospects at a single session in a significant encounter. Lectures give you the opportunity to sell yourself to the group so well that prospects will want to make appointments with the intention of doing something constructive to improve their financial state.

Getting people to attend lectures is always difficult. The direct-mail approach is normally the most highly effective per dollar spent. I personally prefer direct-mail solicitation over newspaper or radio advertisements for the following reasons: (1) a geographic area can be better pinpointed and (2) the quality of the prospect approached is predetermined.

The accompanying sample lecture invitations and reply cards have been effectively used in the past. Like any other illustrations in this book, you may use them as is or revise to suit you and your particular area.

Would you like to get more than dividends from your stock?

_____ Announces...

A Special Forum
on the

WORLD OF LISTED STOCK OPTIONS

TUESDAY, MARCH 29, 19XX
8:00 P.M.

AN OPPORTUNITY FOR YOU TO FIND OUT ABOUT THE RISKS AND POTENTIAL REWARDS

The many ways in which listed options may be used to obtain:

1. ADDITIONAL INCOME FROM YOUR INVESTMENTS
2. PROTECTION FROM DECLINING STOCK PRICES
3. POTENTIAL CAPITAL GAINS
4. FLEXIBILITY IN INVESTMENT TAX PLANNING

Another in a free series of stimulating discussion on intelligent investing in unsettled times and fast-moving markets.

Location: Marriott Inn, Dallas North
LBJ Freeway at Coit Road

Free Options Clearing Corporation prospectuses and study kits will be available.

Reservations can be made by mailing the enclosed card, or by calling _____ (   )
A prompt response is advisable, as seating is limited.

YOUR HOST WILL BE

_____
(Account Executive)

(Please check one or more)

☐ Please reserve _____ seats for the workshop

☐ I cannot attend the workshop, but I am interested in learning how options might benefit me

☐ I would like to receive additional information on the following:

— Stocks   — Mutual funds
— Corporate bonds — IRA
— Tax-free bonds — Money market funds
— Government bonds — Keogh plans
— Commodities   — Corporate retirement plans

Name _____

Address _____

Name _____

Address _____

City _____ State _____ Zip _____

Home phone _____ Office phone _____

Best time to call _____

PLEASE DETACH FOR YOUR USE

MY ACCOUNT NUMBER
IS _____

MY OFFICE
IS _____

LECTURE

Investing For Income in Today's Market: Where Should You Begin?

Needs change. Markets change. Income requirements develop. If you find your investment requirements shifting towards income preservation, attend one or more informative, one-hour lectures for the individual investor presented by_____.

Sequential attendance is not required but we hope you can attend more than one.

LECTURE NO. 1   **FINANCIAL PLANNING FOR THE INCOME INVESTOR**
Tuesday, June 7 — 3 P.M.

LECTURE NO. 2   **TEN RULES FOR THE INCOME INVESTOR, PLUS UTILITIES DIVIDEND INCREASE CANDIDATES**
Tuesday June 7 — 7 P.M.

LECTURE NO. 3   **TAX-FREE MUNICIPAL BONDS**
Wednesday June 8 — 3 P.M.

LECTURE NO. 4   **FINANCIAL PLANNING FOR THE INCOME INVESTOR**
Wednesday June 8 — 7 P.M.

Each seminar will be conducted by Mr. _____ of _____ office. Mr. _____ is a graduate of the University of California at Berkeley with advanced study at the _____ the New York Institute of Finance,

All lectures will be held at:
Lake Merritt Hotel
Crown Room
1800 Madison St.
Oakland

They are free of charge but seating is limited. Please reserve a seat by calling _____ at _____ or by mailing the coupon below.

- -

Oakland, California 94623

Please reserve _____ seat(s) for Lecture No. 1 (3:00 p.m.) _____ No. 2 _____ (7:00 p.m.)

Check here to reserve your seat. No. 3 _____ (3:00 p.m.) _____ No. 4 _____ (7:00 p.m.)

Name _____ Home Phone _____

Address _____ Bus. Phone _____

Investment Course

FEATURING
10 Ways to Increasing Income and Reduce Taxes

TIME: Tuesday, March 29, 19____   7:30 P.M.

PLACE: Key Bidge Marriott

An informative investment course sponsored by _____ will feature methods successful investors use to increase their income and reduce their income-tax liability on invested dollars. It will be conducted by Mr. _____ Vice President of Securities, Inc.

Topics of Discussion

Methods of Increasing Income

Learn why and how conservative investors including many bank trust departments use the option market to increase their return from common stocks. (Option Clearing Corporation prospectus will be given to each attendee).

Learn where the highest return can be obtained from fixed-income investments in the short, intermediate, and long term.

Learn about the most attractive U.S. Government and corporate securities currently being offered.

Methods of Reducing Taxes

Tax-free and *tax-deferred* investments will be thoroughly discussed.

Deferring taxes on utility stock dividends and bonds is possible; learn how.

If you would like to attend, please fill out and return the enclosed card or call _____ at 525-_____ . Be sure to reserve a seat without delay as seating is limited.

LECTURE INVITATION 4

Every year the tax bite seems to have more teeth. But this could be the year you finally do something about it. How?

Tax-advantaged investments let you invest money that would normally feed the tax bite. And they let you postpone paying taxes until a later date. In the meantime, those funds can be working for you. Not for your Uncle.

_____cordially invites you to attend a seminar on the topic of

THE FUNDAMENTALS OF TAX-ADVANTAGED INVESTMENTS

The seminar will be held at

Northern California Savings & Loan, Community Room
425 South Main Street, Salinas

Wednesday, May 18, 1977
7:30 to 9:30 p.m.

For reservations, please return the enclosed card.

LECTURE INVITATION 5

ANNOUNCING...

The Monday Money Luncheon

Every month we conduct a noontime conversation about financial planning for independent women. Complimentary sandwiches and cold drinks are served.

We will discuss how to invest for monthly income, capital gains, tax savings, and whatever financial problems are on your mind.

We welcome the pleasure of your company. RSVP

Place: First Federal Plaze, at Four Corners
Time: 12:15–1:30 P.M.
Date:

_____
ACCOUNT EXECUTIVE
100 First Federal Plaza, Rochester, NY 14614
Telephone (716)

AN INVESTMENT LECTURE SERIES

Tax-Exempt and High-Yield Investments

The seminars will be held on Mondays, December 4 and 11 at 7:30 p.m. at Auntie Mame's, 1080 Valley Rd., Stirling, New Jersey.

Learn about 9 ways to increase your income:

1. **TAX-EXEMPT BONDS** yielding up to **7%**

2. **CORPORATE BONDS** yielding **9¼%** and more

3. **U.S. GOVERNMENT SECURITIES** top quality with current yields up to **8.70%**

4. **GOVERNMENT NATIONAL MORTGAGE ASSOCIATION** Ginnie Maes, yields up to **9.2%**

5. **CORPORATE BOND TRUSTS** (**Bonds** check a month to investor, with yields approaching **9¼%**

6. **MUNICIPAL BOND TRUSTS** tax-exempt yields of **6¾%**

7. **PREFERRED STOCKS** yields to **9½%**

8. **ELECTRIC UTILITY STOCKS** selling to yield over **9½%**

9. **TAX-DEFERRED SAVINGS PLANS**

_____ Account Executive present these seminars.

Attendance is free, but reservations are encouraged. PLEASE RETURN THE ATTACHED POSTAGE-PAID FORM FOR ASSURED SEATING, OR CALL _____ COLLECT AT _____.

Please hold _____ reservations for the investment lectures on December 4 and 11.

Name _____

Address _____

City _____ Zip _____

Phone: Home _____ Business _____

☐ Sorry—I am unable to attend, but please send complimentary information on the investment areas covered in the lecture.

☐ I have friends and/or neighbors interested in attending:

Name _____

Address _____

City _____ Zip _____

Phone: Home _____ Business _____

You are cordially invited to attend a lecture on the

Benefits of a Living Trust

Guest Speakers and Topics:

An attorney specializing in Estate Planning speaking on:

How to AVOID probate and to reduce probate costs
How to REDUCE inheritance and estate TAXES
How to MAINTAIN PRIVACY for your estate

and

Mr. _____
Account Executive

How to DEFER all federal income tax on savings & investment
How to possibly REDUCE life insurance premium costs by 30%-70%

DATE: Tuesday, May 10, 19
TIME: Tuesday 7:30 to 9:30 P.M.
PLACE: Holiday Inn
5520 Wisconsin Avenue
Chevy Chase, Maryland

Please call Jan _____ at 296- _____ for reservations or if this
time is inconvenient, please call for schedule of other lectures.
Spouses also invited.

- -

In addition to my guest(s), I have friends and/or neighbors who would like to attend. Please send complimentary tickets to:

Name _____

Address _____

City _____ Zip _____

Please hold _____ reservations for your lecture on May 10th in the name of:

Sorry—I have a conflict in date(s), but I would like to receive

Name _____

☐ Your research department's opinion on:

Address _____

_____

City _____ Zip _____

☐ Information on receiving tax exempt income

Phone: Home _____ Business _____

☐ An invitation to your next investment seminar

PLEASE DETACH FOR YOUR USE

MY ACCOUNT NUMBER IS _____

MY OFFICE IS _____

WASHINGTON, D.C. 20006
(202)

Why Pay Taxes on Your Savings?

Invest 30 minutes of your time and listen to _____ explain how you can defer ALL TAXES on your savings, accumulate interest tax free, get a guaranteed high rate of return, all with complete safety of your principal. This plan will help you protect that portion of those hard-earned dollars you want to set aside from needless taxation during your earning years. In addition, this plan can complement your Keogh or IRA.

Times:	12:00 Noon
	1:00 P.M.
	2:00 P.M.
	3:00 P.M.
Place:	CALIFORNIA MART
	110 E. 9th St.
	Room A 369
	Los Angeles, Ca.
Date:	March 24, 1977

For reservations and/or information please call (213) _____

YOU ARE INVITED TO An Investment Seminar

Many investors as well as non-investors, are missing valuable opportunities to earn **a** high return on their savings dollars simply because they don't know all *all* the available alternatives. For that reason, and for your benefit, _____ is sponsoring a short investment seminar exclusively for the residents in your area. The class is absolutely free of charge and is designed to give you a practical working knowledge in the following investment areas:

*TAX FREE INVESTMENTS
> What are they?
> How do they compare to taxable investments?
> What are the minimum investments and how do I buy them?
> Bond Funds—advantages and disadvantages.

*HIGH YIELD INVESTMENTS
> United States Government obligations.
> High grade Corporate Bonds.
> Other income producing securities.

*HOW UTILITY STOCKS CAN INCREASE YOUR INCOME
> Investment strategies.
> Characteristics of successful utilities.

*SPECIAL FEATURE:
> How to combine *High Income* with *Growth* to produce excellent long term growth. This discussion will include a look at the current market situation in terms of the economy and specific industries which stand to benefit over the next 12 months. Also, included will be the advantages of covered call *option* writing.

> (Free Option Clearing Corp. prospectus will be given to each attendee.)

The lecture will be held in the Crystal City Marriott, 1999 Jefferson Davis Highway, March 22nd, from 7:30 to 9:00 P.M. The guest speaker will be Mr. _____ a Registered Representative of the New York Stock Exchange. Attendance is free but reservations are encouraged. If you are interested simply return the attached card.

☐ I would like to attend your investment seminar.

☐ I cannot attend, however, I would like further information on the following investment subject(s)

_____

_____

NAME _____

ADDRESS _____

CITY _____ STATE _____

HOME PHONE _____ OFFICE _____

PLEASE DETACH FOR YOUR USE

MY   ACCOUNT NUMBER
IS _____

MY   OFFICE
IS _____

Invest Without Fear of Loss

How would you like to have an investment that is *completely safe*—absolutely no risk. An investment that pays a competitive compounding interest rate—yet *pay no current income taxes*. Have complete liquidity—you can get to your money at any time. Sound interesting?

Many people are discovering this investment opportunity. Invest an hour and you'll probably pay less income tax.

The seminar will be conducted by

The seminar will be held

DATE: February 15, 19
TIME: 7:30 P.M.
PLACE:

Let me know whether or not you can attend. A reply card is enclosed for your convenience—or call _____ at 836-

---

☐ I accept your invitation to an investment seminar on _____ (date)
    with the understanding that there is no admission charge or obligation.

☐ _____   ☐ _____
Name _____
Address _____
City_____ State_____ Zip_____

☐ Sorry, I cannot attend
☐ Please send me information on this program.
☐ I am interested in future investment seminars.

LECTURE RESERVATION CARD 1

Investment Seminar

Please reserve space for me and _____ guests at the investment seminar held on:

Wednesday, May 18, 19 ⎯7:30 to 9:30 p.m.

☐ I am unable to attend, but please notify me of future seminars.

☐ Please send me information on the items checked below.

☐ Corporate bonds   ☐ Tax-free interest from muni bonds
☐ Preferred stocks   ☐ Suggestions for short-term gains
☐ Portfolio analysis   ☐ Selected securities for income
☐ Place me on the mailing list for three months   ☐ Mutual funds
☐ Tax shelters   ☐ Chicago Board of Options Exchange
☐ Growth stocks   ☐ New security offerings
☐ Retirement plans

Name _____

Address _____ City _____ Zip _____

Home Phone _____ Bus. Phone _____

Do you have an account with _____   ☐ Yes   ☐ No

LECTURE RESERVATION CARD 2

Investment Seminar

Please reserve space for me and _____ guests at your investment seminar.

_____ I am unable to attend, but please notify me of future seminars.

_____ Please call me to discuss investments.

Name _____

Address _____

City _____ Zip _____

Home telephone _____ Business telephone _____

Free Lecture Series

Please enroll me in the free investment lecture series and send my ticket to:

NAME _____

ADDRESS_____

CITY _____ STATE _____ ZIP _____

TELEPHONE _____

☐ Check here if spouse or friend is coming and if an extra ticket will be needed.

☐ Some of my friends and neighbors are also interested. Please send extra tickets for:

NAME _____

ADDRESS_____

CITY _____ ZIP _____

NAME _____

ADDRESS_____

CITY _____ ZIP _____

☐ Check here if you have a conflict of dates. We will send you a free copy of our latest research report.

Investment Ideas to Increase Income

☐ **YES,** I would like to attend an upcoming seminar on Investment Ideas to Increase Income.

Seminars are held at the following locations and times. Please check the most convenient.

☐ No preference
☐ Decatur Country Club, Country Club Rd. S.E.
☐   Securities Offices
☐ Tuesday ☐ Thursday ☐ 7:00 P.M. ☐ 8:00 P.M.

NAME (please print) _____

ADDRESS_____

CITY _____ STATE _____ ZIP _____

PHONE _____
       (Residence)   (Business)

☐ **NO,** I cannot attend a seminar but, without obligation, I would like the following:

☐   ten undervalued stocks for 19
☐ Information on tax-sheltered retirement
☐ Advantages of tax-free securities
☐ Information on listed options
☐ Latest research report on the following:

_____

_____

_____

_____

Registration Card

Name _____

Address _____

_____ Zip _____

Occupation _____

Year of birth _____ Phone (day) _____ Phone (eve) _____

Course Title _____ Date _____

Sponsored by _____ Location _____

Where did you hear about the class? _____

Previous investing experience ☐ Bonds ☐ Stocks ☐ Options ☐ Commodities ☐ Funds

Course topics I am particularly interested in _____

_____

Index

298

300 INDEX